A
POPULAR HISTORY
OF
THE REFORMATION

Philip Hughes

IMAGE BOOKS

A DIVISION OF DOUBLEDAY & COMPANY, INC.

GARDEN CITY, NEW YORK

PRINTING HISTORY
Image Books edition published February, 1960

Nihil Obstat: John A. Goodwine, J.C.D.
Censor Librorum

Imprimatur: ✠ Francis Cardinal Spellman
Archbishop of New York
August 22, 1959

The nihil obstat and imprimatur are official declarations that a book or pamphlet is free of doctrinal or moral error. No implication is contained therein that those who have granted the nihil obstat and imprimatur agree with the contents, opinions or statements expressed.

A selection of the Catholic Book Club, March, 1957
A dividend of the Catholic Literary Foundation, April, 1957
A selection of the Thomas More Book Club, March, 1957

COVER BY RAFAEL PALACIOS
TYPOGRAPHY BY JOSEPH P. ASCHERL

RDO. DNO. GEORGIO GARRELTS
QUI EI HAEC OTIA FECIT
AUCTOR ET AMICUS MEMORIA GRATA

ET SODALIBUS QUI IN ALMA ACADEMIA
DE REBUS GESTIS DISSERTANT

Notre Dame du Lac, Indiana
Die festo B. Mariæ Assumptionis MCMLVI

CONTENTS

CONTENTS

A Popular History of the Reformation

CHAPTER ONE

The Traditional Christian Religion

i Fifteen Hundred Years

There are two questions which the ordinary man asks the historian, and they go to the heart of the historians' business. What was life then like? How did life come to be like that? In an ordinary historical atlas for schools which lies open as I write, there is shown a coloured map of western Europe as it was about the year 1500. The seventy-five or so territories into which the vast region is divided that stretches from Lisbon to Riga would, to the general reader, seem somewhat unfamiliar divisions, perhaps. For what the various colours show is not the limits of the rule of the princes and kings and republics of Europe, but of the jurisdiction of its chief spiritual rulers. The seventy-five territories are, in fact, the provinces of the Christian Church. At the head of each is an official called archbishop, and also metropolitan; the province is made up of a number of sees, or dioceses, and each of these is ruled by a bishop. All the millions who inhabit this western Europe of 450 years ago are the subjects, in spiritual matters, of the seven hundred or so bishops whose sees, at this time, constitute the seventy-five ecclesiastical provinces; and there is among these millions, so varied in racial origin, in social condition, in cultural attainment, and in political tradition, a most remarkable unity with regard to religion—that is, with regard to the relations which exist between man and God Who is his creator. This unity has been a fact of life ever since the first sees came into being many centuries ago.

Were the map which I am describing replaced by a religious map of the same territory dated one hundred years later, a new line of demarcation would be discerned, put in to show regions where men had ceased to hold what had, for so long a time, been the universal tradition in these high matters. The story of the appearance of new theories about religion in the opening years of the sixteenth century, of how they gradually came to predominate in various of these ecclesiastical provinces, and of the way in which those other provinces where men stood by the tradition reacted, is the story of the Reformation.

This original unity of religious ideas that obtained throughout western Europe was, first of all, a unity of belief as to the kind of being God is, and about God's plan for the eternal happiness in a future life of man His creature. It was a unity also in its acceptance of a divinely revealed code of conduct— in the universal agreement, that is to say, about what actions are good and what are bad. Finally, the unity extended to a belief that the religion, considered even as an organisation, was a thing divinely founded; to be obeyed, therefore, as God is to be obeyed, whenever its chiefs announced decisions about beliefs or issued rulings about conduct. In all the twelve hundred years that lie between the first conversions of the West to this religion, and the movement called the Reformation, there had been, among those who continued loyal to the Church, very little difficulty in accepting such rulings of authority about matters of belief or morals; but as to the practical fidelity of individuals to the rulings about morals, to the moral code which they accepted as divine, the failure was chronic—as is still, so often, the case with men whose minds high ideals attract, and indeed conquer, but in whom human weaknesses nevertheless persist. *Video meliora proboque: deteriora sequor*.[1] The light words of the pagan poet, Ovid, describe with finality the menace that ever hangs over human history; over the history of the Church also, which is why this must be at times a pretty black history, to the surprise (scarcely scandal!) of those who rarely trouble to think out the full meaning of their own moral failures. And in nothing was this chronic infidelity to the Christian moral law more mischievous than when the great men—the nobles, the kings, and the highly placed churchmen—would definitely flaunt their insubordination or, even more wickedly, strive to make the spiritual power a means to advance their own personal designs.

[1] I see the better things, and they win in my judgment: it is the worse that I pursue.

The history of the Reformation being, in final analysis, the history of a revolution in religious belief, it cannot begin to be understood unless one consents to be, in part, a student also of theology, a student of that sacred doctrine around whose interpretation the rival theologians in the sixteenth century fought so keenly, and not the theologians only, but the rulers of the leading European states. For once the battle was joined—the first purely theological battle—men prepared to take part in it who were moved by impulses and desires that were not theological at all. The political ambitions of the princes; their international rivalry; the social feuds of the nobility; the interests of bankers, traders, and the new industrialists of the economic revolution already in progress—a revolution which must be affected by the general convulsion in belief that was now threatening—all these would play a highly important part in the long fight; but at the heart of it there lay what still lives in the heart of our present weakness, the deep division between men attached to irreconcilable beliefs about God and His will for mankind, the division between the old beliefs and the new. Before we come to the story of the differences, we ought to know what those beliefs were which, at the time when the pioneers of the Reformation were born, all western Europe accepted as the religion of Christ.

We might begin the survey with the recollection that, at the time when the great changes of the sixteenth century began, the mass of the people of western Europe could neither read nor write—perhaps as many as two out of three were completely illiterate.[2] Four hundred years before, the proportion had been even higher—at that time even great kings could not sign their names, as the rude marks still testify on some of the most important documents of European history. For those who were able to read and had the means to buy them, there were, in the year 1500, printed books—and, comparatively speaking, plenty of such. But the art of printing was still a novelty in the early sixteenth century. Luther's father, certainly, would remember the stir made by the first news of the great invention. Down to the sixties and seventies of the fifteenth century the only books were manuscripts, written out by professional scribes and, inevitably, an expensive luxury.[3] And so it had

[2] Ignatius Loyola came of an ancient noble family, but only one of his sisters knew how to write her name.

[3] A Bible would cost ten years of the average priest's income.

always been. Whatever the ideas of the vast majority of mankind—whether illiterate or not—about God, they necessarily
derived in the greatest measure from the direct speech of other
men. So it was in the Europe of Luther's childhood; so it
had been in the far-off centuries when the Gospel work had
first begun, the work of converting mankind to an acceptance
of the truth revealed in Christ our Lord. It was by preachers
that the converts were made, and upon preaching that the
well-being of the Christian intelligence chiefly depended.

There is an abundance of contemporary literature to tell us
what the belief of western Europe was at the time when the
Reformers were born, to say what these Catholic people were
supposed to believe, and to stigmatise what, only too often,
they did in fact believe. We have the learned Latin analyses
and expositions of the theologians who taught in the thirty
or forty universities of Italy, Spain, France, England, and
Germany. We have popular non-technical explanations of the
belief, written in the various national languages for the reading
of the layman. And there is no doubt at all as to its substantial
content and the unity of this.

All believe that the whole universe came into existence
through the creative act of God. Among the living creatures
man is in a class apart, for the spirit that animates him is
immortal. Death is but a stage in his existence. After his disappearance from this world man is meant, in the plan of his
Creator, to live for ever in a life of perfect happiness in the
immediate presence of God. The operation of this plan was,
however, checked abruptly when the first man created turned
against the Creator and defied His will. This mysterious rebellion had effects that were fundamental. All prospect of a future
of eternal happiness was lost, and in man's own being there
was henceforward a dislocation of the harmony between
reason and desire with which God had created him. Henceforth man must always be at war with himself, and after death
nothing awaited him but an eternity without the blessed
vision of God.

But now, all these Christians believe, the essential goodness
of the Creator intervened. A means of reconciliation was found.
For the fundamental, all-wrecking crime of the first man,
atonement would be made by one who was a man indeed—so
that the atonement had a truly human quality, was something
that really belonged to the human race—but one who was, at
the same time, something more than man, who had indeed the

same nature as the Creator. God Himself would become man, and this God-Man, appearing on the earth in a future age, would by some total offering of himself in reparation for the first man's crime restore to the human race the eternal prospects it had lost and provide a means whereby, individually, all men might be reconciled with God and find again a relation of friendly affection with Him.

In the course of time the promise of such a divine saviour was realised, and at Bethlehem, a small town in Judea, not far from the city of Jerusalem, there was born, in the year which we call 4 B.C., of a mother who was a virgin, the divine Saviour, Jesus Christ. The story of His life, the detail of the Good Tidings He brought to mankind, of the way in which He meant these should come to realisation in the individual man—all this is the subject matter of the book we call the New Testament, which all Christians held to be not merely a human account, however valuable, but a book which in some way really had God for its author; a book that was, in the technical sense of the word, inspired.

The central event of the New Testament is the Roman governor's putting Christ to death by crucifixion—on the part of the Saviour a death willingly accepted, an offering of His life to God the Father in reparation for the first sin of Adam and for all the sins of all mankind; an offering of infinite consequence, as the act must be of an actor who was Himself infinite, God. Through that divine sacrifice, always in the strictest dependence on it and never through any means other than this, has salvation, the mere possibility of salvation, come to man. Here, in the infinity of worth offered to God and accepted by God, is the source of the restoration to man of a destiny of eternal happiness, the source also of a new kind of life on earth that is a preparation for, and a foretaste of, that eternal destiny. The Church of Christ—its sacraments, its rites, its guiding teaching—is the means whereby this new life reaches the individual man; the Church is the instrument through which he takes hold of what has been divinely done for him. The saving death on the cross is the fundamental of the whole Christian system, the reality ever-present, the mystery whose operation never ceases; this is the doctrine that is always preached first, from the very beginning of the Church's history.

A man listens to the preaching, is convinced, believes. And he is then initiated into the Church by a rite—he is symbolically washed with water, the ceremony called Baptism. "The Church"—this Greek-derived word is used by the German-influenced languages of Europe as the equivalent for the word which, in the New Testament, designates the believers in Christ taken as a group: the *ecclesia*; i.e., assembly. And it is one of the elements of Christian belief that the Church is not a mere coming together in agreement, or because of agreement, on the part of the believers—it is not their totality, merely, or sum; it is a more than natural thing, is divinely willed, divinely shaped, and divinely endowed, the very membership in which makes the individual one whole with Christ and so a sharer in all that endowment of reconciliation which the sacrifice of Christ has merited. If the Church is a body the members or limbs of which are men, it is also a body whose head is Christ; and the new life, the more than natural life, which is the life of the Church, is the life of Christ, reaching to man through man's being one with Christ in this his mysterious body. From the beginning, then, there is this belief in the nature and the function of the Church, a corresponding veneration for the Church, and a horror at the thought of possible wilful separation from the Church as the greatest of all evils. The faith of the Church is regarded as indefectible; that is to say, all believe that the Church as a whole can never believe anything to be the teaching of Christ which, in point of fact, is opposed to what He taught. From the very earliest days the appeal of the teachers to the testimony presented by the general unanimous belief, as conclusive evidence that what is taught is what Christ taught, is constant.

In this Church, provision is divinely made for good order, through officers called, in the Greek of the New Testament, *episcopoi*—in English, bishops. Literally the Greek word means an overlooker, a superintendent. The bishops it is who govern the local groups of believers, they preside at the meetings for worship; it is they who baptise the converted and whose presence or authorisation is the guarantee, for the believer, of a true Eucharist. To be recognised by the bishop, to live in obedience to him, is for the believer a most concrete assurance that he is one with the Church divinely founded. The importance of this authority, as a factor in the religious life of the believer, it is scarcely possible to exaggerate. Practical veneration for the bishop's office is one of the surest marks of the true believer.

Divinely founded, or divinely authorised, ritual acts are

believed in as means essential to the new life, to the realisation of all that incorporation in Christ can be. Baptism, the initiating rite, has been mentioned. No less important is the rite called the Eucharist, which from the beginning was the chief business of the weekly assembly for corporate worship.

The pattern of the daily life of the believers who in these first centuries constituted the Church of Christ eludes us at more than one point. This is not surprising, for almost nothing has survived of what they wrote save works, or fragments of works, occasioned by some special crisis or other. The human intelligence is always active, and there were seeming contradictions in the Gospel message that challenged the believer, obscurities in the sacred books that perplexed and teased. There was need, also, to reply to the criticisms that came from the world without: that the new doctrines were antisocial, nonsensical, immoral; that the believers were traitors to the state. Whence a theological literature to resolve the believer's difficulties, and an apologetic literature to meet the critical pagan; and constantly, in these ever-continuing discussions between the believers, we meet the interposition of the bishop, the ruler who is also, because ruler, the teacher, who does not argue but decides, with the common belief, the universal teaching, the tradition, for his measure. There is one bishop, above all, of whom we hear as deciding with authority, and not for his own local flock alone: the bishop of the imperial city, Rome; and, at certain periods, it is almost all that we hear of this bishop. Rarely is there any mention of him, but always he is deciding as with a sovereign authority and without any need to produce credentials. Not even to assemblies of bishops, against which at times, he sets his will, does he give arguments to prove that he is in the right.

These assemblies of bishops—councils of the Church, they came to be called—are an institution that develops during the last hundred years of the long war against the Church on the part of the Roman Empire, the world-wide state in which the Church had come to birth. In the first years of the fourth century (A.D. 313) the emperor—it was Constantine—declares himself a believer. The war of extermination is at an end. In its place come state protection and patronage, genuine zeal on the part of the christianised ruler, and a natural assumption that henceforth the state will have rights with regard to the Church and exercise some control. Within one hundred years of the conversion of Constantine the pattern of Chris-

tian-Church Christian-State relations is set which will be a
main feature of all European history thenceforward. The state
finds its first opportunity—sees the occasions for its duty to
intervene as protector, the emperors would say—when the
controversies reawaken about the mysterious truth that Christ
Who is truly man is also truly God. Partly because the state
intervenes, these controversies—not the doctrine controverted
—now begin to have a new social and political importance.
The councils of the Church which succeed one another in
the three hundred and more years after the conversion of Constantine are leading events in the history of the empire no
less truly than in that of the Church.

But while the sole anxiety of the Church is that truth shall
not be falsified or obscured by admitting its enemies to rights
within the Church, the emperors are also interested in civil
peace, ever willing, where the reconciliation of opposing views
cannot be hoped for, to arrange compromises, ever willing to
devise (and to impose) ambiguous formulae which both the
believer and the heretic[4] can sign, which will allow the heretic
—and his view—the same status within the Church as the true
believer. To the war between the Church and the pagan emperor bent on destroying the Church, there has succeeded a
war with the Christian emperor determined to use the Church
in the interests of the state: and where the Christian emperor
really survived, in the end he won. So it was in the East.

While this second long war is in progress—it is henceforward continuous for hundreds of years—two forces are slowly
operating that transform the political thing called the empire,
and the social organisation too. That empire was still, in the
time of Constantine and the first General Council (held at
Nicea in 325), a state that included all western Europe as
well as northern Africa, Egypt, Syria, Asia Minor, Greece, and
the Balkans. But at that time only the East was anything like
wholly christianised. In the West, outside the cities, the populace even in Italy was still pagan. Upon the task of converting these country folk the zeal of innumerable apostolic men
had been already at work for a hundred years when, from
about the beginning of the fifth century (from about the year
407), there came, to complicate the task, the very varied
movement that bears the general name of the Barbarian Invasions. For a good hundred years and more, Visigoths and

4 Literally, the man who picks and chooses—where the true Christian believes all that the Church teaches.

Ostrogoths, Vandals, Suevi, Burgundians, Franks, and "Anglo-Saxons" descended upon the lands we know as Spain, France, Italy, Britain, and Western Germany. From the Rhine to Gibraltar and to Sicily the emperor's authority was, by the year 500, no more than a name. But amid all the fights and destruction, the endless change and counterchange, the missionary work went on.

The new Western world which emerged, the world of the first half of the Middle Ages, was to be a world where countrysides were vastly more important than towns—which indeed shrank to vanishing point—and where life was a very primitive thing and a great contrast to life in the centuries-old urban civilisation of the Hellenic East where the Church was born and for four hundred years had its first developments. This world of peasants and country-bred, fighting warrior-lords and barbarian princes was an all but illiterate world, and the language it spoke was moving ever further and further away, not from the tongue of Cicero only, but from anything that resembled grammatical Latin. In this new Western civilisation the bishop, as such, came to have a civic importance and to be a social power, beyond anything which his brother in the still civilised, imperially governed East could have imagined. And the bishop was more and more becoming a great lord in temporal matters; his spiritual children were also to be, in great part, his subjects.

At this moment when a religion that had grown up in an urban world was about to face the problem that the world was now to be a rural thing, there providentially appeared that essentially rural institution, the monastery. To the work of converting the rural populations the new institution of monks was the most valuable auxiliary of all. These retreats where dwelt the men consecrated to prayer became, willy-nilly, centres of Christian preaching and also, increasingly, centres of social salvation. In the map of seventh-century France, for example, the monasteries are what the towns are in the maps of today. And the great abbots were becoming rulers in civil matters just as much as the bishops.

Life in this vast Western backwoods—on this vast frontier—was hard and cruel, of course; filled with all the violent crime one cares to imagine. But with the bishop and the monk—and through them—there came to it and nevertheless were established (or re-established) the elements of the culture of the great days: building in stone, and sculpture, and painting, music, knowledge of the literary Latin language, something of the great literature, and "the holy Latin tongue," oratory, the splendour of organised ritual, the copying of books. And more than all this, of course, infinitely more, there came the thing that ultimately made all the difference: belief that Jesus Christ Who was God had died to save man from his sins and to open to him the life of eternal bliss; belief that to all men it was God who ultimately mattered; that for all there was a day of doom, so that kings themselves could not escape the judgment of God; that sins must be repented, or else . . . ; belief that charity was the noblest virtue of all—a belief whose reality was proved in the universal veneration of the saint, the believer who had lived a life of perfect charity, and especially of the martyr-saint who had sealed his Christian life by fidelity to Christ amid the torments of a cruel death; belief that the Catholic Church, whose bishops, priests, monks made all this known, was God's creation, the visible organ of revelation, the visible guarantee that all this was true; the Catholic faith, and the practice of the divine, grace-conferring rites technically called sacraments.[5]

Western Europe emerged, after four hundred years, and more of the "backwoods" phase, as a mass of small lordships, knit by the contractual bond of homage and protection to overlords and then, through these, to the half score of lords called king, chief of whom was the German king, who was styled the emperor. This king came to be elected by the leading princes of Germany; and this summit of temporal dominion had enjoyed a seemingly supreme consecration ever since the day when the pope had crowned the most famous of all the barbarian rulers, the Frankish king, the emperor *par excellence*, Charlemagne, 25 December, 800.

In this network of political relationships, where with possession of land there went always some political authority, and where all possessed of land were either lords or vassals, and often both—vassals to those from whom they held the land, lord over those to whom, in turn, they had made over parcels of what they held—church organisation and the organisation of what we should call the state, authority of ecclesiastical chiefs and political authority, the twofold jurisdiction of which the same identical population were the subjects, were

[5] Baptism, Confirmation, Penance, the Holy Eucharist, Holy Orders, Extreme Unction, Matrimony.

by now inextricably interwoven. Prelates as prelates, and not as lords of some principality, exercised control in matters of ordinary life over the subjects of the lay lord—nay, over the lay lord himself—who might be the temporal lord of the prelate. On the other hand, the lay lords might exercise a control in matters that went close to the very essence of church life.

In the course of these centuries when civilisation itself had to fight hard to survive, there had inevitably come to each of these twin powers much that properly belonged to the other. On the whole the Church had perhaps lost more than it had gained. For it had lost, in a very notable degree, the control of the appointments to bishoprics and to abbeys. The very papacy had for a time been the prize of the robber-barons who were lords of the environs of Rome.

The men thrust in this way into high ecclesiastical positions were only too often, in culture and in morals, indistinguishable from their patrons. The latest historian to treat of the history of these times (i.e., the years 888–1057) has ventured to call his book *The Church in the Power of the Layman* —the title states the very essence of all that was wrong. The struggle on the part of the popes to wrest the Church from the lay grasp, to restore the primitive condition of religion mistress of its own life—a struggle which began in the generation that saw the Norman Conquest of England, and in which the popes were only partially successful—was long and exhausting. So much so, that the end found the very victors all but bankrupt spiritually. In whole provinces of the Christian world, in Germany very notably, religion was wounded all but mortally by the new scandals inseparable from this civil war in spirituals.

Germany—the fact is supremely important to a student of the Reformation—had been the scene of all the major conflicts that filled so many of the years between the excommunication of Henry IV by the pope, Gregory VII (Hildebrand), in 1075 and the death, in defeat, of the emperor called Lewis of Bavaria in 1347. But it was in France that the most recent contest of this kind—recent to a Catholic of the generation of Luther's father, let us say—had taken place. At this time (1398–1405) the lay power was the group of lords of royal blood who ruled France in the name of its imbecile king, Charles VI; and the papal power, making one of the most resolute resistances of all time, was the Aragonese, Peter de Luna, known as Pope Benedict XIII, but acknowledged as pope by only one half of the Church. For in the year 1398 two rivals were claiming the allegiance of Catholics as pope.

Indirectly, this last extraordinary and scandal-breeding state of things can be traced back to an earlier conflict between the popes and the rulers of France, in the closing years of the previous century—a conflict, as always, about royal claims to control over church rights and church property, and about papal claims to admonish and correct kings for ways of ruling that were sinful. The protagonists were, both of them, personalities of the first order, Philip IV of France (usually called Philip the Fair) and Pope Boniface VIII. In 1303 the pope died, broken physically by the brutality of the assault, but, to the end, unyielding. Two years later a Frenchman was elected pope, and thenceforward, for seventy-three years, all the popes were Frenchmen and all governed the Church from France, or rather from their own tiny principality, the enclave of which Avignon was the chief town.

The last of these French popes, Gregory XI, was brought to return to Rome in 1378 largely through the influence of the holy woman whom we know as St. Catherine of Siena. That same year he died. In his place an Italian was elected at which time mobs surrounded the Vatican, uttering threats of death should another Frenchman be made pope. The Italian was crowned—Urban VI—publicly acknowledged by his electors, and then these same cardinals, after some stormy months of disagreement with the man they had elected, left Rome, repudiated the election, and at Fondi, a little town sixty or seventy miles from Rome, held a second election at which they chose a Frenchman. He called himself Clement VII and took up his abode at Avignon. So it was that from 1379 to 1409 there were these two rival lines of popes. Peter de Luna, called Benedict XIII, was this Clement's successor.

Towards the end of this thirty years' rivalry the mind of the chief supporters of both the lines began to be turned wholly to the problem, not of victory over their rivals, but of bringing the schism to an end. Their principals, the rival popes, were less interested, once elected, in this holy purpose. But in 1408 the joint efforts of their cardinals induced both the popes to agree to negotiate in a personal meeting. When the two aged men, however, with the infinite ruse of the senile, successfully evaded their pledges, the disgusted cardinals of both deserted their masters, came together in council at Pisa (1409), declared the two popes no popes at all, and proceeded to elect to

THE TRADITIONAL CHRISTIAN RELIGION 23

the "vacancy" a Franciscan cardinal, Greek by birth. Christendom now had three popes instead of two.

It was the initiative of the emperor Sigismund that finally brought back the traditional government. He compelled the pope of the Pisa line[6] to summon a council that met at Constance, in Switzerland, in 1414. This council first deposed, for his evil personal life, the pope who had summoned it; and he submitted to the council's act. Then the pope of the Roman line, Gregory XII, sent envoys to the council who, in his name, reconvoked it, as it were; and to the council he had thus convoked, Gregory gave his resignation as pope. The third of the rivals—still the Aragonese, Peter de Luna, the representative of the Avignon line—refused to treat with the council, calling upon all to disperse, as rebels against his authority, condemning them as schismatics and excommunicates. His following had by now shrunk to the mere handful of servants and officials who dwelt with him in the rocky fortress of Peñiscola on the Mediterranean coast of his native land. The council ignored Pedro's very existence and proceeded to elect, on November 11, 1418, Martin V, whom the whole Church accepted and acknowledged as pope.

It was now one hundred and twenty-two years since the quarrel between Philip the Fair and Pope Boniface VIII had begun. In all that time the supreme ruling authority of the Church had been operating under the strain of wholly abnormal conditions. It was also sixty-five years to the day to the date of Luther's birth. In those sixty-five years the destruction wrought by the long abnormality would by no means be wholly repaired. And new troubles, deriving doubtless in part from that long crisis, would arise, troubles as deadly to the understanding and practice of true religion as anything produced by the schism. The prospect, at the time Luther was born, was black indeed.

In the four hundred momentous years between Pope Gregory VII (1073–85) and Martin Luther (1483–1546), more than one constructive development of permanent value had been accomplished, notwithstanding the chronic preoccupation of the popes; i.e., that fight to preserve the independence of the Church in spiritual matters just spoken of. Under the

[6] Who was not the Greek elected in 1409, but his successor, an Italian, Baldassare Cossa, who had taken the name of John XXIII.

active patronage of the popes the first universities, for example, had been founded. Of these there were now, in 1517, thirty or more.

The beginnings of this particular departure had coincided roughly with the appearance of a new type of monk—the friars; these were priests whose houses were founded, not in the depths of the countryside, but in the newly reviving towns, and whose vocation was the active work of the preacher and the missionary. It was a calling which brought them into continuous contact with the whole life of their time as they passed from town to town and from village to village in their extensive preaching tours. Two of these orders of friars, the Dominicans and the Franciscans, are, as names at least, familiar to all who can read. The first of them was especially important because it was founded as a society of theologically trained preachers, a society in which study was considered a religious duty and where the rule was so arranged that, after prayer, all else made way for the activities of the student preparing to be a preacher: classes, private reading, and the rest. Whoever entered this order, it has been said, enrolled himself in a university as a student for life.

Within a generation the Franciscan order, founded about the same time, had followed this example, and from these two societies the nascent university movement gained immediately a host of students and a wealth of teachers of the very first rank. Four names in particular stand out in the first hundred years of this alliance of the friars and the universities; in chronological order, among the Dominicans, the naturalist-philosopher-theologian we know as St. Albert the Great (1195–1280) and the philosopher-theologian St. Thomas Aquinas (1225–74); among the Franciscans, St. Bonaventure (1221–74) and John Duns Scotus (1266–1305). There were two other orders of friars, more important, perhaps, in the later part of the Middle Ages, the Carmelites and the Austin Friars, both of whom were occupied with this same work of preaching and teaching. It was to the last-named order that Luther himself belonged for a critical fifteen years of his life. By the time Luther was born there must have been, in one country and another, the best part of 100,000 of these various kinds of friars, the preachers of almost all the sermons on which the layman depended for his religious education, the priests who heard the great bulk of the layman's confessions. Few were the towns where there was not at least one house of friars with its great public church attached; churches of a new kind that were, in effect, great preaching halls. In most towns of any size there were both Dominicans and Franciscans. In great cities all four orders were to be found.

The four great friars whose names have just been set down were not lecturers merely. They wrote extensively, and their works were of such fundamental character that for centuries they were the basis of all philosophical and theological education. To this day St. Thomas Aquinas is the principal intellectual influence in the Catholic Church; and there are experts prepared to say that, even yet, the fullness of his *personal* contribution to thought has scarcely begun to be understood. What all these scholars did in their writings—and many lesser men followed their example—was to present vast syntheses wherein, in orderly, systematic fashion, the various truths of the religion of Christendom were explained and their relation to the divinely inspired Scriptures carefully traced. The same method and learning were employed to explain the meaning of the rites of religion, and especially to explain the seven major rites which, by their nature, were a class apart— the rites called sacraments. And in the expositions which these doctors gave of the Christian virtues and the vices opposed to them, there was provided all that a man could need of guidance in the use of his religion, considered as an instrument to bring him nearer to God in this life and to keep him united with God in faithful friendship. The character and high intrinsic worth of these works are facts, readily verifiable by whoever will enter the great libraries of today and take down the volumes from their shelves, works at whose completeness and competence—practical as well as speculative —we must still marvel.

How did it come about that, in these ages which produced such classic works, the very evils against which they were offered as a remedy were so flourishing that a man might feel tempted to say it is these, and not the theological accomplishment, that characterise the Christianity of that time?

This, again, is a long and involved story. These great theologians, in their explanation of doctrine, in order to give any explanation of it at all, needed to know the meaning of the words and the science that governs the construction of sentences—they had to be conversant with the human knowledge called Grammar; they had to be able to analyse not only the literary form of what lay before them but its content—i.e., to make use of the human knowledge called Logic; they had to go further still, they needed some more than philological understanding of important key words, such as nature, substance, and person, for instance—they had to make use, that is to say, of the human knowledge called Metaphysics. Without such tools of natural knowledge anything more than a surface understanding of what the words of the Divine Scriptures mean is not possible; and it is entirely out of the question to attempt a solution of the major difficulties that many key passages of the text present.

Later we shall hear Luther pour scorn on the theologians' use of philosophy as an obsession with knowledge that is merely human and bound to distort the knowledge that is revealed. Yet without a training in the human sciences it would not have been possible for Luther to arrive at his criticisms of the theology he found in possession, nor to arrange them for presentation once he had formed them in his own mind.

These auxiliary sciences are, indeed, no more than natural knowledge. And in the pursuit of natural knowledge there can be no guarantee of infallibility. And while, where philosophers differ in the solutions they propose for philosophical difficulty, or in their exposition of a philosophical doctrine, all of them may be wrong, it is just not possible that all can be right. The first great weakness in this splendid achievement we call the Scholastic Theology is that the masters were not in accord about the philosophy that was so pre-eminently their auxiliary. And in the second generation a genius arose who, for philosophical reasons, called in question some of the major positions recently established—John Duns Scotus' critical examination of St. Thomas; which itself, as a scholastic activity, is but the repetition of St. Thomas critically examining his own contemporary St. Bonaventure, or the great mind that dominates the whole history of the Christian intelligence, the fourth-century doctor St. Augustine. The academic world, the philosophical and theological schools of the thirteenth and fourteenth-century universities, was by no means akin in spirit to the modern institution where the student's only hope is to cram into his memory other men's digests of masterpieces the direct study of which—it seems taken for granted—must always be beyond his powers. That older academic world is now revealed to us as seething with a passion for fundamental analysis and criticism. In the midst of the fourteenth century a second genius arose, of the philosophical type called, technically, critical. This was the Englishman, William of Ockham (?1280–?1349). He, too, was a Franciscan. Presently, between the third or fourth generations of Thomists and Scotists and these new Ockhamists—between the *Via Antiqua* and the *Via Moderna*, as the two came to be called—there was a kind of civil war within the academic life of Christendom that paralleled the civil war between the Christian Church and the Christian State.

The general tendency of the philosophical ideas of the *Via Moderna* was to reduce the sphere in which the human reason could expect to know with certitude. Such a truth, for example, as that the human soul is immortal, which St. Thomas Aquinas had held to be demonstrable by the natural human reason, was now declared knowable by religious faith alone. The time came when a theologian of the new school might, as a thinker, find himself holding that a truth was not necessarily reasonable, while as a believer he held that it was necessarily true. The new school, moreover, gave itself more and more exclusively to the study of its own theories of knowledge and, in its numerous teachers of less than Ockham's genius, to sterile discussions of mental subtleties. To the ordinary man it might easily seem, as the fifteenth century went by, that the fashionable Scholasticism could only lead to a semi-scepticism and to a life devoted to futilities. Except as the natural ally of the new developments in the knowledge of nature, this critical philosophy seems to have lost contact with the life of the time.

Nor was the *Via Antiqua* any closer to the needs of the day. Thomists, in these fourteenth and fifteenth centuries, debated endlessly with Scotists about the matters that divided them, and both schools fought the *Via Moderna* endlessly. Moreover, the *Via Antiqua*, the Thomists especially, made little attempt to study the new knowledge—whether scientific or literary—and to reform its methods accordingly. The metaphysical doctrines of Aristotle, for example, were fundamental in the thought of the *Via Antiqua*. They had never been accessible save in translation. Now, from the fifteenth century, not only were the original texts available, but teachers of Greek also. All this these scholastics ignored, as they ignored the reappearance of the works of Plato, of whom the West had hitherto never known anything of real importance.

It is of course all but ridiculous thus to set out in a couple

of pages a criticism of so vast a subject, to seem to weigh the
faults, define their magnitude, and assess the blame. But to
the educated of the generation in which Luther was born,
scholasticism was all but finished, a target for their mockery
as something pedantic, pretentious, futile, a matter of jargon
fighting jargon. Did not another of the same generation,
Thomas More, say about one aspect of the philosophy of these
days that it was about as useful as milking a he-goat into a
sieve?

Theology, considered as the scientific exploration and explanation of the truth divinely revealed, and as man's guide
in his relations to God, was by now in a bad way. Perhaps
the most striking evidence how theology was losing its influence was the neglect of the theologians on the part of those
personages we have come to call the mystics; and, still worse,
their hostility, not for particular theologians, but for the very
science, and the implication met with in the writings of the
mystics that the study of theology, and expertise in the science, is more likely than not to be a hindrance to the soul's
union with God. Such a mystic, turning from the direction
of the theologians, began (in fact) to be his own teacher,
making his own experiences in prayer his final guide.

The quasi-totality of all these men, Thomists, Scotists, Ockhamists, of mystics as well as theologians and scientists, were,
however, at one in their religious belief, whatever the depth
of their dislike for "approaches" to the belief that differed
from their own. Nevertheless, unity could not survive indefi-
nitely a state of things where believers were in chronic disagreement about matters so intimately connected with belief.
And of course in every generation there were some who re-
belled against particular items—fundamental items—of the belief itself. Sometimes these rebels were theologians whose solution for difficulties or explanation of the mysteries landed
them into positions not compatible with the traditional teaching. Others were mystics who arrived at their new ideas
through endless solitary brooding over such anxieties as the
state of the Church, the obvious unlikenesses of current practices to the simplicities of New Testament times, or the
chronic contrast (experienced by them as by all other men)
between the high ideal with which, perhaps, at times they had
experienced something like direct contact and their surrenders
to the common weaknesses of mankind.

Through all the Middle Ages, moreover, strange under-currents persist, strange combinations of religious ideas with moral aberrations, sometimes Manichee, sometimes pantheist, half magic, half fraud, and in part incipient natural science; real cults, the devotees loosely organised and practising bizarre rituals, attached at times to spurious versions of the Christian Scriptures and to a whole fantastic legendary of super-human and semi-diabolic power, half tyrant over the lives of its clients and half their slave. Along with this underworld there also persisted, through these centuries, a Christian attachment to spurious revelations which promised a speedy-coming apoca-lyptic age, the kingdom of the Holy Ghost, when all the saints —all who now accepted the new Gospel, the Eternal Gospel, to name the most famous of them—should triumph over the indifferent and over their own present oppressors and reign for ever with Christ. What lasting trouble came to the Fran-ciscans, in the first century after their foundation, through the association of a handful of zealots among them with the Eternal Gospel, is one of the commonplaces of the history of the time.

To all who were responsible for the maintenance of a healthy public opinion with regard to fundamental morals, in an age when all men practised a religion of some kind and when all recognised as obvious the connection between mo-rality and religious belief, the activities of such dissidents, whether these were academics or of the more freakish types, was a perpetual anxiety. When the devotees of these sects were rounded up and proved to hold these odd beliefs—or confessed their belief—they were handled very severely. Ca-tholicism and belief in an infallible church are identical. A Catholic who considered himself free to believe as he chose was a contradiction in terms. When his attention was drawn by the Church to some discrepancy in his belief it should have been instinctive to thank his corrector and to rearrange his ideas. To do other than this was to make his own will his guide to God, asserting, "For me, reason, or truth, is what I choose to make it." It was obstinacy defiant before the Di-vine, an outrage such as called for the removal of the offender from among living men. This is not an apology for the pro-cedure, but a description. It is not a modern way of regarding the problem. But it was a way that was universal for centuries, and among Protestants after the Reformation just as truly as among Catholics before it. These obstinate, self-willed-in-matters-of-belief Catholics were the heretics. Their ultimate punishment was to be burnt at the stake.

Moreover, to complete the tableau of the forces ever active against the unity of belief during these centuries, everywhere during the Middle Ages there was the Jew, as trader, physician, banker, often hated and treated brutally, the victim of countless lying tales, but always necessary to the social life. And there was the Saracen also, as mysterious as the Jew and, like the Jew, simultaneously courted and feared. Here were non-Catholics whom, however, no laws for the repression of religious dissidence could touch. It was the essence of such laws that they were for the correction of Catholics. Were the medieval Jews and Saracens really a menace to the long-rooted Catholicism? Who shall say? But from time to time there were hostile reactions provoked by a fairly general subjective certitude about the danger.

ii *The Faith in Practice*, 1500

Etienne Gilson has written, in *The Unity of Philosophical Experience*, that it was one effect of the internecine strife of fifteenth-century Scholasticism to leave the ordinary man "fed up" with the whole business of employing the mind about ultimates. What was the religious practice of the ordinary man about the time when Luther was born? Of a man like Luther's father, and his friends? Of the lawyer who was the father of Thomas More? Of the farmers and peasants and artisans who made up the mass of the Catholics?

The little parish churches, large enough for the tiny communities in which the mass of mankind then lived, survive by the tens of thousands in all the countries of western Europe. And of the external part of religion, of which they were the scene, we know a great deal. The buildings survive and even a part of the fittings, sometimes the very altar, the niches where stood the statues of the patron saints, the screen that separated the sanctuary from the place where the worshippers knelt, with the crucifix that surmounted it and the images of the Blessed Virgin and St. John; the niche for the holy oils used at baptism and at the last rites for the dying, the stoups that held—and hold—the holy water with which on entering and leaving the church the worshipper crossed himself, the consecrated bell that hung in the tower and warned the hamlet of the hours of service. The very books used at the altar and in the choir, the illuminated manuscript missals and graduals, the antiphonaries and psalters survive by the thousand, sometimes in the museums of our great cities and in the libraries of wealthy collectors, sometimes to this day in the very church for which they were bought. In a hundred archives we can find the remains of the once mountainous collection of parish accounts and of the reports on the state of the parish compiled from time to time for the bishop by his various officials at their visitations.

And with all this mass of evidence we can compare the innumerable pictures of parish life preserved in the literature of these past centuries, in the prose tales and in the poetry.

And to one feature all this evidence witnesses with unquestionable unanimity—that the religion, everywhere, was what is nowadays called Roman Catholicism, and that, so far back as we possess evidence at all, it was always this. Who, it may be asked, ever doubted that fact? The discussion nowadays ranges rather about the question: How far were these populations really instructed in their religion? How far did they understand what all this ritual, for example, meant? How far did they, in the practice of their religion, put first things first? How far was their belief pure; that is to say, free from superstition? And closely connected with the enquiry into such matters is the important question of the professional capacity of their clergy.

The Middle Ages—if one ventures on the nonsense of writing a generalisation about one thousand years of human activities—present, at every stage, to the student who observes their life, the most staggering contrasts where, reasonably enough, he might expect to find harmony, logical relation, differences merely of degree. Have other "ages" been, in this respect, unlike the medieval centuries? Be this as it may, no one will fail to marvel at the contrast presented by the supreme competence of the teachers of theology in the great universities and the degree of theological knowledge possessed by the rank and file of the parish clergy. The fact is that the average priest never saw a university, and for his professional training the medieval Church was never able to organise any kind of system at all. And the vast majority of the clergy trained in universities, the doctors of theology and the doctors of Canon Law, passed from their schools to form the great army of professional administrators whom every bishop then needed to employ in the administration of sees where what are now journeys of a couple of hours might then call for weeks of laborious travel.

This utter difference in kind between the mass of the parochial clergy and the clergy who ruled the clerical estate, who inspected its life and the way it conducted its cure of souls, and enacted the very frequent laws for its reformation and improvement, was surely one of the major weaknesses of Catholicism considered as a world-wide system, as the greatest institution of European public life, as the source of all morality: to say nothing of the first importance of the Church, as a thing divinely founded for the continuance, through space and time, of the mission of the Divine Saviour. As regards the relative importance, vis-à-vis the Church's mission, of the several functions of the parish clergy—the explanation to the parishioners of the truth divinely revealed, the administration of the saving sacraments—this is hardly the place to say anything, except to recall that these are so related that one cannot conceive a healthy state of religion where either is regarded as relatively unimportant. And it is true that for the valid administration of sacraments much less training will suffice than for the adequate exposition of the Gospel. It is also true that the less sophisticated the auditory, the simpler the sermon the better. It is not, of course, true that to preach simply is itself a simple matter. But even the simplest of mankind require more than a bald repetition of principles or facts already baldly known, if their notional apprehension is to be transformed into the apprehension that alone produces assent that is effective as living act.

The evidence seems to be conclusive that the average priest was not able really to preach to his parishioners. What sermons, in the real sense of the word, they ever heard were preached when the friars visited the village. Did every village church enjoy the opportunity of such sermons? How often? These questions stare us in the face, and so far we cannot answer them. Without, ever, a first foundation of systematic instruction, without the systematic reminder and development of this which is the business of the preacher as catechist, with nothing more than a kind of lore handed down from one generation of half-educated priests to another, and so to the faithful people, how shall the religion of the ordinary man, who has no books from which he may supply his deficiency, who more often than not is unable even to read, how shall his religion be to him a reality, unless he is beyond the average faithful and constant in prayer?

All this population was baptised with the complex ceremonial of blessings, exorcisms, anointings, catechism of fundamental belief and profession of faith that had come down from the earliest ages of the Church. They received the sacrament called Confirmation at the hands of the bishop and about the age of fourteen were admitted to receive Holy Communion—the actually present, true body and blood of Jesus Christ, God as well as man, under the appearance of a wafer of unleavened bread. Before receiving this sacrament they prepared themselves by a confession of all their serious sins, which together with their sorrow for these as offences against the all-loving Creator, and the words of the priest to whom they made their confession—"I absolve thee from thy sins, in the name of the Father and of the Son and of the Holy Ghost" —constituted the sacrament called Penance. Leaving aside, as far too lengthy a business even to summarise, the question of the frequency with which Catholics received Holy Communion in previous ages, it needs to be said that in these later medieval centuries the Catholic almost invariably received the Sacrament once a year only, at the time fixed in the year 1215 by a famous General Council, the Fourth Council of the Lateran. It was the law of this council that all Catholics should at Easter make their sacramental confession to their parish priest, and in their parish church receive Holy Communion —this under pain of excommunication. Few facts of church history are more disconcerting and more difficult to understand than the infrequency with which, in these medieval centuries, this sacrament was received.

When these Catholics came to marriageable age, they must observe the somewhat elaborate laws against alliance with near relations (the impediment of consanguinity) or with those closely allied to them through marriage (the impediment of affinity), and they knew that their marriage, once it was consummated, was dissoluble only by the death of their spouse. Marriage, again—i.e., the contracting act of the man and the woman making the marriage—was a sacrament. Wherever this took place, with or without witnesses, the effect was that the two who made it were henceforward man and wife. The Church, however, for centuries now, had a ritual for the contracting of marriage, which included, as well as the contracting words pronounced by the spouses-to-be, the priest's blessing

of the matrimonial ring and of the married couple. This ceremony was then followed by the special Mass *pro sponso et
sponsa,* during the most solemn part of which the bride was
led to the altar by her husband and solemnly blessed. Marriages that took place otherwise than according to these public
rites, secret or *clandestine* marriages, were strictly forbidden
and the participants held to penance.

On every Sunday and on another thirty or so major feast
days, holy days (whence our word holiday), all these Catholics went to their parish church to assist at the Eucharistic
rite which was the central part of their religion, the service
called the Mass; a service indeed of praise and prayer and
thanksgiving, but essentially an action, a sacrifice, really offered by the priest, offered in the name of the Church, and
also offered by him as the human agent of the real offerer,
the Divine priest, Jesus Christ Himself; a sacrifice in which
the victim was Jesus Christ. The Mass was Christ once again
offering Himself to the Father as a propitiation for the sins
of the world, not in order to *merit* forgiveness for them, as at
Calvary, on the cross, but in order to provide particular men
with a means of making that forgiveness their own, in order
that the merit won by the cross should be applied. Sunday,
from the earliest times, had been with Catholics what the
Sabbath was—is—to the Jews; the day of the Lord, consecrated
by the testimony of the whole community present at a ritual
worship, and by their abstinence from ordinary toil. To neglect to assist at the Mass on Sundays and on these special
feast days was held a serious sin, as also was the neglect to
observe the law forbidding ordinary work on all these days.

Around the church there were placed statues of the saints
and, painted on the walls, pictures that told the story of the
great events narrated in the Scriptures or in the lives of saints.
One very favourite subject was the Last Judgment, Christ at
the last day of all, judging all mankind. Very notable among
the saints were the special patron of the particular church or
village, the saints traditionally associated with that countryside, above all others, a saint in a class apart, Mary, the mother
of the God-Man Jesus Christ.

These churches, generally, were the great pride of the village, for their statues and pictures and silken hangings, for
some specialty in a vestment, or in the chalice and other sacred
vessels. Countless inventories survive to provide evidence of
these riches. It is characteristic that, in the critical beginning

of the Reformation in England, what fired the smouldering resentment of the peasantry against King Henry VIII was not the dissolution of some hundreds of monasteries but the rumour that the king was now about to abolish hundreds of parishes, destroy their churches, and confiscate their little treasures of plate.

The churches were maintained by the revenue from the lands settled on them when they were first founded, and the priest lived partly on this and partly on the dues, called tithes, which his parishioners paid him. These tithes, and the endowment for sustenance, were the right of the parish priest. Very often indeed it happened that the priest who actually served the church was not, and could not hope to be, the parish priest. In an earlier time, for one reason or another, the benefice had been granted to some college or monastery, so that this religious corporation was henceforward the parish priest, to whom went the whole of the income minus a certain sum, agreed between the benefiting corporation and the bishop of the diocese, which was paid as a salary to the priest who actually did the work, not the *rector* of the parish but his *vicar*. The vast majority of the rural clergy—who, in turn, were the mass of the parochial clergy—were poor men, scarcely any better off than the average of their parishioners. Poor, untrained, isolated, taxed by the bishop, taxed by the pope, and taxed also for the king's benefit, serving the same parish, very usually, for a whole lifetime, little more than a peasant among peasants, this is the man whose professional shortcomings drew such bitter words from his better-situated university brethren, once these had thrown off "the yoke"; nor have the historians treated him any more kindly who have written the panegyrics of those more learned—but not always more charitable, for all their learning.

There is one particular matter where the historians have judged the parish priest very severely as a general cause of scandal. For many centuries it had been the law that priests must not marry, and since the beginning of the twelfth century marriages contracted by a man in holy orders were, by the fact, null and void—i.e., since some 360 years before Luther was born it was just not possible for a priest to marry, even in the most clandestine fashion conceivable. The allegation has been fairly general among historians that with the bulk of these rural clergy their obligations in the matter were disregarded—that they notoriously cohabited with women to whom they could not be married. Certainly there were such priests, and many of them, and casual references to them and to their children in the literature of the time are common enough. Was this the shocking thing it would be to Catholics today? Were they the inevitable grave scandal such priests would be today? It is hard to think so. Again I refer to More, answering Tyndale on the state of the clergy and speaking of priests doing public penance for these offences as almost an ordinary feature of life. Were such priests the rule? This no one has even begun to demonstrate. And the extent of this grave disorder varied greatly from one country to another.

To all these populations, urban no less than rural, the church calendar was a document of the greatest practical importance. Around the system of feasts and fasts the whole of social life turned for centuries. Of all the feasts, the greatest was Easter, the annual commemoration of the triumphal resurrection of the Divine Saviour two days after his sacrificial death on the cross. The commemoration of the passion and resurrection were spread over the whole week from Palm Sunday to Easter Sunday, and the risen life of the Saviour was commemorated through all the next forty days, to the feast of His ascension into heaven. Ten days later the cycle came to an end with the week of feast days that recalled the great day of Pentecost when, strengthened by the marvellous descent of the Holy Spirit, the Apostles of Christ came forth from their hiding place and began the preaching of the Gospel. The Catholic prepared for this long and joyous liturgy of feasts by an equally long period of penitential fasts—the season called, in English, Lent. During the forty days of Lent the use of flesh meat was forbidden and the butchers closed their shops. Only on Sundays was more than one meal eaten. And on every Friday in the year there was the like abstinence from meat and, on perhaps a score of other days too, an obligation to fast. Fasting, almsgiving, and prayer were traditionally the "good works" spoken of in Holy Scripture as characterising the life of the good Christian. This community of ideals and community of observance, no less than the community of worship and the community of belief—and not any remarkable efficiency of disciplinary action—was what made the unity of Christendom a real thing and what kept it in being despite the various "civil wars" that have been mentioned, to say nothing of the real wars between the various Christian princes;

despite, also, the chronic weaknesses (of which those times were at least as conscious as are those who now write their history), weaknesses sometimes all but inherent in the system, but more often due to the stupidity and the sin of those who governed these spiritual communities.

With the subject of fasting seasons and of the feast days that were the holidays, too, of these centuries, the occasion of all manner of communal jollification, we approach that important line where religion is not merely the private affair of the individual relating himself to his Creator, but a force that works upon all social life and is in turn worked on by it. In a world where there was but the one religion and where all publicly professed this religion and were, at least outwardly, devoted to it; where, at every turn, every man had to reckon with the fact of religion, as either a help or a hindrance to his plans—every shade of local feeling, every kind of human impulse, the ideas of music, of poetry, of sculpture and painting which at any time were fashionable, the fears as well as the hopes, the vices as well as the virtues, the whole life of the time, indeed, was bound to find some reflection in religious practice. The popular genius for comedy and for farce, for example, found scope in the religious plays where on feast days such great events as the birth of the Saviour were represented—a comic or grotesque, or unseemly, interpretation being readily placed by the playwright on some of the sacred characters and their acts. The like irreverence, which the modern can find shocking and which authority at the time by no means approved, is often apparent in the religious paintings and carvings. Again, the popular songs of the day were used as the themes for the music to which the *Kyrie, Gloria,* and other texts of the Mass were set. Protestations by authority, edicts, and threats fell on deaf ears. For reasons that will be given, the reaction of authority to what should have been its main concern had long been merely mechanical. To its empty, minatory gestures few, by the end of the Middle Ages, paid any attention whatever.

That familiarity of this sort with sacred things, personages, histories, rites, on the part of an illiterate population possessed of the bare rudiments of religious truth and as material-minded as workaday people tend to be, should breed a distorted version of religion is not surprising—making primary in its own religious life what, of its nature, is by comparison of little importance; giving to mint and cummin[7] the place that belongs only to the weightier things; and by its ignorant misuse of religion transforming the very nature of what it professes to reverence, until it ends by piously venerating what, in point of fact, are degrading superstitions. There was in these centuries, it cannot be denied, a cult of the saints for ends that were purely material, some particular saint being venerated and invoked about whom nothing was known by the devotee except that—so it was held—this saint duly invoked, some particular material benefit was speedily experienced. Or the supposed benevolence of the patron was understood to be linked to a particular set of words, or to the repetition of this a particular number of times, or to the petition being made before a particular image of the saint, or on particular days. Or saints were invoked for such things who had no existence outside the legend, which came down from no one knew whom, and the prayers of their devotees. The Reformers, not surprisingly, had much to say about this caricature of religion. That it was widespread, very general, we can learn from a witness of such uncontestable authority as Thomas More, when in his controversial writings he deals with the Reformers' deductions from the facts. The very Mass became associated with the like material superstitions, people endlessly speculating on the ratio of Masses said to benefits received, for example, and passionately anxious for certitude that the Mass said had achieved what they hoped.

Allied with the genuine and reasonable cultus of the saints, there was an amazingly lively devotion to their relics; and this, too, had its corrupt and superstitious counterpart. There were bogus relics in plenty, against which people were warned, and there were relics which were taken as genuine which it is hardly credible that reasonable men can ever have believed to be what they were said to be. There were relics, presented as genuine, that nowadays dared scarcely be named, or one would be thought to be inventing an unseemly, irreligious jest, but relics for which those more down-to-earth, or cruder, or less mealymouthed Catholics professed an intense devotion. Again let the reader turn to Thomas More, familiarity with whom will soon convince him that, in this matter of popular religion, to move back five hundred years is to meet a humanity very often unlike our own. And when the all but incredible

[7] Matthew, xxiii, 23.

coarseness, not of Luther's language, but of Luther's mind with regard, say, to marriage is to be discussed, let this open pious joy in these highly unlikely relics be recalled.

Abuses in the matter of praying to the saints were general, and abuses of the cult of their relics. More makes no difficulty about the fact. What he does deny is the insinuation that these abuses were official practice, and he suggests—how rightly—that there is an obstinacy in the ignorantly religious that no human power seems able to overcome. Witness those pests of our own day, the inventors and circulators of chain-prayers, at the root of whose industry lies that "pertinacity" which, of old, was held to constitute the essence of the here-tic's crime. As to the Reformers' suggestion that these devotees thought that it was the actual statue that rewarded them, More dismisses it as a lie invented by his opponent for the occasion.

There remains another superstition that calls for notice, for it had the most frightful consequences as long as it endured —the belief in witches.

By a witch is to be understood one who, through a pact with the devil, has acquired a more than human knowledge of events and more than human powers over the world of nature. A witch, if benevolently minded, can be a source of help all round; if malevolent, the witch is evidently a terrible scourge—supposing always that there are such creatures. Belief in their existence is, seemingly, as old as humanity itself. It is still undoubtedly active; and, not uncommonly, among men and women whose belief in the witch's power is the nearest they ever get to belief in God.

The long history of the mass of superstition that grew up around the possibility that believers, by a conscious apostasy from God and a deliberate offer to the devil of the honours and the obedience due to God alone, by a kind of profession of faith, in fact, in the devil as God, could attain to more than natural powers must be read in the books that tell it. What interests the historian of the two centuries that immediately precede the Reformation is that, with the beginning of the fourteenth century, under Pope John XXII, the attitude of the Church to the long-standing fear and hatred of the people alleged to be witches began to change. For this pope made accusations of witchcraft matter for the papal inquisitors into charges of heresy, the ground for this legal development being that witchcraft had for its basis a pact with Satan.

From about the year 1400 these accusations begin to multiply; and there are continual conflicts about the trials between the rival authorities who claimed jurisdiction over them, the royal courts, the courts of the bishops, and the Inquisition. We are now in the great age called the Renaissance, but the men who keep their head while this fanaticism spreads and develops are few indeed. The belief that the world is full of witches and that these are easily recognisable and must be put to death, as a duty to God, is all but universal. And the superstition will receive fresh life from the Reformation and will reach its height in the countries dominated by Calvinistic forms of Protestantism. All men, then, know of the witch and her dealings with Satan, the pact, and a host of witless obscenities; of the witch's "familiar," the petty spirit who is her companion, disguised from men's sight as a cat or a toad; of the reunions of witches for the worship of the devil, to which they fly through the air by their diabolical powers; of the blight they cause to crops, and the plagues with which they destroy cattle; of the way they cause those whom they dislike to wither away, etc., etc.—all this based on rumour, breeding fanatical panic fear (and, very explicitly, the fear of consequences should one not accept the accusations as true directly one hears them) and a hideous sanctimonious ferocity in the punishment of the accused.

In the year 1484 the newly elected pope, Innocent VIII, instigated by two expert witch-hunters, two German Dominican friars who had long served the Inquisition in the Rhineland, published a bull to regulate the whole business of these trials and primarily to decide once and for all that these accusations were to be dealt with by the Inquisition alone. But in this solemn document, in the preamble, the pope recited the whole tale of what the witches were said to be and their employments, and accepted the tale as true: all the nonsense, all the obscenity, all the stories of practical malevolence, the totality of the legend that for a hundred years nearly had been driving men mad with fear in every corner of Europe. And three years later the pope's two advisors combined to publish a kind of *Summa* of the subject, a huge handbook for Inquisitors, the *Malleus Maleficarum*, in which the whole legend is carefully set out, and the law, and the procedure—the torture, the obscene examinations, etc., etc.

iii *The Rulers of the Church*

No one at all familiar with the careful control of the life of the universal Church characteristic of the papacy for generations now, who scans the list of disastrous developments that mark the history of the Church in the fourteenth and fifteenth centuries, can help asking the question: What, meanwhile, were the authorities doing? Which brings one immediately to a second question: What were the authorities in a position to do? In few matters is the contrast so startling between Catholic life then and now as in the papacy's actual exercise of its powers and in what lies between the papal desire to make changes or reforms and the chances of any practical realisation of the desire.

Since we cannot, every few pages, go back to the primitive Church and trace thence the development of each problem and of the solution appropriate to it, down to the generation of the first Reformers, let us now go back no more than four hundred years, to the election in 1073 of the pope whose name is proverbially associated with the classic struggle to free the Church from the control of the lay princes, to St. Gregory VII. We first note that his victory was incomplete, that it was largely an external victory, that although the worse abuses never returned—just as the darkest days of social life never returned—the lay prince remained, at heart, unconvinced that he should not have the decisive voice in, for example, the nomination or election of the great ecclesiastics. The papacy itself—after the crisis of the reign of Alexander III (1159–81) —was indeed safe, but the endeavours of the princes to secure the sees and the great abbeys for the candidate of their choice never really ceased: and very naturally, for the bishop and the abbot were great feudatories, responsible for the social welfare of vast areas, for the contentment of their populations, repression of crime, administration of justice, collection of taxes when such were levied, raising of troops to serve the prince in time of war. So long as kingdoms were organised in this way, and so long as the resources of the Church, vital for its mission of charity, and the prestige of the Church too, were linked with the way kingdoms were organised, just so long must this chronic duel about ecclesiastical appointments continue—unless the princes and the pope could arrive at some working agreement. And this, in the end, was what happened.

The princes recognised the pope's right to appoint, and the pope (usually) appointed the man of the princes' choice.

It would be most useful here, were it feasible, to say something of the atmosphere of that Curia Romana in which and through which the popes transacted their business with the universal Church, to note (were we able) how it varied if not from one pope to another, certainly from one age to the next; to compare the comparatively simple administration of such monastic reforming popes as Gregory VII and Urban II (1088–99) with the rapidly developing bureaucracy of, say, Alexander III; and this, again, with the more or less finished product of such a creative legist as Innocent IV (1243–54). And it would need to be noted for how great a part of the twelfth and thirteenth centuries the pope was an exile from his city of Rome, driven forth by the turbulence of the citizens or of his unruly baronage allied, it might be, to the imperial enemy. By comparison with these days, "the seventy years captivity" at Avignon is for the papacy a time of unusual peace. It is a period, also, which has a great unity from the character of the seven French popes who there succeeded one another: lawyers of very high capacity, for the most part, administrators, all of them, with clear ideas of their goal— and of the means appropriate to attain it.

Had organisation for its own sake been their aim, these popes could scarcely have managed better. They built up a marvellous governmental machine in their city of Avignon, the most evident sign of whose efficiency to the Christian world was its system of taxation—money, and still more money, being called for to maintain the wars in Italy for the protection of the Papal State. The Church itself was now organised like a state—to the general resentment of the official ecclesiastical world everywhere, outside the Curia; and to the resentment, more or less instructed, of the layman too. Once crisis came, this bitterness would reap a full harvest. Crisis came, of course, when for nearly forty years rival popes contended for the allegiance of Catholics; forty years of practical plans for reunion, of drastic theories about the right of the Church to coerce the pope and to depose the pope; of opportunities for princes to break down the operation of the wonderful Avignon machine, to wrest more rights of appointment from these popes-in-difficulties, to wrest also from them special arrangements about monies due to the pope from the princes' own people. All came to a head in the long years of the Council of Constance

(1414–18), which ended with a series of treaties—the first concordats—between the newly elected pope whom the whole Church acknowledged and the rulers of England, France, Spain, and Germany: extensive surrenders on the part of the pope.

These are not pleasant subjects for the Vicar of Christ to be haggling about with Christ's faithful people. But for a long time now the marvellous competence of the professional administrators had been producing its common—not inevitable—result. The apostolic spirit—the *élan intérieur*—had been steadily disappearing from the whole corps of the rulers of the Church. The diminished personalities of the popes of these times are only too close a reflection of their anaemic view of their pastoral office. And once free of the menace that would reduce their primacy to a mere chairmanship—the objective of the so-called Conciliar Movement that had developed in the time of the schism, and now dragged on for a good thirty years after Constance—the main energies of the popes went to repair the losses the Papal States had suffered; to rebuild Rome itself, in whose streets the grass had grown for years now, where wolves lived in the ruins, coming out at night to prey on the corpses of the recently buried dead. This work of restoration, the accompanying struggle to maintain their independence in the Italy of the Sforza and the Malatesta, and the new everlasting struggle with their cardinals—all this, again, was a distraction inseparable from another temporal care that was certainly a part of their duty: leadership, namely, in the great revival of letters. How to lead this, to be the patron of all that was best, and yet escape, not indeed the renascent paganism, but such a preoccupation with all these glories that made the labour to promote them the main business of everyday? Here was a problem that none but saints could have solved: to be so detached from the good, in serving the good, that the needs and interests of the better and the best do not suffer; and though there were some men of exemplary lives among the popes of the Renaissance, they were none of them saints.

The Roman Curial system, as it operated by the close of the Middle Ages, is easily described in its principles. All matters of policy were discussed by the pope and the whole body of his cardinals in the assembly called the consistory. The consistory was also the highest of all the church courts, where sentence was given by the pope in person. It was in the consistory, again, that the creation of new cardinals took place and appointments were made to vacant sees. Lawyers appeared before it to plead in the great suits of the day, and the ambassadors of the various princes to enlist support for their masters' policies, to ward off censures, to make amends for offences when it was thought wiser to withdraw from some anti-papal course.

The high importance which, by the end of the fifteenth century, the cardinals had long enjoyed dated from the year 1059, when Pope Nicholas II decreed that for the future the cardinals were the sole electors of the pope-to-be. These elections, since 1274, had, by law, taken place in what came to be called the conclave—by which is meant that the electors, with a handful of secretaries and servants, were completely segregated from the outer world, in a walled-off portion of the papal palace. While they were free to choose whom they would, they almost invariably chose one of their own number.[8] For the first two hundred and fifty years after the decree of Nicholas II the number of the cardinals at any given time was very small, rarely more than twelve. There was no obligation on the pope to create any special number, or indeed to create any. With the coming of the Avignon popes the number began to grow. In 1352 there were 26, at the election of Martin V in 1417 there were 36 (the creation of the three papal rivals, Gregory XII, Benedict XIII, and John XXIII). In the conclave of 1484 there were 32, and thence the number grew steadily until, in 1587, Sixtus V fixed their number at 70. A majority of two thirds of the cardinals present in the conclave was needed to elect the pope (since the third General Council of the Lateran, 1179).

The cardinals, in these last centuries of the Middle Ages, were a much greater power than modern times have known. The popes not only consulted them on all matters of high importance, but, by custom, very often were guided in their decisions by the opinion of the majority; and in the consistories the general opinion of the cardinals about proposed additions to their number could be decisive even against the expressed desire of the pope. The cardinals enjoyed, in addition to their share of the revenues of the college which they formed,

[8] In the fourteenth century Clement V (1305–14), Urban V (1362–70), and Urban VI (1378–89) were never cardinals. All the popes since the last-named have been chosen from among the cardinals.

a well-defined share of the general income of the Roman See. The most extraordinary sign of their importance, and of their own view of their place in the Curia, is the practice that developed at elections of popes, from 1352, of the cardinals drawing up a kind of pledge, which each swore to observe, that if elected he would renounce certain rights, or admit the cardinals to a larger share in the administration, or to a more generous share in the revenues. These were the so-called capitulations, which it was usually the first act of the newly elected pope to disavow as being necessarily wrong and unlawful.

One natural effect of the extraordinary prestige which the cardinals enjoyed was that their own sovereign tended to use them as agents at the papal court—for the promotion of his own interests—and to subsidise them liberally, if not with actual cash, then with nominations to valuable abbeys and sees to which he had a right of appointment. And next, the princes made great efforts always to have one at least of their subjects created cardinal. The history of the consistories from the middle of the fifteenth century onwards is filled with struggles between the popes and the Catholic princes about such demands. Popes, now, could no longer take it for granted that a cardinal's first loyalty was to the Holy See. They began to protect themselves by creating some near relative a cardinal and using him for their confidential business. And about the same time that these new developments first showed, the popes began the practice of giving the cardinal's hat to prelates who were diocesan bishops and who continued to function as the bishops of these sees after their creation, rarely coming to Rome save for the ceremony of their creation and then for the election of a new pope—there were, indeed, cardinals (and very famous cardinals) who never appeared at Rome even for these important purposes. Wolsey, for example, never saw Rome in his life; not even the conclaves of 1521 and 1523, in which he was so passionately interested, drew him to Rome.

From the mid-fifteenth century each conclave tended to be the occasion of something like a battle between the cardinals associated with the various states of the Italian peninsula. From the end of that century the battles were still more serious and the cardinals in conflict as the agents of such nascent powers as Spain and France and the Empire. Their nationality now began to matter extremely. One of the features of contemporary church history has been the progressive increase in the proportion of non-Italian to Italian cardinals. One hundred or so years ago, at the election of Pius IX (1846–78), the Sacred College was all but wholly Italian, with a great number of the Italian bishops of sees within the pope's own dominions. What of this question of nationality in these bygone centuries when the cardinals were powerful enough to dispute the administration of the Church with the very popes?

The seven French popes of 1305–78 created, in all, 134 cardinals—111 of these were Frenchmen, Italy had but 16, there were two Englishmen in the list and five Spaniards. At the time of the resettlement of Constance (1417), of the 36 cardinals who took part in the election of Martin V, 20 were Italians. Under the next five popes (1417–71) the Italians were a minority, but from the election of Sixtus IV, in 1471, they gradually came to dominate in the Sacred College. Not, of course, that 21 Italians in a conclave of only 27 meant an easy victory for some Italian cardinal. The Neapolitans, the Venetians, the Milanese, the Romans—by comparison with what now obtains, these were distinct, and sometimes bitterly hostile, nationalities.

The cardinals were immensely powerful lords in Holy Church, and each had his train of clients, great wealth, and an influence that reached far beyond the borders of Rome and even of Italy. Yet the cardinalate as such was a purely human office, the creation of many generations of popes. The divinely appointed rulers of the Church are the pope and the diocesan bishops. Of these last there were some 700 at the end of the fifteenth century. What of them?

The jurisdictions of these 700 bishops were very unevenly distributed over the various states of western Europe. In Italy, the only part of the old Western empire of the Romans to be at all extensively christianised, the primitive idea still obtained of a diocese so small that the bishop might almost seem able personally to know all his subjects. There were, in fact, as many as 277 Italian sees. In those lands where the effect of the destructive centuries had been more severe and where the movement of conversion and the establishment of sees had gone hand in hand with the development of the new feudal civilisation, where the bishops were, from the beginning, territorial magnates, vassals and nobles of the new kingdoms, the pattern was very different. In France, for example, there were 118 sees; in the peninsula to the south of the Pyrenees (where, from the year 711, the main business of life for centuries was the destruction of the Moorish kingdom) there were 57. In all the vast area nominally subject to the emperor, there were only 65. In England and Wales there were 21, in Scotland 13, Ireland 34, in the three Scandinavian countries 27; Poland had 16 bishops, Hungary 19, and the lands on the eastern shore of the Adriatic, christianised since the fourth century, 41.

Enough has already been said about the way in which religion and the life of every day had for centuries interacted, the one upon the other, to dispense the writer from any need to explain further why so high a proportion of the men who were bishops at the time when Luther was born were, to our notion of things, as far removed as might be from what the word bishop suggests to us. Lords secular, they then were, no less than lords spiritual; all but invariably chosen (in practice) by their own sovereign; high officers of state, often enough, at the same time that they were bishops—in Germany the actual rulers of the state, sovereign rulers in all but name. The big man, socially and politically, of the whole countryside, wealthy, magnificent in the formal etiquette of his movements, ruling his diocese through a host of officials, professionals of the Canon Law, with his tribunals for offences of the spiritual order, and his prisons: even when the bishop was not (as too many were, under such a system) a man for whom the appointment was little more than a title to an income, even when the bishop was a good professional administrator who personally ruled his diocese, the distance that separated him from his clergy and his flock reduced the great title Father in God to little more than legal jargon, words with no more reality than the adjective in the phrase, "Dear Sir," with which all our letters begin.

This, I fear, reads very savagely, and yet the evidence that such prelates were then so common as to be the type is constant and general. It is notoriously dangerous to quote reformers of any sort—political no less than religious—as necessarily exact when they describe what they desire to see changed; and it is also notorious that in the Middle Ages the wildest language was habitually used, conventionally used, and, it would seem, of obligation, once the mind turned to consider an enemy. The chroniclers, the satirists, the preachers, the bulls of the popes, the indictments of the criminal courts of the bishops and the princes—in all of these, and in all kinds of circumstances, we can note in this respect the same abandon, the same swollen list of crimes alleged, and the same litany of denunciatory texts from the Scriptures, all in a kind of conventional, ritual gesture. With which in mind we can recall the judgment of a once famous French legist, Cardinal Jean Lemoine, writing in the early fourteenth century a commentary on the Canon Law, and in this piece of highly technical scholarship pausing to remark, apropos of bishops—his subject at the moment—"Nowadays, none of them, or very few unhappily, are ever to be found leading their flocks to the pasture. What is to be noted is that all of them think only of shearing the sheep. Finding food for the sheep is not what occupies them. It is the wool that they are interested in and not the sheep."

Only too often the bishop was an absentee; he might, at the same time, hold more than one see; and while he held two or even more sees, he might have the additional anxiety that he had been promised a fourth when it should become vacant; absenteeism, pluralities, expectatives are the triple scourge of the episcopate, terms that recur continually in the writers of the time, abuses of so long standing that they must have seemed to be as old as religion itself, so much a part of things that it would probably always be the same. And, in cold fact, the Church in western Europe had not, by its sin as it were, lately declined from some golden age. It had come into being in those centuries of iron, when semi-savages dominated its world, and if after hundreds of years it had largely converted the savages, it had had to struggle from the first against itself becoming barbarian, and the struggle was not yet over.

These bishops who held more than one see did not, of course, achieve their good fortune merely by the pleasure of their sovereign. For this, all of them needed and had obtained from the pope a special dispensation. What, on the other hand, an absentee bishop could mean to a diocese we can faintly guess from the welcome given to Cardinal Borromeo—St. Charles Borromeo—when in 1565 he took possession of his diocese of Milan, the first Archbishop of Milan to live in the diocese in a hundred years. Milan was by no means the only great see to suffer in this way. Sometimes the non-resident bishop did not trouble to get himself consecrated; sometimes he went for all his life not even ordained priest. There were also sees which, for a hundred years and more, had descended from uncle to nephew and had become a kind of family property. Needless to say that the nobility found these high ecclesiastical posts a wonderful opportunity as provision for their younger sons, and presently kings used them as a means to maintain their bastards. In every court of Europe during the fifteenth century one comes across specimens of these various scandals sooner or later. Not all bishops, of course, were like this, but there were so many like this that few people can have been ignorant that such existed.

And I pass over the matter of bishops who, in despite of all law, managed to have families of their own and to provide for them out of the wealth of the Church. No more need be said of this grave scandal than that it reached the very papacy, when, arrived in their later life at the supreme see, elderly men could be so little embarrassed by these relics of their *jeunesse orageuse* that they brought them forward, acknowledged them, ennobled them, married them well, and spent a not inconsiderable amount of their diplomatic energy in efforts to work them into the families of the reigning princes.

CHAPTER TWO

The Reformer's Europe

How was the life of western Europe organised politically in
these last years which we may call the Eve of the Reformation?
There is no aspect of human life that can be safely ignored,
in even the slenderest account of the event. Political history
is among the factors that are primary. Princes, and the interests of their states, will play a large part in this story.

At the time when Luther was born (November 11, 1483)
there were two great monarchies which, for nearly five hundred years, had dominated what it is tempting to call—but
scarcely correct—the international life of Europe: the empire
—Germany—and the kingdom of France. The bitter rivalry
of these two powers is to be the leading feature of European
history for the next 160 years. Both will be shaken to the
foundations by the religious revolution in one or other of its
phases. A third power, whose importance had been obscured
for nearly a hundred years by misgovernment and civil war
but which will presently reappear and play a leading part in
these struggles, is England. Finally there is the country we
today call Spain. In 1483 it is only just emerging as a potential
power since the succession, in 1474 and 1479, of the married
heirs to the kingdoms of Castile and Aragon, whose territories
took in the whole of the peninsula except Portugal and the
Moorish kingdom of Granada. Italy, except as a term used in
literature, had no existence. The northern plain, and the long
peninsula running thence to the south, and the three great
islands were the territory of a dozen independent and rival
states. The three scantily populated Scandinavian kingdoms
were, like Scotland, of scarcely any importance at all in

European affairs. The chief interest of Poland was the menacing barbarian state to the east; and, to the south of Poland, the kingdom of Hungary was the last line of European defence against the aggressive Turks. In the opening years of the sixteenth century—the birth years of the Reformation—it is the Turkish empire that is the most powerful of all the European states, by reason of its armed forces.

Let us examine more closely, with some elementary comparative statistics, the relation of the more important of these states to the general international position.

The leading power is France, with an area of something under 200,000 square miles and a population of perhaps 16,-000,000. No king has anything like so many people under his rule in one single, compact territory. The new Spanish kingdom is about the same size as France but has only one half its population. England, the southern two thirds of the island of Great Britain, is little more than one fourth the size of France, and its population is probably no more than 3,000,-000. Of the four leading powers, the empire is, *in theory*, the greatest, with perhaps 300,000 square miles of contiguous territory and perhaps 20,000,000 people in all. But the empire, as we shall see, is a case apart. In Italy and its three islands of Corsica, Sardinia, and Sicily—about 120,000 square miles—the subjects of the several ruling powers number perhaps 12,000,000.

Western Europe has a total of 60,000,000 people, where today the calculation (all but accurate, where these sixteenth-century figures are never more than learned conjecture) gives something like 280,000,000. The Reformation world, so very scantily peopled, is also a much larger place than ours, for it then takes months to travel distances that we can cover in a day. This is a first point on which to meditate at some length if we are to make the necessary effort to realise that life then and now was so different that it is tempting to say the two are wholly different.

Of the 16,000,000 people who dwelt in the great contiguous domain of the King of France, he was the absolute lord —that is to say, there was no one of them, nor any group of them, who possessed the right to oppose a negative to the royal policies, whether in the internal ruling of the country or in its relations with other countries. From the moment we say this we must, however, begin to qualify all our summary sentences. The historian of these ages who warns us that the boundaries of the various states were never so precisely, and one might say so definitively, settled as in modern times is careful to warn us also that the scope of the ruler's power and of his subjects' right was usually no more clearly defined. There could be overlapping jurisdictions claiming obedience from the same set of men. And, without any man's mind being disturbed by the fact, there might be in the one state several nationalities. Nonetheless, it is not impossible to answer fairly and simply, and with no substantial distortion, the concrete question: How far, in any given state, was the ruler master of the lives of his people, and what was the basis of his authority over them?

The King of France was the lawful ruler because he was the last king's lawful heir. Monarchy in the sixteenth century was all but universal, and in almost every land this meant hereditary monarchy. And in the history of all these monarchical states there had been one feature common for centuries, the continual discussion about the powers of the king and the privileges of his subjects; discussions, and on both sides vigorous efforts to maintain or to extend what was claimed. Under weak kings the nobility and the towns achieve a privileged position, exemption from the control of the king's officials, it may be, or the right to say how much they will contribute to national expenses. The strong kings, on the other hand, never cease in their efforts to drain all political reality out of such privileges. In every country of the West the medieval centuries are a time of constant interaction of this kind between the ruler and the more powerful of his people. And one of the foundation facts of all these countries needs to be borne in mind; namely, that in the primitive organisation with which they emerged from the Dark Ages, the possession of land, originally a concession from the ruler, while it entailed the responsibility to maintain peace and justice, necessarily carried with it a wide autonomy. The duke, the count, the baron, the bishop, for all that he was the king's man, had enjoyed, by the necessity of the case, by immemorial custom, and by universal consent, considerable independence vis-à-vis his overlord the king.

Gradually, in the course of the eleventh to the fifteenth centuries, as the long social crisis gave place to more settled times, as the first signs of political and administrative genius appeared, nourished on faint reminiscences of the ancient law of Rome, the kings managed slowly to make their own imme-

diate, personal authority the chief reality throughout their
kingdoms; over the vassals of their great feudatories no less
than over their own immediate vassals. This had taken place
almost everywhere in western Europe by the end of the
fifteenth century except (a fact of the utmost importance) in
the lands to the east of the kingdom of France. Here the
supreme overlord, the German king, called also the emperor,
was by this time but a nominal chief; and his feudatories
were, in fact, independent sovereigns.

The King of France ruled through his council; that is,
through the great officers of state, the chancellor, treasurer,
constable (for the army), admiral (the navy), and four secretaries of state. There was no law to bind the king, defining
who should compose this council or to say that the king
should follow their advice or even ask it. And in the Parlement
of Paris—which was at once a court of law and an administrative body—the king had the best of instruments for the defence
and extension of the royal jurisdiction against all others,
whether of the underlords (who will increasingly be no more
than the nobles of the kingdom) or of the Church. The nobles
were already beginning to be little more than a caste: wealthy
men well-dowered with estates in land, their families enjoying the greatest possible social prestige and many hereditary
privileges in matters of law and taxation. But, so far as real
power over others went, the nobles were gradually yielding
place to the corps of royal officers. More than any other country of the time, France was governed by such officials. It was
the king who named them, and to the king alone they were
responsible. They were not minor politicians, nor royal favourites, but professional legists and administrators, trained in the
Roman Law. As the laws of the kingdom were the king's sole
act, so the taxes were what he chose to levy. There was no
manner of consultation of the subjects, not even of the nobles,
in the ordinary government of the country. And by "the
country" we must understand, at the beginning of the sixteenth century, the whole land of France. For the last of the
semi-independent dependencies had by now been united to
the kingdom since King Francis I married the heiress of the
last Duke of Brittany. One family alone remained who could
at all seem to challenge the royal power, the Bourbons, descended from a younger son of the thirteenth-century king,
St. Louis IX. Their lands formed a great T in central and
southern France, with the city of Clermont roughly where the

arms crossed, the arms running 100 miles to east and west and 150 to the south. This semi-royal family was to go over to the Reformed religion midway through the sixteenth century and then to give to France one of the most famous of its kings, Henry IV, who ruled from 1589 to 1610.

The semi-island kingdom of England, so very much smaller than any of the other powers of the time, forms a striking exception, in the way it was governed, to what now obtained everywhere else. The Englishman of today, were he back under the Tudor régime where the role of the state, it has been well said, was that of the prying steward of some great nobleman, would think himself subjected to despotism indeed. But nowhere else in the world were there, in the sixteenth century, such checks on the power of the ruler; nowhere else had a subject the Englishman's opportunity lawfully to criticise and to oppose the ruler's projects of laws; and nowhere, except in England, did it so rest with the subjects to say how far they should be taxed. England's regularly functioning Parliament, and Parliament's control of taxes, made it a country apart; and no less remarkable, as a force that worked against despotism in the ruler, was the national system of law, the Common Law of England, "the one system of Christian law to come out of the Christian Middle Ages," and perhaps the greatest of all the forces that differentiated the English way of life from that of the rest of Christendom.

In England there was no noble caste. The only nobles were the men actually summoned, or with the right to be summoned, to the House of Lords, and their wives. A nobleman's children, even his heir, were commoners. And the nobleman's privileges in law were very few; in the matter of taxation he had none. For centuries now the whole criminal justice of the country had been in the king's hands, and trials, also, of all suits about a subject's rights. Nor were these English nobles at all numerous. By the end of the fifteenth century there were not more than 50 of them, dukes, earls, viscounts, barons. And when at a Parliament they came together in the House of Lords, they were usually outnumbered by the spiritual lords, the 21 bishops and the 31 abbots, whose voting strength was never diminished by the fact that some were under age. The lay lords present usually numbered about 40.

Below the nobles, in point of social prestige, and yet well above the common people, was that most important class, so hard to define, the gentry: the owners, for centuries, of great estates which they rented out as farms; a class often inter-married with the nobles, made up in great part of the descendants of the younger sons of nobles, and the class from which, in every generation, the new nobles were taken; the class from which the king chose his unpaid, untrained local justices, who were the foundation of law and order throughout this kingdom where (as in all states then) there were no police and, what is more surprising in the sixteenth century, not even the beginnings of a standing army. The gentry also made up a good proportion of the members elected to the House of Commons.

By the time the so-called Reformation Parliament was summoned in 1529, the House of Commons was made up of 308 members, 74 from 37 counties, four from the city of London, and 230 from 115 other cities and boroughs. The counties varied greatly in size and population. Wales was not represented until 1536, nor Cheshire. Durham had to wait for its representation until the seventeenth century. In the county, the qualification for a vote was the possession of a freehold worth forty shillings annual value—which is as much as to say that, of the farming population, only the substantially well-to-do had a vote. London at this time was a city of perhaps 100–120,000 inhabitants. The total of the next three largest cities, York, Bristol, and Norwich, would be scarcely 30,000. Five thousand inhabitants was then a large population for a city or a borough. Of the 115 towns represented in Parliament, were there even 25 as large as this? The right to a vote in these "urban" constituencies varied greatly, as did the number of voters. What seems beyond doubt is that the elections were the business of the body that governed the town, in practice an oligarchy of the most prosperous storekeepers and the manufacturers. Also, the town was generally so small that the local great landlord—especially if he were a noble—could influence its "political" life without difficulty.

Finally, the king's government usually took a hand in the election, if only by sending a general message about the kind of men it wished to see elected—this to the sheriffs of the counties as well as to the mayors of the towns. And in places where the lands were royal property—the boroughs in the far-spread Duchy of Lancaster, for example—or seaports, the government actually chose the man to be elected. Hence the question whether a particular Parliament was "packed" needs to be considered with the fact in one's mind that all parlia-

ments were more or less "packed" at this time, the fact that
the government could always more or less procure the election of the men it wanted to see in the House of Commons.

Of the detailed procedure in the House of Commons we
know very little. That the initiating of bills on public matters lay with the crown—as today it lies, in practice, with the
cabinet—we might take for granted even if we had no evidence.
There was freedom of speech—always with the possibility that
a man might have to explain his language to the king's council
and even be sent to the Tower to reflect on his hardihood.
There could be obstinate opposition to the king's projects—
which were put forward in the House by the members who
were also of the king's council—and the opposition could prevail. To beat it down or to coax it into acceptance, the king
himself might come into the Commons' chamber and explain
his intentions.

Parliaments met whenever the king thought fit—which in
the reigns of Henry VII and Henry VIII and Elizabeth was
rarely enough. There was usually one session only—of five or
six weeks at the most—and then the Parliament was dissolved. Henry VIII's fourth Parliament, which was elected in
1529 and sat until 1536, was a revolutionary innovation and
none too popular, with the Commons especially, who found
themselves inconveniently brought up to London each winter
for an expensive six or eight weeks. On the other hand, such
frequent contact of the same men, year after year, in the public business of the House of Commons would breed a new
feeling about the real importance of their class in the government of the country, and a corporate sense too.

Parliamentary life was a reality—it was by no means a matter of merely assenting to the king's decrees. But with the
day-to-day administration of the government, and criticism of
this—one of the chief activities of the modern Parliament—
these Tudor parliaments were very rarely concerned. Administration was the king's affair, and its centre was his council.
Here there sat, along with some of the great nobles, clerics
trained in the Canon Law and the classic Roman Law and
lay professionals of the same sort. We can observe in the mentality of this body and in its procedure—especially in its examinations of those accused of offences against the state—
something of that enthusiasm that is to be seen at this time
all over Europe to build up a strong central government whose
will shall be for the subject the supreme and final law. When

clerics who have spent years in this business are promoted
to be bishops, and when such bishops come to form the greater
part of the hierarchy, we can be prepared to see surrenders
of church rights to the royal will that, in themselves, are
scarcely credible. The local administration—the execution
throughout the country of the laws and of the council's instructions—is not the business of trained professionals, of sal-
aried royal officials; in England these do not exist. The work—
unpaid—is done by the local gentlemen, the Justices of the
Peace. And the activities of these local agents are closely
supervised by the king's council, all complaints made about
them most carefully scrutinised, and exemplary punishment
meted out to offenders.

To return to the Parliament: its principal function was to
vote the king an important part of the money his administration needed, the duties on imports and on exports, and special
taxes for special occasions. And since the English king was
not above the law, but "under God and the law," and since
he could no longer, for long, "live of his own," all kings must
sooner or later summon a parliament—and learn how to manage it.

As there is free speech in the Parliament, so is there also
in the king's courts of Common Law—the King's Bench, the
Court of Common Pleas, and the court of the Exchequer. The
trials are public and the accused knows his accuser and the
witnesses against him, and can interrogate them, as well as
put his own case; and no torture is used on the witnesses.
Decision as to fact does not lie with the royal judge, but with
the jury of the accused man's peers. The English are very conscious of these differences from what obtains elsewhere, very
proud of them as something characteristically English, somewhat scornful of new, superior foreign ways, and determined
to hold to their own.

Spain—the dominion ruled by Ferdinand and Isabella, *los
reyes católicos*, in the year 1500—is a much more complicated
subject to present; and a subject of very high importance for
whoever wishes to understand the Reformation century at all.
France, as a single kingdom, is a greater power, it is true; but
the figures who dominate the whole sixteenth century are two
successive kings of Spain, Charles V (1516–56) and his son
Philip II (1556–98). Between them they rule for eighty-two
years, and they are the consistent, active enemies of all that

the Reformation stands for. Their militant Catholicism is a
kind of instinct with them, as it is with Spain itself, a country
whose history is a mystery unless we bear ever in mind that
it is the one country of western Europe where Mohammedan-
ism ever really got a hold—in the years following the invasion
of 711—and that from the moment of the national reaction
against this victory the fight to expel the Moors and re-
establish Catholicism scarcely ceased for seven hundred years
and more. In the course of those centuries the various Catholic
states, expanding gradually as they drove out the Moors, came
by marriage and by conquest to coalesce. By the middle of
the fifteenth century there were but three kingdoms, Portugal,
Castile, and Aragon. In 1469 the princess who would five years
later be Queen of Castile, Isabella, married the heir to Aragon,
Ferdinand. When he succeeded to that kingdom in 1479, the
Spain of today was created. Only in the south did the Moorish
kingdom of Granada detract from the unity, and in 1492 this
too yielded to the armies of the united nation.

Of the two constituents, Castile was by far the larger, twice
the size of Aragon. But Aragon, with its long Mediterranean
coast line, had had the more adventurous part in international
history. For a good two hundred years and more it had been
the great naval power of the western Mediterranean. All the
islands of that sea, save Corsica, were now its possessions. Its
seaport of Barcelona was one of the world's great cities. And
in the opening years of the sixteenth century the armies of
Ferdinand conquered, from the lately victorious King of
France, the mainland of southern Italy, the so-called kingdom
of Naples, all Italy from the heel and toe to within forty miles
of Rome along the Mediterranean coast, and up to sixty miles
beyond that, on the Adriatic. The King of Spain was thus, by
the time any German—Luther, for example—needed to be
troubled at the thought of this, lord of a good half of Italy
too. Through all the next two hundred years the history of
Italy is inseparable from the history of Spain.

And the history of Spain is inseparable also, for all that
time, from the history of the countries we now call Belgium
and Holland and Luxemburg. It was not that any King of
Spain ever conquered these Low Countries but that one of
their native rulers, the man who was Duke of Brabant and
Count of Flanders and Count of Holland and the rest, and
also—his most magnificent title—Duke of Burgundy, had married Juana, a daughter of Ferdinand and Isabella. When her

only brother predeceased her father and mother and an older sister too, the succession to Spain passed to Juana, and thence to her son by that Duke of Burgundy, Philip the Handsome (1482–1506), whom she had married. That son was the sovereign we know as Charles V: Duke of Burgundy (and so ruler of the Netherlands) at six years old; King of Spain at sixteen, of Sicily too and of Naples; and to become, at nineteen, something more still—the emperor. What were his powers, in reality, over the people and the resources of his Spanish kingdom?

The grandfather whom Charles succeeded had, in the course of his thirty-seven years as king (1479–1516), done much to give Spain a smooth-running, orderly system of administration, and Charles, in a reign of roughly the same length, was to do as much again. In both the kingdoms of Castile and Aragon, the mid years of the fifteenth century had been a time of great disorder, with weak rulers and a turbulent nobility, and everything seemed to be pointing to a coming age of legalised anarchy. To control the nobility of Castile, Isabella allied herself with the towns, and Ferdinand was later to do the same in Aragon. The fortresses of the nobles were reduced, crown lands recovered. And then a new link was forged between the crown and the nobles, when the king secured, as a hereditary right, the grand mastership of the three great military orders of Spain.

The two countries, although governed in all things by the joint action of their married sovereigns, retained nevertheless their own laws and customs. They were still distinct kingdoms at the end of the fifteenth century, and their future relations (should Ferdinand and Isabella not die simultaneously) seemed, in the early years of the sixteenth century, somewhat doubtful.

In both countries there were, to complicate the task of the monarch striving against the anarchy that threatened, elected chambers whose opinions could not be ignored—the Cortes. In Castile, by the time of Ferdinand and Isabella, the clergy and the nobles no longer took any part in the Cortes. And where once fifty towns had sent *procuradores* to represent their interests, now only eighteen were so qualified. The consent of the Cortes had once been required for the validity of all new laws. But from 1505 the king's mere authority was recognised as sufficient to make laws, to interpret, and to amend them as he thought fit. In Aragon the Cortes remained much more of a power. Here there were four chambers—clergy, greater nobles, lesser nobles, cities—and the consent of all four was essential for new laws and for new taxes. In the Cortes each man had the right to complain about grievances, and there was no rule to limit the length of his speech. The principle was also admitted, "No more money until complaints have been remedied." And the king was bound to summon the Cortes, once at least in every two years. There were Cortes, also, for the two states associated with Aragon, the kingdom of Valencia and the county of Catalonia. In what kind of spirit a reforming king of Aragon might expect to be met can be gathered from the words spoken to him by the *justicia* as he imposed the crown, "We, who are as good as you, swear to you, who are no better than we, to accept you as our king and sovereign lord, provided you observe all our liberties and laws: but if not, not."

The actual administration of the realm was the work—yet once again—of a council that was largely made up of highly trained lawyers, with local agents (*corregidores*) to control the numerous self-governing municipalities. What gave strength to this new centralising activity, and made its success certain, was the growing prestige and popularity of the monarchy, as the evident source of the new peace and prosperity.

Spain had two other problems that were peculiar to it and of the utmost gravity, and to deal with them its kings developed a special institution. The problems were the presence in the kingdom of large numbers of Jews and of Mohammedans. The special institution was the Spanish Inquisition—and it came eventually to be of very great importance as a constituent force making for royal absolutism. This Spanish Inquisition was a court set up in Castile, first of all, by Pope Sixtus IV in 1478 at the request of Ferdinand and Isabella. What they hoped to do through this new court was to track down the (allegedly) large number of Jews who, having been converted to Catholicism and accepted baptism, or, being the descendants of such converts, had since secretly reverted to Judaism and, behind the mask of a normal Catholic life, were living again as Jews. Many priests were said to be of this sort. For years now there had been a great deal of unrest about this menace, and from time to time there were demands that the state should "take some action." The bull of 1478 gave the King of Spain the right to name the judges and effectively put this ecclesiastical institution—whose real objective, as an ecclesiastical court, was not punishment, but the conversion of the sinner—under the control of the state. When the machine began to work, appeals and complaints from its victims poured in to Rome. The pope, thereupon, withdrew some of the authority he had granted. The kings protested violently and announced that they would ignore the pope's commands. The crisis ended with the pope surrendering to their threats and restoring all that he had first granted. From now on it was all but impossible for the pope to interfere with the working of the Inquisition. The surrender was the beginning of a state control of the life of the Church such as was never seen in any other country in the world. After the conquest of Granada in 1492, the Moors presented to the kings a curious facsimile of the problem they already had to face in the Jews. They first organised great preaching missions to convert the Moors, who were now Spanish subjects, and conversions followed, many sincere no doubt, but just as certainly many conversions that were prompted by very real fear. These unfortunates, Catholics outwardly, Mohammedans at heart, were obviously matter for the consideration of the Inquisition. In 1492, to simplify the problem, all Jews had been banished from Spain, and in 1502 the Moors too were banished.

The legal penalty for one who, having been won over from heresy or infidelity, relapsed was death by burning. There were now to be many such executions—not, indeed, so many as the legend has it, but enough to bring it about that, for masses of people, the words Spain and Inquisition and cruelty are synonymous.

The boy of sixteen who in January 1516 became King of Spain had, for ten years already, been, as Duke of Burgundy, the ruler of the Netherlands, where indeed he was born and beyond which he had as yet never traveled. This, his original inheritance, was the most valuable of all his possessions. For within the very limited area, perhaps 25,000 square miles, there dwelt something like 4,000,000 people, the wealthiest community in Europe and, after Italy, the most generally cultivated. Here were the cities that had been, for centuries now, the chief industrial centres of the world, with weavers, metalworkers, craftsmen of the fine arts, printers; the greatest seaport in Europe, Antwerp, and the centre of its financial life; a most flourishing university, Louvain; and in Brussels the most splendidly organised court of the time. The Low Countries, or the Netherlands—the plural form is to be noted—were a group of states united only in this, that they had, each of them, the same ruler, ruling by hereditary right. It had taken a good hundred and fifty years for this French family, the dukes of Burgundy, descendants of a younger son of King John II (1350–64), to gather these various lordships into its hands; and how to govern the whole in the interest of the ducal policies had never ceased to be a major political problem. It was indeed a land of towns—many of which were quasi-autonomous—and, in outlook upon the life of the time and in culture, it was the wealthy middle-class burghers who set the tone. But this middle-class society, dominant because the principal cause of the wealth, was nevertheless set in a monarchical and highly aristocratic state, the first state to make the splendours of court etiquette an end in itself, a profession, as it were, or a career. And this dynasty did not cease to be foreign, nor its aims to be primarily dynastic, never truly "national"; and so always the dukes remained an object of suspicion to these subjects who yet so loyally supported their rule and were so proud of the dynasty's magnificence.

In each province there still survived the body called the Estates, whom the ruler must consult and through whom the government was carried on; and to preside over the province, in the name of the dukes, there was the stadholder—always a high noble, and appointed by the duke. Since the year 1463 there had also been a kind of central body, the States-General, in which all the provinces were represented, whose business was to levy general taxes and to make general laws. But this body was more a congress of plenipotentiaries than a general government. None of its decisions could have any effect except in so far as the several states accepted them. The States-General was in no way sovereign. Nor was it elected—the duke appointed all its members. Nevertheless, it was ultimately to develop a life of its own. For in 1531 Charles V set up at Brussels a really effective central administration to which all the Low Countries were subjected: there was a Council of State, for general policy; a Privy Council, to judge disputes between the provinces; and a Council of Finance. All the members of these three councils were appointed by the duke, and for life. In the Council of State the nobility were given places. But the members of the other councils were, for the most part, the professional legists and administrators whom the middle class were producing everywhere and the universities training. Presently, as the great national crisis developed in the time of Philip II, there were to be serious conflicts between the States-General and this administrative bureaucracy.

This monarch who was the master of the Spains, of a good half of Italy, and of the Netherlands might be master indeed, in comparison with the contemporary kings of England. But he needed to be a wholly different kind of monarch according to whichever of his realms he was dealing with, and above all a man gifted with endless patience, if not with universal sympathy. And the man in whom this rich array of power was first constituted, King Charles I of Spain, became, within three years of his inauguration, something more. In June 1519 he was elected King of Germany and emperor—Charles V. He thereby became the sovereign of the Austin Friar who, all but two years earlier, had loosened the first stones of the avalanche now about to carry all central Germany before it, Martin Luther.

The Holy Roman Empire—"not holy, nor Roman, nor an empire" (it was to be written)—was already no more than a splendid name, a titular dignity borne for the last four centuries of its existence by the longest line of hereditary mediocrities that history records. From 1438 to the end, which came in 1806, all the emperors but one were Habsburgs; and of them all, Charles V was the only emperor possessed of any real power. He was the only one of his line who had any resources beyond the hereditary lands of his family in Germany. Charles, Duke of Burgundy and King of Spain, was an emperor with means of his own; the armies of Spain—never to be defeated in a hundred years of European wars—and the commerce of the Netherlands. And even Charles V, as sovereign of the Holy Roman Empire, achieved nothing. Indeed his military adventures as emperor brought him, at the end of his reign, as near to disaster as might be. The actual rulers of the 20,000,000 or so inhabitants of Germany were the princes who nominally were the emperor's vassals, the various dukes, margraves, counts, archbishops, bishops, abbots, knights—to the number of more than 400—and the various free cities. Each of these, in his own dominions, was master absolutely. In one sixth of the territory the ruler was a bishop or abbot.

Three of these prelates, the archbishops of Cologne, Treves, and Mainz, were members of the college of electors with whom lay the choice of the emperor. The other four electors were the King of Bohemia, the Margrave of Brandenburg, the Elector of Saxony, and the Count Palatine. The election of 1519, when Charles V was chosen in succession to his paternal grandfather, the Emperor Maximilian I, was the last for two hundred years in which there was any real doubt as to the outcome. It was a rare opportunity, and various electors made fortunes by taking magnificent bribes from all sides.

The empire as such had no government or administration. Periodically the emperor summoned the Reichstag—usually called, in English, the Diet. This consisted of a House of Electors, a House of Princes, and a House of the imperial towns. There was no constitution; there were no rules and never any certitude, save that nothing would ensue from the deliberations and the decisions taken, save what the individual princes or towns chose to put into operation. The decisions of the Diet were of the nature of treaties negotiated between independent sovereign states.

What did so powerful a king as Charles V gain by being elected to this sham imperial dignity? He certainly kept out his rival, the King of France, whose authorised presence across the Rhine would have been ruinous to Habsburg interests. And not to be elected would have entailed the humiliation that the King of Spain, the German prince whose hereditary lands were almost one fourth of the empire and more extensive than the territories of the next dozen most important princes combined, would be, in Germany, the nominal inferior of some petty duke. The 70,000 or so square miles of Habsburg territories—Austria and the rest—whose capital was Vienna, Charles never, indeed, ruled. He speedily made them over, after his election, to his younger brother Ferdinand, who was soon to be King of Bohemia and King of Hungary and, many years later, to succeed Charles as the Emperor Ferdinand I (1558–64).

Of the eleven states that made up what nowadays is the Italian Republic, the largest was that kingdom of the Two Sicilies which was part of the dominions of the King of Spain. Here alone, in Italy, had there ever been anything like a feudal system and a beginning of parliamentary government. By the time Ferdinand of Aragon had made himself master of the kingdom in the opening years of the sixteenth century, this tradition had already faded away, and in the next half century more and more did the administration take on the

form of a well-centralised despotism. At the other extreme of
Italy, the Duchy of Savoy was still governed, in part, by a
collaboration of the ruler and the Estates; and although in
the states of the Church there were no States-General, the
Estates of the various provinces still continued to function.
In both of these jurisdictions, however, and in Naples too,
these were not meetings of deliberative assemblies but rather
a conference about the taxes between the ruler and those upon
whom would fall the task of raising the money. The three
states of Milan, Florence, and Venice were despotisms—small
compact areas (though Venice had also a "far-flung empire"
in the islands of the Greek archipelago and in the Levant)
where a single will ruled: the harsh brutal rule of successful
condottieri at Milan; the masked control of the millionaire
banking family at Florence—the Medici—soon, after a long expulsion, to be permanently installed there as Grand Dukes of
Tuscany; at Venice an oligarchy, the rule of the wealthy merchants, presided over by the doge, who more and more dwin-
dled into a magnificent ornament of state. Separating Venice
from Florence and the states of the Church lay four small
states of considerable strategic importance, Mantua, Modena,
Parma, and Lucca. Between Savoy and the Mediterranean was
the maritime republic of Genoa, no longer a rival whom Venice had need to fear, but of high commercial importance nonetheless, and lord of the island of Corsica.

In no part of Europe was the Reformation, as a theological
movement, to have less direct effect than in Italy, even after
Calvin had been installed at Geneva, a bare fifty miles from
the frontiers of Milan. But one of these Italian princes was
the head of the Catholic Church, and, on the other hand, the
cosmopolitan republic of Venice was to show itself—to the
constant anxiety of the popes—remarkably indifferent to the
presence of foreign Protestants on its territory, even actively
anti-Catholic Protestants, and the city was a centre whence
Protestant literature circulated throughout the north of Italy.
Moreover, Italy never ceased, throughout the sixteenth century, to draw men of the well-to-do, educated classes from
every part of western Europe. And from one or other of the
Italian states came all the popes who were the target of the
Reformers' zeal, while these Italians were, of course, the leaders of the movement to destroy the Reformers and their work.

CHAPTER THREE

Revival and Restoration
1495—1530

i *The* Devotio Moderna: *Ximenes*

The story of the Reformation cannot profitably be written if
attention is restricted to those countries where Protestant and
Catholic were locked in combat, as though European religious
life during this century had shrunk to this duel. One most
important event in the history of the struggle, for example,
is the council of Trent, and the work done here was very largely
the fruit of the scholarship of Catholic Italy. If the Reformation be regarded, in part, as the outcome of the religious
condition of Europe in the preceding hundred and fifty years
and more, then side by side with the history of what the
Reformers achieved there needs to be set the religious history
of that European world where, for one reason or another, the
Reformers had little influence or, indeed, no influence at all.
There needs to be considered, for example, the story of the
singularly fruitful religious revival in sixteenth-century Spain
and of another renaissance of Christian life in Italy—a rebirth
of the spirit for the heroes of which the contemporary crisis
north of the Alps might as well not have existed. Again, the
Catholic religion in those very lands of the north had never
been left wholly defenceless, in the critical hundred years between Constance and Luther (1418–1517), against the serious evils that have been described. The Reformation—allowing for argument's sake all the claims made for it—was by no
means the effect of a voice raised in a spiritual wilderness. It
is in relation, not to the undoubted abuses alone, but also to
generations of effort at reform that its history must be read.

Never, in all those years when so much was going so steadily
from bad to worse, had there been lacking, throughout the

Church, earnest men and women whose fidelity to the Gospel ideal reached high sanctity and radiated far beyond its first beginnings, the saints' humble anxiety about their own short-comings and sins. These holy souls were the means of renewing the fervour of the convents to which they belonged and of the very congregations. They were apostolic preachers of surpass-ing eloquence, who trudged for a long lifetime all the roads of Italy and France and Spain. There was no country that could not point to the presence of good bishops at some time or another, prelates who recalled their clergy to the observance of the ancient standards and, founding colleges, prepared a better state of things for the future.

The greatest names are but a handful, perhaps,[1] but what a power many of these were, each in his own time for a whole generation and over whole countries: St. Vincent Ferrer and St. Catherine of Siena and St. Antonine of Florence, among the Dominicans; St. Bernadine of Siena, St. John Capistran, St. James of the Marches, and St. Colette, among the Francis-cans; St. Francis of Paola, St. Frances of Rome, and St. Bridget of Sweden, among the founders of new orders; St. John Kenty and St. Casimir in Poland; in France, St. Joan of Arc and the beatified monk-pope, Urban V; in the Netherlands, St. Lydwine and Jan Ruusbroeck; in Italy, saintly cardinals like Niccolo Albergati, Domenico Capranica, Juan Carvajal. In England there were the mystics, Richard Rolle and Mother Julian of Norwich. The Benedictine monks were revived through such great reforms as those associated with the abbeys of Melk in Germany and St. Justina of Padua. In the Low Countries the ancient system of Canons of St. Augustine came to new life in the congregation of Windesheim, to be the cen-tre through all the fifteenth century of the new so-called *Devotio Moderna* and to be immortalized by a single book,

[1] The Catholic Church, as is well known, is accustomed to propose for public veneration the lives and the personalities of deceased Catho-lics who have lived and died in heroic fidelity to the will of God. These are the personages to whom the Church officially gives the title "Saint." It is only given after the most lengthy and elaborate investigation of all available evidence. The Church also allows a cer-tain locally limited cult of those proved to have lived this life of heroic virtue but whose case has not yet progressed to the final stage of canonization. These personages have the title "Blessed." From the period 1476–1521 there have been found, so far, seventeen saints and fifty-nine worthy of veneration as "Blessed."

which to this day is read by millions of all beliefs, the *Imitation of Christ*, the work of one of the canons, Thomas à Kempis. And with this same *Devotio Moderna* and Windesheim there is closely associated a wholly new order whose work lay in a new type of school for boys, the Brothers of the Common Life. From these schools came Nicholas of Cusa (1401–64), who, as an official reformer of church life, is one of the really great men of the fifteenth century. Here the career of Erasmus had its first beginnings. Another of their pupils, Jan Standonck, was the second founder of the austere College de Montaigu in the University of Paris, a house of residence for clerical studies, which Erasmus also will know (and detest), St. Ignatius Loyola too, and—Jean Calvin. The old university was itself the scene of a most vigorous reformation of life in the closing quarter of the fifteenth century—a reformation whose chief purpose was better priests.

Meanwhile, these are the first years of the conquest of the world by the new invention of printing. From the pens of scores of writers in every country of the West a host of works goes now to the presses: prayer books, guides to the spiritual life, books to aid parents to instruct their children in the faith; the *Art of Living Well*, the *Art of Dying Well*, *The Paradise of the Christian Soul*, such titles alone will tell the aims of this new apostolate. Another very popular line is the printed collection of sermons. More than one hundred of these are known from Germany alone. The Bible, too, is printed again and again, translated into the vernacular languages in which all this other literature is written—Italian, Spanish, French, German—but, a spectacular exception, there is no Bible printed in an English translation.

In the centres where all this new world of piety is developing, new forms of devotion are gradually appearing, to the Blessed Sacrament of the Eucharist, for example; to the Heart of Jesus crucified for love of men; to the mystery of Christ's nativity; to the sorrows of Mary, His mother; and, side by side with the Rosary, there begin to appear the first of those Stations of the Cross, which for centuries now have been one of the most familiar of Catholic aids to a devoted life.

One of the most remarkable books yet written about these critical years, which its author (like many another) sees as *The Waning of the Middle Ages*, has familiarised two generations of readers already with all that is decadent in their religious life. The substantial truth of what is there related will hardly be denied; and no reader can fail to notice, and to be moved by, the author's sympathy, both for the ideals that were so rarely realised and for the poor struggling human beings who so often failed. But not all piety was morbid in these admittedly terrible years.

It is from the world of these faithful people, ever attentive themselves to follow still more closely the life to which the gospel calls them—monks, friars, clergy, nuns, laymen, and lay-women—that the most serious cries never cease, demanding that the church reform itself. The princes' call for reform is too often tainted with the wish to increase their control of the life of the Church; the universities' interest in reform is allied to the desire that more church wealth—better benefices—should be guaranteed to the clerics whom they educate. It would not be surprising that in the bourgeois demand for reform there should be something of a desire to loosen life from the guiding lines thrown round it by the clergy. But when the devout souls insist that abuses shall cease, it is in order that a caricature of religion shall no longer—through authority's apparent indifference—seem to be authority's own ideal of religion; it is in order that the divinely appointed means of salvation, the divine Gospel and the divine sacraments, shall stand out in all their simplicity, available to all men, and immediately available, and not fenced from life by "protections" which are now only hindrances. This demand for reform never ceases, from all sorts of men and women through the two hundred years or so that follow the move to Avignon. And the popes are not only conscious of this, they agree with the critics and the saints. For the greater part of all that time a mass of admonition never ceases to descend from them upon the faithful people and their shepherds.

Verba et praeterea nihil. Not even the calamity of the schism is able to provoke any great constructive scheme of reform. Nowhere in the ecclesiastical world is there a sign of such a phenomenon as St. Gregory VII: holiness, intelligence that sees where the root of the trouble lies and that is able to devise the appropriate remedy, energy, and courage that never fails, an utter indifference to all that is meant by "the world." The Hildebrands, the Napoleons—the Churchills—who sometimes make their appearance in the great moments when catastrophe threatens a whole world, are inexplicable phenomena for whom the reasonable man is devoutly grateful and whom he will take as they are, "warts and all." To ask, as we study the catastrophes of the past, why the ordinary run of mankind did not show themselves the peers of these wonder men—to expect this simply because it was the peers of such that were called for as life neared the brink—this is surely folly. Upon one man alone, of all these generations, can we discern anything at all resembling the mantle of Hildebrand. This was the Spaniard, Francisco Ximenes de Cisneros.

Ximenes, as in English he is generally styled, was for twenty-two years (1495–1517) Archbishop of Toledo and primate of Spain. And in that time he effected a very thoroughgoing amendment of most things that were wrong in the lives of the clergy and laid the foundations of a better system that endured long after he had passed away. In this Spanish reform we have the rare spectacle of wholehearted Christian zeal, in both the prelate and his sovereign, turning to good account the unnatural domination of the Church by the state which, everywhere else, was one main cause why the abuses endured. The joint sovereigns of Spain were Ferdinand and Isabella, and it was the queen who was the mainstay of Ximenes' intelligent and very firm reforms—the sole reigning sovereign of the time of whom it can be said that her life was wholly good.

Ximenes was sixty when he took up his task. He had begun life as a member of the secular clergy and a canonist. For a time he had lived in Rome as an advocate in the highest of the papal tribunals, and on returning to Spain he had for years ruled the diocese of Siguenza, which, along with the see of Seville, had for its bishop one of the great personages of Spain, Cardinal Mendoza. Then quite suddenly, when close on fifty, Ximenes threw up his administrative career and became a Franciscan, in the most severe branch of the great order. He was first a hermit and then a preacher, and in 1492 he was called to court by the queen to be her spiritual director—this, apparently, at Mendoza's suggestion. Three years later he took the cardinal's place at Toledo. In 1507 he was himself made cardinal and Inquisitor-general.

No field of Catholic life escaped Ximenes' zealous and experienced attention—his own Franciscan order, the other religious orders, the diocesan clergy, the innumerable chapters of cathedral and collegiate churches, the very bishops. He had the monarchy behind him in all that he did, and into the monarchy's hands Rome was more and more allowing a vast control of ecclesiastical life to slide. One order that resisted all his efforts to recall it to its first fervour, and that used against his commands all the machinery of delay which the Canon Law could offer, found itself finally suppressed, with the property of the irreformable houses transferred to more deserving causes. Ximenes' reformation of the secular clergy was crowned by his great foundation of the University of Alcalá, which provided for clerical education "at all levels." The crown of the new university was the faculty of theology. There was no faculty of law (although the Canon Law had its place in the school of theology) and there were two colleges of liberal arts. In the college of theology there was a Thomist chair and a Scotist professorship also, and a professorship in the theology according to the *Via Moderna*. More striking than this was the provision for the new study of the ancient fathers of the Church, and therefore for the teaching of Greek and Hebrew and Syriac. The foundation began in 1498, but it was ten years before the university was really functioning. And the cardinal lived to see printed, just four months before he died, the great polyglot edition of the Bible that he had planned years before. Here in six great folio volumes are printed, in parallel columns, the Hebrew, Greek, and Latin versions of the Old Testament, and the Greek and Latin of the New, with the needed critical apparatus and a Hebrew dictionary.

Meanwhile, from the presses of the university came a flood of popular books on religious subjects in all the languages of the country, Castilian, Catalan, Valencian. It is while all this apostolic employment of the Catholic intelligence is in its first spring freshness that, away in the Basque country to the north, the lad is growing up whom we know as Ignatius Loyola.

And as to the apostolic note—the very essence of Ximenes' whole life—it must be recalled how the year 1492, which saw him drawn from his Franciscan preaching to a new vocation at the court of Isabella, the year of the conquest of Granada, is also the year of Columbus' first voyage to the new world that is to be called America. And of all the successive discoveries that now set western Europe wondering and debating, none is more immediately challenging than the problem of converting to the Catholic faith these millions whose very existence has only been known a matter of months. No priest had sailed on the first voyage when the great discovery had been made. But with Columbus on his second expedition there went a friar of the new order of Minims and two Fran-

ciscans, despatched with the mission in order to work for the
conversion of the natives. From this moment there went with
every expedition a company of priests and brothers, Franciscans first, then Dominicans. In 1504—twelve years after the
first voyage—the pope created the first American sees. By 1513
there were four bishops at work, two in Santo Domingo, one
in Puerto Rico, and one on the mainland in what is now
Panama. This missionary work gave additional force and a new
reality to the movement for the reform of Christian life already sweeping through Spain, and especially to the reforms
in the monasteries.

ii *Erasmus*

Luther, at the time when those famous Ninety-five Theses
of 1517 began to make their way from one northern university
to another, was utterly unknown to that world of men, zealous
for religious reforms, that he was about to convulse. It was
a world where the personality of Erasmus of Rotterdam
reigned without a rival, scholar and supreme stylist, the man
who, for a generation, influenced educated Europe as no other
living man before his time or since—and Erasmus influenced
that world chiefly by his passion to reform what was amiss in
the general presentation of the traditional Catholic religion.

Erasmus, in this year 1517, was a man touching his fiftieth
year, or perhaps three or four years younger than this. What
had made him famous was the publication, within ten years,
of three books that were "best sellers," witty yet serious discussions, perfectly written, of the burning topics of the day,
above all of the very urgent subject of true religion and the
superstitions that now disfigured it. Erasmus, after his first
schooling with the Brothers of the Common Life at Deventer,
had entered, somewhere about 1487, the priory of the Austin
Canons at Steyn.[2] One year later he took the solemn vows
that bound him for life, and in 1492 he was ordained priest.

This priory of Steyn was not one of the Windesheim group.
But it was not a relaxed monastery, and the complaints which
Erasmus had to make about the life there centre on the crude
habits of the brethren and on their indifference, and even
hostility, to the sight of any priest interested in the use of his
intelligence. It seems certain that, at Steyn, Erasmus was

[2] Close to the town of Gouda, where his boyhood had been spent.

neither taught nor learned any philosophy or theology. The duties of the daily services in the Church once at an end—they would occupy, no doubt, a good four or five hours—he was free to give himself to the classical studies which so passionately attracted him, and above all to the cultivation of a good Latin style.

It is interesting that—to judge from his letters—Erasmus in his early twenties appears wholly unconscious that he is a witness of the waning of the Middle Ages. Nor does he give any hint of spiritual turmoil, of anguish caused to a young man thrust against his better judgment into an uncongenial observance. The whole of his later theological writing, it has been said, was inspired by the sense of every man's need for a religion that is personal and interior. That as a young religious he ever felt this need we have no evidence at all. As yet Erasmus appears perfectly happy, once he is left with his classical authors, writing his little treatises on style, where already the barbarians are well scourged, or (a most stilted exercise) on *The Contempt of this World*—with never a reference, in this, to Thomas à Kempis or to the Bible; while Valla and Poggio Bracciolini and Aeneas Silvius Piccolomini (who became Pope Pius II) are studied no less diligently than Virgil and Horace and Juvenal.

In the same year that he was ordained, Erasmus entered the service of Henry of Bergen, Bishop (and also Prince) of Cambrai, as a kind of secretary for public affairs. Three years later, in 1495, he persuaded the prelate to allow him to go to the University of Paris, and so there began a connection with the famous school which continued for the next ten years. The university, whatever its fame, was in a wretched condition in this year 1495. The students of philosophy were formed on mere abridgements and digests of the important texts, biblical studies had all but disappeared, while in the school of theology the petty doctors of the time did little more than repeat mechanically the lectures given years before by their own masters. It was the *Via Moderna* that dominated, and the general effect was to indoctrinate the student with the fatal idea that the last word had been said on all the great problems of theology and that this was to be found in the books now set before him. Each professor was a pope in his own subject, and the main feature of academic life was the bitter feuds between these popes and between the schools where the professors were of the secular clergy and those manned by the religious orders.

If we add to this that Paris, the greatest city in the Western world, was also the scene of the most incredible disorders of church life, and that in these years a battle royal was in progress between the reform party and the disorderly, it is not hard to understand the venom with which Erasmus habitually described the spiritual treason of clerics and religious, and the incompetence of authority before these scandals.

In 1498, after three years in the schools, Erasmus took his bachelor's degree in theology and the next year, in the company of a distinguished Englishman who was his pupil, William Blount, Lord Mountjoy, he crossed the English Channel. It was the first of many such crossings, but in the nine months of this first stay his whole outlook on life was changed. For at Oxford he made the acquaintance of John Colet, then lecturing, after a wholly new fashion, on St. Paul's Epistles, and in London he met Thomas More. Colet, the only son of a wealthy merchant, was almost the same age as Erasmus, and it was the passion of his life to reform the clergy through a thorough reorganisation of clerical education. Upon Erasmus, Colet had the greatest possible effect. He persuaded him, it would seem, that the much-desired renovation of the general life of the Church had nothing to hope from the plans of the monastic reformers; and, secondly, Colet convinced him that Scholasticism was over and done with. What was needed was an entirely new approach to theology. Theology must be based on Scripture alone, and the books of the Bible must be studied as a whole, as the books of living authors and not as mere quarries of useful texts.

Henceforth Erasmus was in no doubt as to the purpose of his life. He was not called to be a prince in the world of letters, but a Christian apostle. The ancient classical literature gradually ceased to be the main interest. In December 1504 he wrote to Colet that it was to sacred letters that he proposed henceforward to devote himself. He was to meet, in his mission, opposition and slander at every step of the road—always, of course, from his brethren in the priesthood and from the professors in the universities. The mere contrast, evident on a first reading of anything Erasmus wrote, between his own distinction and their loutishness, between his fine scholarship and their pedantry, his enormous success with the educated laymen for whom, first of all, many of his books were destined, and for whom his closest friend, Thomas More, may stand as symbol—these were inevitable sources of trouble to the scholar. And, when attacked, he fought back.

In these years when he was building up his great reputation, Erasmus was continually on the move. Luther rarely left his native province. Once only did he visit a foreign land. But Erasmus, between 1500 and 1517, had spent nearly three years in Italy and much more than three years in England during the four or five visits he had paid. Oxford and Cambridge were as familiar to him as Louvain and Paris. His earliest important book was a collection of proverbs—rather of light essays to which proverbs served as a text. It was called *Adagia* and was first published in 1500. Eight years later it reappeared, greatly enlarged, the lightly written commentary of a scholar who was a man of the world on human life in all its phases. Between this date and the author's death, twenty-eight years later, there were no fewer than sixty editions of this book, and another seventy-five by the time the sixteenth century was out. It was translated, in whole or in part, into English, Italian, German, and Dutch. In 1504, *The Christian Soldier's Manual* was published, of which more will presently be said. In 1505 he edited Lorenzo Valla's hitherto unprinted *Notes on the Latin Version of the New Testament*, and thereby inaugurated a new kind of Scripture scholarship. In 1506 he published in association with More, a Latin translation of some of the satirical dialogues of Lucian, a work which the Renaissance world had already taken to its heart. This was an opportunity for Erasmus to renew the drastic censure of abuses in religious practice which had appeared in the *Manual*. For Lucian was a sceptic who mocked at the superstitions of paganism and at paganism itself as a superstition. "Nothing could be more useful than this work," Erasmus wrote, introducing Lucian's dialogue called *The Fake Prophet*, "for those who would like to unmask and to silence the impostors of our own day who deceive the common people with tricksters' miracles, sham religion, bogus pardons for sin, and other such marvels." And More took the same line about the fables which universally disfigured the current lives of saints and the legends about hell. Lucian's satire, he thought, will deliver the reader from the superstition which, disguised as religion, is gradually creeping in from all sides and is the cause of needless anxieties—all the work of "pious" minds who fear that truth will be ineffective unless it is propped up by lies of this sort.

When Erasmus in 1511 was More's guest, he spent some time composing a satire of his own in which he returned to this extremely serious danger that piety, so called, was, for many people, turning the Christian religion into superstition. The new book was called *Moriae Encomium*—i.e., *In Praise of Folly*—and Erasmus showed himself a very Lucian as he analysed and described how it is the fools who, in the end, get their way and reach the heights of success in every walk of life. This was the most resounding triumph of Erasmus' career as a man of letters. Few of us indeed, even among the well educated, are nowadays on such terms with classical Latin that we can experience the gaiety with which the sensible minority read this tract, the very pope, it is said—Leo X—laughing at the brilliant shafts which never missed their target. What can be admired by all, in the excellent modern translations, is the subtle skill with which the pretence of panegyric is maintained and a devastatingly serious criticism of serious matters is conveyed under an unparalleled continuity of light-heartedness. What, almost alone, is usually remembered of the book is the attack on the monks as religious leaders—heavy scolding, nagging, in the sixteenth-century translation, bad-tempered, bitter, and ultimately tedious.

The *Moriae* was still making its way round Europe when in 1516 its author published three works of a different sort. These were a new Latin translation of the New Testament, a critical edition of its Greek original—now published in print for the first time[3]—and a critical edition of the letters of St. Jerome.

Such was the amazing succession of books which, by the year 1517, had given Erasmus his place as the great luminary of the Christian world. Of them all, it is the *Enchiridion Militis Christiani*—i.e., *The Christian Soldier's Manual*—which best reveals this great man's ideals and methods as an apostle and reformer of Christian living. "I wrote the *Enchiridion*," Erasmus explained to Colet, "in order to correct the common mistake of those who think religion is a matter of gestures and rules about material things that go beyond what even the Jews observe, and who are marvellously negligent about piety itself." More briefly, in the last lines of the book, and with something—surely—of effrontery, he tells the

---

[3] The Ximenes edition was actually in print already, but out of respect for the Holy See it was not published until officially passed at Rome.

reader that his purpose is "to show the way which leadeth straight unto Christ." One of the scholars most conversant with the life of these times has written that the book is "the manifesto of a new reform movement," and so, in effect, it proved to be. Not that Erasmus had any new interpretations of doctrine to offer: the purpose Erasmus had in mind was to bring relief to the layman whom none had troubled really to instruct about religion and who was worried out of his mind by the confusion and the threats of terrible penalties which were the most obvious features of that life where the clergy were, ex officio, teachers and rulers. "I did see the common people of Christendom to be corrupted, not only in their ways, but in their ideas. I considered the most part of those which profess themselves to be pastors and doctors to abuse the titles of Christ to their own advantage . . . preaching men's inventions and alleging them to be God's commandments . . . indulgences, financial substitutes for penance, and such like . . ." This Erasmus wrote in the preface to a later edition, answering his critics.

The *Enchiridion* might run, in translation, to as much as two hundred pages such as these. The bulk of it is moral exhortation and, what reads very strangely today, the whole literature of the ancients is called upon for stories and allusions to the heroes of old whereby the pious Christian may strengthen himself in the daily fight. And, though the name of Christ is far from absent, it is as the greatest teacher and exemplar of morality that He is presented, and not as the Divine Redeemer. It is not so much sin—the offence against God by the conscious preference for the bad, by the deliberate surrender to evil—with which Erasmus deals, which must mean death unless it is forgiven, and which cannot be forgiven without repentance; but with the flaws which disfigure the moral character.

There is nothing here about the supernatural world, about the need of grace, of the sacraments as the channels of grace, about the so-called "eminent" good works,[4] the "evangelical" counsels.[5]

There is, in all this, much apparent justification for the criticism that what Erasmus preached was non-dogmatic re-

[4] Prayer, fasting, and almsdeeds.

[5] Voluntary poverty, perpetual chastity, entire obedience—the framework of that particular form of Christian life to which monks and nuns are dedicated.

ligion and a piety that was mere matter of ethics. Yet Erasmus believed that Christ was God, that man (through the first man's sin) was the child of sin and needed for his salvation a forgiveness that only God could give. He believed the Catholic doctrine that the sacraments actually produce the graces they signify, the doctrine of the sacrifice of the Mass and of the real presence of Christ in the Holy Eucharist. And he knew that his hearers believed all this as firmly as he believed it. He could take all this for granted. And in estimating this somewhat coldhearted exposition (and its author) we need to remember the world of faith in which, and for which, it was written—of faith all too often dormant, it is true, and embarrassed by the presence of a spurious "faith" in the impossible and the unseemly, but faith never denied. Erasmus is not the prophet of some new sect of "Ethical Christians"; he is a priest who uses his vast classical lore to make his message more attractive, more effective, because this classical lore is what the fashion of the day most loves to read.

Of all the means by which a Christian man may defend himself, none is so potent as "fervent study or meditation of the divinely inspired holy scriptures." Here is "the true source" of that "philosophy of Christ"—a phrase dear to Erasmus— which is the supreme guide of life. Erasmus will defend his book against the critics by saying that it is no more than an attempt "to gather the sum of Christ's philosophy out of the pure fountain of the gospels and the epistles and the most approved interpretations." And it is "with the hidden spiritual sense of Scripture, which lies underneath the literal sense," that a man needs to be familiar. It is this which is the best of all protections, whence the direction, "Of the interpreters of Scripture choose them above all that go farthest from the letter, which chiefly, next after Paul, be Origen, Ambrose, Jerome and Augustine."

The greater part of the book is taken up with warnings about the right use of religion, about the dangers that come from misunderstanding that in all the external acts of worship—"ceremonies," Erasmus calls them—"the letter killeth, it is the spirit that giveth life." What he has in mind are such matters as devotions to the saints as expressed in pilgrimages to their shrines and in reverence to their images; such discipline as fasting and abstinence from meat; the monastic discipline of silence and wearing a special dress; the three monastic vows of poverty, chastity, and obedience; the use of blessed water, blessed candles, and tokens of the saints; public prayers and hymns. All these are but means to an end, not the end itself. These means that are visible and grasped by the senses, Erasmus will instruct his disciple, tend to be regarded and used as ends once their relation to the invisible world of God is allowed to fade from the mind. "Thou believest perchance all thy sins and offences to be washed away at once with a little paper or parchment sealed with wax, with a little money or images of wax offered, with a little pilgrimage going. Thou art utterly deceived and clean out of the way . . . I had liefer have thee hate once thy vicious manners within and in deed, than to defy them before a priest ten times in word . . . Paul forbiddeth not thee to use the law and ceremonies, but he will not that a man be bound to the law and ceremonies which is free in Christ: without these things peradventure thou shalt not be a Christian man, but they make thee not a christian man; they will help unto piety and godliness, even so yet if thou use them for that purpose. But and if thou shalt begin to enjoy them, to put thy trust and confidence in them, at once they utterly destroy all the living of a christian man."

Erasmus does not here pause to correct the error that indulgences do not forgive sins—perhaps he shared it. Nor does he seem aware that something more than hatred of the bad thing willed is needed if a man seek *forgiveness* for his sins. As to the commentary on St. Paul, we may note a serious difference between this reformer of 1504 and the more radical Germans who are soon to follow. Erasmus is saying that mind (or heart) must correspond with act if these religious practices are to be fruitful. The Reformers properly so called will teach that even the best of such acts, done with the best of intentions, is without influence upon man's salvation.

When Erasmus was attacked for what his book had to say about the bishops, the clergy, and the monks—the good, observant monks—it was an easy matter to reply that it was only their practical misunderstanding of the Christian life that he criticised, and the evil done when they passed this on to the laity whom they influenced. And this is strictly true. The references to monks, for example, in the *Enchiridion* are few. But Erasmus had spoken of them—and he said explicitly that he was speaking of the good monks, those whom people "commonly took for angels"—as the classic examples of what was chiefly wrong in Catholic life at this time: neglect of the spirit of Christ's law, an exaggerated view of the importance of "ceremonies" and of the obligation to observe these. Nothing mattered so long as the monks could "say over every day as much as they could of the psalms scarce understood, even in their literal sense." Most monks thought that the disciplinary rules peculiar to their particular order were more important than the precepts of the gospel—charity in thought and speech, for example.

And in the last pages of the book, returning to his purpose in writing it, he says that charity had urged him to write it as a help to his friend, now "recovering from vices unto virtue"—the charitable fear that he might at this stage fall victim to "that superstitious kind of religious men" who go about in the hope of capturing such for their order, exhorting, threatening, and flattering as though "without a cowl there were no christianity." Monasticism as such, Erasmus then says roundly, is not piety: it is no more than a particular way of life, profitable or not according to a particular man's temperament, in itself neither advisable nor inadvisable. In the preface to the edition of 1518, answering his critics, Erasmus is less philosophic in tone. "Would to God," he says, "that it were provided and ordained by a law that no man should be taken in such snares afore he were thirty years of age." These modern Pharisees, who "wander about to make novices both by sea and land, shall never fail of young men lacking experience whom they may allure into their veils and nets, and also deceive. There be a great number of fools and simple souls in every place."

It is not surprising, given the reluctance of great interests to see themselves publicly criticised, and given the habitual carelessness with which so many men read, that the reservations of Erasmus, his warnings about what he did *not* mean, were less regarded than the fact that here was a man bold enough to attack the ordinary habits of the class in power and capable of a mortal blow against its prestige. Erasmus was to be "the man to whom all Europe turned at the crisis of religious conflict as to an umpire." Meanwhile his every word was construed as hostile to the existing order by an overwhelming number of his own. On the other hand, his various books sold as such serious books have rarely sold; and all over Europe, from Spain to Poland, there was presently a whole "sect" of "Erasmians," a host of unorganised individuals, cultured Catholics, of regular piety after the model of the *Handbook*, clamorous for reform, hostile to superstitions, sceptical about "Devotions" and monasteries, expectant of change.

iii *The Italian Saints*

The average man is not a scholar. Nor was Erasmus unaware of this. The "common man" for whose relief, ultimately, he laboured was usually scarcely literate. Erasmus realised that a reformed priesthood was a first condition of a more religious laity and he hoped to effect this relief through the medium of a better-instructed clergy. There were others, more or less his contemporaries, who also went to the common man —directly. By their fervent preaching, and still more by the evangelical simplicity and heroic practical charity of their own lives (of whose unusual quality they were seemingly unconscious), they won the common man back to the fervour he had long since lost, and renewed in him the power of his neglected belief.

At Rome, for example, in the last months of the reign of Julius II (1503-13) a group of pious men organised themselves into a kind of guild which they called the Oratory of the Divine Love. The idea was not new. They were refounding in Rome a good work inaugurated under that name in 1497 at Genoa and due, indirectly at least, to the influence of the mystic, Catherine Fieschi-Adorno, whom we know as St. Catherine of Genoa.[6] The members of the Oratory at Rome met for their various religious exercises at the church of SS. Sylvester and Dorothy; they bound themselves to a frequent reception of the sacraments, they preached (those who were in Holy Orders), and they gave themselves systematically to such works of charity as the care of the sick in the hospitals—the actual, physical comforting of the sick—visiting the prisons, and care for the poor of the Roman slums. Among the first members of the brotherhood were two great personages of the papal court, the secretary of Leo X, Giacomo Sadoleto, Bishop of Carpentras, one of the leading humanists of the time, and John Peter Carafa, Bishop of Chieti and one day to be Pope Paul IV. Another was John Matthew Giberti, secretary of the Cardinal de' Medici who would in 1523 become Pope Clement VII, and a fourth recruit was a young Venetian

---

[6] She died at Genoa in 1510.

noble Gaetano da Thiene, late a prelate of the household of
Julius II, and soon to be ordained priest.

From this association, whose purpose was the spiritual well-
being of its members, the most remarkable developments
were soon to come. Meanwhile it needs to be said that their
dedication, "of the Divine Love," was not merely a pious
phrase—it connoted very definitely a particular spiritual principle and a way of life flowing from this. The principle was
that expressed in the long apostolate of the Genoese mystic,
St. Catherine, that the most powerful agent for personal holiness was for the soul to be consumed with a wholly disinterested love of God. This idea, in a variety of expressions,
was to dominate the spiritual life of Italy for generations
henceforward. It is the theme of innumerable books with
such titles as *The Art of Uniting Oneself with God*. It obviously called for, from the start, a dedication that was un-
limited, a wholeheartedness on the part of the dedicated that
mere natural enthusiasm or emotion could never produce or
maintain. It could only be the fruit of God's own love working
upon souls who placed not the slightest hint of self as an
obstacle to its infinite influence.

One of the conditions—if this incorrect word be allowed—
for the divine friendship to progress is wholehearted devotion
to the needs of one's fellow men. *Greater love than this no
man hath, that a man lay down his life for his friends*, was
the lesson taught at the very beginning of the Christian religion. The disciple of St. Catherine, through whom the Oratory came to Rome, Ettore Vernazzi, has a great name as a
founder of hospitals. And in the writings associated with the
saint these charitable works are described with a realism such
as to convince the aspirants that only a more than human
love will suffice to carry them through. "You will find among
the sick," the saint supposes the Spirit to say, "creatures
soaked in filth of every sort, crawling with vermin, smelling
revoltingly. There are some whose only words are of despair,
arising from the terrible calamity that has befallen them. It
will seem to you as you go into these places, that you are
going down into the graves . . ." And they are warned that
pure love for God is not compatible with any interest in the
gratitude of these unfortunates. All over Italy, in the lives of
all the saints of the time, in the story of the religious orders
and of the guilds of pious laymen, there is no more regularly

recurring feature than this, their personal care of the sick
undertaken as an act of the love of God.

A reformation which begins purely as a re-forming of self,
which wastes no time on the motes in other men's eyes, and
which proposes such a charitable devotion as this for a regular
life employment takes us at a bound as far from Erasmus and
his school as we may care to think. Let us briefly mention
the names of the leaders and list in very summary fashion
some of the fruits of their fidelity.

The first, and perhaps the most remarkable, was the appearance of a new kind of religious order, and the personages
connected with the first experiment are Gaetano of Thiene
and a Dominican of Lombardy, John Baptist Carioni, commonly called Battista da Crema, from his birthplace near Milan. The Dominican was renowned throughout the north of
Italy as a preacher and venerated as a man of unusual holiness.
He was also the author of several books whose titles tell something of his special approach, *The Way of Open Truth, Self-
Knowledge and Self-Conquest, The Interior Mirror.* It was one
of his maxims that talk about reforming the Church was a
waste of time: the reality was the personal problem of reforming one's own life; and, for this business, helping grace was
ready for all who were willing to surrender to it and begin.
Battista shared the ideas of St. Catherine of Genoa, and when
some time after the foundation of the Oratory at Rome, Gaetano returned to his own country[7] it was Battista who brought
to a definite resolution and plan Gaetano's desire to organise a
group of priests whose spirit should be that of the Oratory.
So, with the powerful co-operation of Carafa there came into
existence, in 1523, the first congregation of Clerks Regular—
priests bound by vows, but neither monks nor friars. Their
work was to be the ordinary pastoral ministry of preaching,
administering the sacraments, caring for the sick and, above
all, for the poor: to be merely the kind of priest priests should
be. They did not propose to be more than this, but they said
Mass daily, and the daily Mass was the central point of their
day. And to those whom they served they recommended frequent and even daily communion. They had no enclosure, did
not wear any special dress nor use any special means of devotion.

In their own training the principal instrument was to be

[7] In 1517, to Vicenza. Gaetano, born in 1480, ordained in 1516,
died at Naples in 1547. He was canonised in 1671.

that "methodical prayer" which for some twenty years and more had been spontaneously developing in various parts of Europe—the regular daily hour, at least so much, of personal communion with God; a practice which, once more, had some relation to the ideals of St. Catherine of Genoa. From this time on, this special way of prayer was to be an integral part of every new order, to enter into the life of the older orders too; and finally, when the Council of Trent called the seminary into being for the spiritual formation of the ordinary clergy, the daily hour of "methodical prayer" was to be the foundation of that new formation. If it be allowed to isolate any particular innovation of these years and to say that from this came the renovation of Catholic life, it is surely this exercise that must be so remarked.

What especially marked the order founded by Gaetano was its extraordinary poverty: all property was given up, all benefices surrendered for example (Carafa resigning the two sees which he held), and the order was made dependent on what was given, resolved to make it a rule not to beg. From the Latin name of Carafa's bishopric, these priests came to be called Theatines, and for the next sixty years the name was proverbially used to mean a priest of strict life. The order grew very slowly. After nine years there were but a score of Theatines. But as preachers in the streets of the great Italian cities, as apostles of the hospitals and the gaols, as confessors, they made a mark wherever they went. And presently they became an obvious stock from which the popes could draw reforming bishops: more than two hundred before their first century was out.

Battista da Crema was also a means in the foundation of the second institute of this type, whose founder, Antonio Maria Zaccaria, came from the Lombard city of Cremona. He was of noble birth and a physician, trained in the University of Padua. His first director, once he began to practice at Cremona, was a Dominican who gave him the means to base his life on the study of St. Thomas, and presently the young man's leisure went to teach children the rudiments of their religion, and then to preaching: the sufferings of Christ crucified, the need for penance. Then his mentor died, just as he had convinced Antonio that he ought to receive Holy Orders. It was now that he turned to Battista, and in 1528, twenty-six years old, he was ordained. Battista now brought into his life the Countess Ludovica Torelli, a young widow who had experienced to the full what the Renaissance could be for a woman of noble family. Her father was murdered during a ball; she lost her husband, was then married to a man who had murdered his first wife and who treated Ludovica vilely, until the dagger of a relative despatched him too. Now, at twenty-five she had dedicated herself to works of charity. Her great support, under Battista's influence, was the Epistles of St. Paul. And this was the foundation on which Antonio also had built. Presently a scheme emerged for two foundations in Milan: of priests to do the same kind of work as the Theatines, and of nuns to care for orphans and refugees from the streets. The priests were officially the Clerks Regular of St. Paul, but the church assigned to them was St. Barnabas, and they became and have ever since been called the Barnabites. They were perhaps more flexible in their approach than the Theatines, and the streets of the city were the scene of their processions, their pageants—for they neglected no means of teaching—and their never-ceasing exhortations. Their churches were reputed, above all, for the silence that reigned and for the solemnity with which the liturgy was carried out; and it was here that there began the devotional exercise of prayer before the Blessed Sacrament exposed in the monstrance and surrounded with all possible ceremony.[8]

It was a third nobleman, the Venetian Girolamo Miani, who brought the third of these orders into being. He had been a soldier, and in the war of Venice against the League of Cambrai (Pope Julius II, the Emperor Maximilian, Louis XII of France, and Henry VIII of England) and after a brilliant defence of Castelnuovo he was taken prisoner. What he had to endure as a prisoner of war was more degrading than one of his birth might have expected in those days, and after a deliverance which he considered miraculous, an answer to prayer, he gave up his military ambitions—and his all too typically loose soldier's life—and vowed himself to works of charity among the poor of Venice. He set himself to study theology, and at thirty-seven he was ordained. For the next twenty years he busied himself with the foundation of orphanages, and presently, in order to give stability to the work done, he and his companions organised themselves as Clerks Regular—not without the advice and assistance of Carafa,

---

[8] Antonio Maria Zaccaria died early, in 1539. He was canonised in 1897.

whom the troubles that followed the sack of Rome in 1527 brought for some years to Venice.

The chief house of the foundation was in the little town of Somascha, near Bergamo, and these priests have always been known as Somaschi.[9] From the care for orphans, the work of the Somaschi gradually extended to a general interest in charities for the poor, hospitals, homes for the aged, refuges for converted street walkers. And from their obvious duty to instruct all these unfortunates they came to share the preaching apostolate of the Barnabites and the Theatines.

In this same north of Italy, Brescia and its environs, there was developing in these same early years of the sixteenth century a charity whose object was the education of poor girls, the work of a pious lay woman, Angela Merici, of Desenzano. It was only after twenty-five years of this work that the society revealed to her in a vision began to take shape—an "order," curiously akin in its novelty to the new Clerks Regular, for these ladies took no vows nor did they wear a special dress, and they continued to live with their own families. But by 1537 they swarmed in Brescia and all the neighbouring villages. Angela placed the work under the patronage of St. Ursula. From these associations there was to develop, in the years following the death of the foundress, the first order of women dedicated to the education of girls, the Ursulines.[10]

The best known to us of these new institutes of Clerks Regular, the Society of Jesus, barely existed as yet, even in the prayers of Ignatius Loyola. At forty years of age he is still valiantly working his way through the University of Paris, already the saint, devotedness itself, and very mistrustful of Erasmus. Meanwhile—to round off the record of mystical Italy in the years 1514–30—a Franciscan of the Observants, Matteo da Basci, now led yet another great return to the absolute rule of St. Francis; and in so doing he produced, all unwittingly, the great order we know as the Capuchin Friars Minor. Matteo

[9] Girolamo Miani figures in English calendars as St. Jerome Emilian. He was born in 1481, converted somewhere about 1510, ordained in 1518. He died of the plague at Somascha in 1537. Clement XIII canonised him in 1767.

[10] St. Angela Merici was born in 1469. The date of the vision is 1506. Clement VII, who gave her an audience in 1525, would gladly have seen her transfer her apostolate to Rome. The foundation date of the institute is 1535. The saint died in 1540, and was canonised in 1807.

was a young lay brother of twenty-eight or thirty when he signalised himself by his extraordinary devotion to the sick when the plague struck the city of Camerino in 1523. He next began to long for a hermit life and to live in the absolute destitution of St. Francis. There was a strong initial opposition from his superiors and appeals to the pope. At Rome, Carafa—the name recurs in all these movements—was very helpful to Matteo and his friends. Once the needed permissions were granted, these reformed friars began, in the small towns of central Italy, the same kind of apostolic work which the new Clerks Regular had undertaken at Rome and Venice and Milan: street preaching and care of the poor in the hovels where they lived. "They preached the Holy Scripture," said the contemporary chronicler, "and especially the Holy Gospel of our Lord Jesus Christ, exhorting everyone to keep God's commandments"—the words so often used in the earliest descriptions of the Theatines, Barnabites, and Somaschi. Great devotion to the Bible, to prayer, to the sacraments of Penance and the Holy Eucharist, regularity in what we have come to call by the dismal-sounding name "mortification," characterised all these varied groups of active Catholics. And the stories of their first endeavours sparkle with a kindly, open simplicity and optimistic, cheerful trustfulness that recall the Franciscans of the Fioretti. "A joyous heart is more easily made perfect than one that is cast down," the saint was to say who, better than all others, typifies this attractive school of Christian guidance, the Florentine Philip Neri, who, a generation later, was to be the apostle of Rome itself—nay, of the very Curia Romana.

CHAPTER FOUR

Luther. The First Protestants
1517—1532

i *Luther's Catholic Days, 1483–1517*

Nothing could less resemble the setting in which Erasmus or the Italians just described came to realise their vocations than the background against which the contemporary genius of Martin Luther was displayed—six thousand square miles of rural Germany. This was, in the main, the territory known as Electoral Saxony. It contained—geographically, but not politically—the university town of Erfurt, which, with twenty thousand people, was one of the leading cities of Germany, but scarcely another town that could muster even five thousand inhabitants. Wittenberg, the capital of the Elector and also the seat of a university, was a mere village of two thousand. The vast bulk of the men and women, the priests and the layfolk, with whom Luther had first to deal, as a Reformer, lived in hamlets of only a few score families each. Wittenberg is perhaps sixty miles southwest of Berlin—in Luther's time an insignificant village—and Eisleben, where Luther was born on November 11,[1] 1483, is as far again from Wittenberg, roughly southwest. Erfurt is fifty miles to the south of Eisleben, and thirty miles west again is Eisenach, in the mountainous Thuringian country that affords as great a contrast as could be desired to the flat sandy plain through which flows the Elbe and where Wittenberg is situated. Luther once made a famous journey to Rome; he made other famous journeys in Germany, to Heidelberg and to Augsburg in 1518, and to Worms in 1521. And that is almost the sum of his displacements from the bucolic little world that bred him.

[1] St. Martin's Day.

Luther's parents were poor at the time he was born. The father was a copper miner, but presently he became a wealthy man. Luther was the only child they managed to rear. Of his childhood and adolescence we know very little more than the places where he went to school, Mansfeld (then his home town), Magdeburg (where the Brothers of the Common Life were his masters), and Eisenach, with which town he associated his only really happy memories of early years. His parents, he tells us, bred him with great severity. Punishments for trifles, severe beatings were the order of the day. At eighteen he began his university studies at Erfurt—then the greatest university in Germany, with two thousand students. He followed the usual course in the liberal arts and philosophy—under good masters—took his baccalaureate in 1502 and his master's degree three years later. By this time he had begun, at his father's command, to study law. Then came the first great event of his life of which we can be certain: he threw over all his father's plans for his future and announced that he proposed to become a monk—a friar of the order called the Hermits of St. Augustine, the dominant force in the religious life of Erfurt and in the university also. He was then nearing his twenty-second birthday.

Luther has himself told us what brought about this unexpected change of mind. Riding back to Erfurt after a visit to his home, he was overtaken by a terrible storm. It was so severe that the rider feared for his life and, calling on St. Anne to help him, he made a vow that if he came through safely he would become a monk. The date of the storm was July 2, 1505, and on July 17 Luther entered the Augustinian monastery at Erfurt as a candidate for his new career.

The unusual circumstances under which this young man came to take so momentous a decision make it a matter of the greatest regret—to the historian—that almost nothing is known with certainty of the kind of man this young Martin Luther was. It is, of course, the reverse of helpful to guess about this from what he afterwards became or achieved. We do know that his academic record was brilliant and that the student's life was good. We also know that he played the lute and that he sang well. A promising recruit—so far as all this goes—for the Austin Friars. As to the prudence of the young man's decision and of the order's acceptance of him within a few days of his making the decision, we can do little more than raise our eyebrows and try not to judge the joint action in the light of what happened later—by which is not meant the Reformation, but Luther's personal trials as a friar of the order.

The next stages of Martin Luther's ecclesiastical progress—he is now under obedience to his religious superiors—are (to us) so remarkable as to be almost incredible. Nowadays there would be a period of weeks before the candidate was ceremoniously clothed in the friar's uniform dress—the religious habit, as it is called; then he would serve two years as a novice, learning the rule and the details of the new life, free to leave without any formality at any moment that he chose, while the order was equally free to tell him to go; after these two years he would take vows—promises publicly made to God to give up all rights of ownership, to observe perfect chastity, and to obey his superiors according to the rule of the order; today these vows would be taken for a period of years only—four, it may be, or six; at the end of this period of temporary vows, the religious, if still of the same mind, and the order also, would repeat the vows but make them now as binding him for life. Between this first putting on of the dress of a friar and the irrevocable act of perpetual vows there is nowadays an interval of six to eight years. In Luther's time the law was different. The vows when first taken were for life, and they were taken after a single year as a novice. It needs also to be pointed out that whereas today it is a matter almost of routine that one who has taken even the final vows can be dispensed from them on sufficient reason—if a priest, he can be transferred, so to speak, to the ranks of the non-monastic clergy—in Luther's time such dispensations were extremely rare.

That Luther took his vows within a year or so of entering the friary at Erfurt is not what most startles the modern Catholic, but the speed with which he was next advanced to the priesthood, and the relation of this progress to his studies. For he was ordained on April 3, 1507, barely nine months after his religious profession. Nowadays, for one who, like Luther, had already completed his philosophical studies, there would be an interval of four years after the profession, during which theology is studied. At the end of the third year the aspirant would be ordained sub-deacon, during the fourth year he would be made deacon, and at the end of the fourth year ordained priest.

Luther's formal theological studies began after his ordination to the priesthood. They seem to have lasted something like a year and a half. For in the autumn of 1508 he was transferred to the Augustinian house at Wittenberg and appointed to lecture in the new university—founded only six years before—on the Nichomachean Ethics of Aristotle, his theological studies continuing meanwhile. In March 1509 he took his first—i.e., bachelor's—degree in theology, and just one year later returned to Erfurt to lecture on theology in the house of studies of his own order. After another eight months came the violent interruption of Luther's journey to Rome.

The Augustinian Hermits in Germany had been for some years undergoing a reorganisation, sanctioned not only by their own general superiors but by the pope. Among the houses hostile to these arrangements was Luther's monastery of Erfurt, and now (with a confrere whose name has not survived) he went to Rome on the hopeless task of presenting once again the case that had been judged with finality and found wanting. The two set out in November 1510. They would make their path to Rome afoot, and the return journey also.

It was the spring of 1511 before they returned. In the summer Luther was again sent to Wittenberg—a house that favoured the new order of things and of which Luther, in 1512, was made sub-prior, the second-in-command. He was also made responsible for the preaching in the monastery church, and in October he took his degree as doctor of theology. He was now on the verge of his thirtieth year, and next year, taking up his work as professor in the faculty of theology in the university, he would, all unconsciously, begin the movement we have learned to call the Reformation.

What that movement will chiefly be, in Luther's intention, is not a crusade to reform the moral lives of Catholics, clerics as well as layfolk, but rather a crusade against Catholicism itself, observant, conscientious, dutiful Catholicism, now considered to be a corruption of the Gospel of Christ. And on his own showing, according to his own account, the origins of his stupendous conviction lie in his own personal experience of the ineffectiveness and the mischievousness of Catholicism as a solution offered him for his spiritual troubles, and in his own divinely guided discovery of the true meaning of the religion of Christ. It is Luther, and not his opponents, who brings into court, as an important consideration, the experiences, the spiritual crises which he experienced in his life as a monk. By the time the Wittenberg professorate opened he had been a monk nearly seven years (1506–13). He had still seven years (1513–20) before the pope's excommunication cast him forth; i.e., four years during which his new ideas germinated (1513–17), and then three years as the monk agitator, liberator, prophet. What had the monk's life done for him, or to him, in the years between his profession in 1506 and the lectures now beginning at Wittenberg in 1513?

There are very serious obstacles in the way of those who would like to know all about Luther's life or exactly what kind of man Luther was. There is, of course, the presence of the conflicting Luther legends, those which have come down through the great army of his followers, and the others which are a tradition among the people whom he left. We can safely ignore both of these obstacles. The Reformation did not begin when a young monk found in the monastery library a book whose very existence none suspected—the Bible—and straightway began to read it. Nor did it begin with the same young monk's inability to overcome his own immoral habits.

One really formidable obstacle is the vast amount of Luther's own writings—113 volumes[2] of published works, in German and in Latin, and of correspondence.

Another serious problem, of a different kind, is that for many important matters Luther is himself our only witness, that he is not a disinterested witness, and that his testimony is often a reminiscence thrown up in some chance conversation the better part of a lifetime after the event. We do not by any means really know the Luther of 1507–13. We do, however, know well the Luther of 1521–46. How far can we use this knowledge to control or check the account which this later Luther gives of the kind of life the earlier Luther lived? Luther's own character is of the greatest importance to the historian of the Reformation—he was himself so very much the whole Reformation in the early years—and his character is extremely complex. The admonition of Oliver Cromwell to the portrait painter is classic—to paint the warts also. Luther has unconsciously painted himself, and he has left nothing out. Is everything in that portrait equally true? What is true is that every event of Luther's life, and almost everything he ever said, has been a battleground where the historians and biographers, friends and foes to Luther, have fought ever since.

[2] Erlangen edition.

Nay, the fight began in Luther's own life, the fight within his own party as to which was the true "Lutheranism."[3]

In the crucial four years, 1513–17, Luther, as professor of Theology at Wittenberg, lectured turn by turn on the Psalms, the Epistle to the Romans, and the Epistle to the Galatians. Study of these lectures reveals that by the time he entered the field as critic of the indulgence system—i.e., by the winter of 1517–18—he had already reached conclusions of his own on matters far more fundamental. He was already a Lutheran, whether he realised this or not.

Of the three series of lectures, that on St. Paul to the Romans is the most important. These lectures were never published in Luther's lifetime; but, rediscovered[4]—first in a student's copy and then in Luther's own manuscript—some sixty years ago, they have done much to give new life to the never-ceasing study of Luther and to the debate as to what it was that he accomplished. In this epistle—one of the longest items in the New Testament, after the Gospels and the Acts of the Apostles—St. Paul is setting out the Christian theology of justification, in an argumentative way.[5] His opponents are Christians who, like himself, are converts from Judaism but who have not been able to understand that the religion they have now embraced is something new, that the former things have passed away, that since God became man and, as God made man, died upon the cross in order to reconcile man with God there is a new way for man with God. The apostle, in this letter, has to set out the new way and at the same time to show it in contrast with the old, which is now no more. It is not surprising that this epistle is, proverbially, one of the more difficult books of Scripture—even though it be not the particular epistle of St. Paul to which St. Peter refers, "Wherein are some things hard to understand, which the ignorant and un-

---

[3] "The quarrel as to the authentic Luther first flared up when Melanchthon and Luther confronted one another with different versions of the doctrine of justification." Zeeden, *Legacy of Luther* (1954), p. 26.

[4] They are not finished lectures, but the detailed notes actually used by the lecturer (it would seem).

[5] Justification: the divinely ordained process by which man, from being God's enemy, becomes God's friend.

stable wrest to their own destruction, as they do also the rest of the scriptures."[6]

St. Paul, in the courteously worded introductory phrases of his letter, speaks of his long-standing desire to know personally these Christians at Rome, for the mutual encouragement of the faith they have in common, and also of his desire to preach to them. He then goes on to say, "I am not ashamed of the gospel; for it is the power of God bringing salvation to every one that believeth, to Jew first, and then to Greek. *For the justness of God is revealed therein, from faith unto faith, according as it is written, 'The just man shall live by faith.'* "[7] The words I have italicised should be noted. Around Luther's explanation of them the whole Reformation was to turn. This book that I am writing is not an account of Luther's life but of his part in the Reformation. Also, a critical analysis of his lectures on the Epistle to the Romans is the business of the theologian, not the historian. And a history so summary as this can do little more than set out what is new in Luther's explanation of St. Paul's mysterious words, or rather what is at variance with the explanation hitherto accepted.

Luther, at the time he began to lecture on St. Paul, had already a serious personal problem calling urgently for solution. He had grown up with a vivid realisation of God as the law-giver and the meticulous avenger of every breach of the law—God the punisher of man's sins. The phrase "God is just," had only this one meaning for Luther as he grew up, and no one he met or consulted ever said anything to suggest that the words ever meant anything else. It became, then, the main anxiety of Luther's life that somehow the just wrath of God in his regard should be assuaged. Despite all his exercises of piety, he never reached a stage where he was free from all inclination to do what was wrong. Unreasonable likes and dislikes continued to trouble him and sometimes to overcome him. And though his counsellors bade him have confidence that the sins for which he was sorry were forgiven—since, to the best

[6] 2 Peter, 3:16. The translation is that of the Westminster version from the Greek, authorised by Cardinal Griffin, as is the next quotation.

[7] Romans 1:16, 17. The quotation is from the prophet Habacuc, 2:4—i.e., from the Greek translation of this: the original Hebrew reads "faithfulness," not "faith." To show that all is not plain sailing in these matters we may note that Monsignor Knox translates this quotation, "It is faith that brings life to the just man."

of his ability and knowledge, his repentance was sincere—there never came to Martin Luther a consciousness of this forgiveness, something that he could feel. It all remained a matter of words spoken to him, of mental propositions to which the reason must assent but which did nothing to quieten the imagination, to still the fears and anxieties. This is the account of his troubles while a friar as Luther gives it. And since this pious young monk (for it seems he was indeed "a diligent observer of all holy duties") felt no different for all his pious activities—his good works, in the technical sense of the words, and a phrase soon to be a matter of world-wide discussion—these pious activities, he concluded, could make no difference to the way God regarded his sin-inclined self. "When I was a monk," he wrote in later life, "I used immediately to believe that it was all over with my salvation every time I experienced the concupiscence of the flesh, that is to say an evil movement against one of the brethren, of envy, or anger, or hatred, or of jealousy and so forth. I used to try various remedies; I used to go to confession every day, but that didn't help me at all. For this concupiscence of the flesh was always returning, so that I could never find peace, but was everlastingly tormented, with the thought 'You have committed such and such a sin; you are still a prey to jealousy, to impatience and the rest. It did you no good to receive Holy Orders, and all your good works are just useless.' "

What should have been done for Luther by his guides in the monastery while he was passing through the years from twenty-one to thirty? What could have been done by them for a man who seemingly was anything but teachable, an instinctive debater, who can say?[8] What we do know, and what matters, is that in the end the monk found a remedy himself. And if one modern historian's summary of the discovery is correct, it was what Luther ought (one might think) always to have known, the basic truth indeed of all the Christian centuries; for, according to this scholar, to Luther meditating on Romans 1:17 it suddenly came home that "God is nothing but sheer goodness, which is always giving itself." And another of our own contemporaries, a Catholic, will say, what may startle, that for the monk Luther this was indeed news. "For

---

[8] *Ad contradicendum audax et vehemens*; a hostile contemporary was to record this as the opinion of Luther's fellow friars of the house at Erfurt, the reason why they chose him to argue their case at Rome, then three years short of thirty.

Luther"—and for how many others? And how had a Catholic come to be in this extraordinary ignorance? One of the features of the violent controversies, fifty years ago, about the origins of Luther's ideas and about his own good faith was the publication of an elaborate chain of quotations, from the earliest times down to Luther's own, which showed that what he declared he had never heard of before his own discovery, had been the opinion of every theological writer who had ever had to explain the words "justice of God."

In his lectures on this epistle, then (to list some of the young professor's untraditional ideas), Luther teaches that the righteousness, by reason of which the one-time sinner is now accepted by God as reconciled, is no more than a righteousness cast around him by God, imputed to him, behind which, or apart from which, the sinner himself remains exactly as he was before the divine acceptance justified him; and that what brings about justification is faith, and faith alone, by which term is meant the sinner's confidence in God's word announcing the promise and the fact of salvation. No "good works" done by man can at all avail towards his salvation. Man himself is never anything but sin, for even after baptism there remains in him that tendency to do evil, which is itself sin and so vitiates every action done by man. All man's acts are sins, then; and continue to be sins, even after justification; but, in the case of the justified, God does not hold this sinfulness against them. As to those acts by which man deliberately sins, these also, even though forgiven, are not destroyed. "I used to think that they were taken away entirely, and not merely externally," Luther would say. What actually is taken away is nothing more than the liability to penalty. The sin itself remains. Moreover, it is not possible for man to observe God's commandments. So that "we are deservedly always not just, and must ever be in fear of sentence and need to pray that this 'unjustness' be remitted, or rather that it be not held against us."

There is no place in this scheme for natural goodness, and even the most virtuous of the philosophers of the old pagan world were necessarily damned. There are no such things as small sins and no such thing, in God's sight, as human merit. Finally, Luther teaches that God not only permits sin but that sin cannot be committed unless He commands it; "it does not follow," he goes on to say, "that God wants the sin to be committed, although He wills that it should take place." The

reason why God wills that it should happen is the opportunity
thus provided for a manifestation to man, through the spectacle
of the divine anger punishing the sinner, of how hateful sin
is to God. This is what Luther calls "the deeper theology."
And in the service of this terrible divinity, whom man is meant
to serve in fear and trembling, the peak of virtue is the resignation to his decrees of those who think themselves predestined by Him—irrespective of their actions—to the eternal
torments of hell. These lectures on the Epistle to the Romans are the earliest exposition of Luther's mind on the
questions that will occupy him for the rest of his life—the exposition which, once launched, will occupy all western Europe
too.

This is not in any way meant as a description of these lectures on St. Paul. It is no more than a note to show, from
Luther's earliest important piece of work, how far he had already moved from the teaching in which he had been bred
—from the Catholic religion—and how far he had developed,
if not a system of his own, at least the main ideas that would
later be worked into a systematic relation. And he is as yet
no more than a junior lecturer in this Catholic university,
wholly unaware that he is about to astonish the world by the
way he will conduct a campaign against one of the leading
abuses of the day, the contemporary preaching of indulgences.

How Martin Luther came by these new interpretations, this
fundamentally different theology of the relations of God to
man, of the forgiveness of sins and of salvation, historians are
by no means agreed: Ockhamist influences (or reaction
against these), reading of the German mystics of the previous
hundred years and more (or misreading of them), and so on.
But the ultimate solution is Luther's own. One of his modern
admirers has written that he " 'lifted himself by his own boot-
straps' from one world to another." Which does not exclude
Luther's explicitly worded belief that the cardinal point of it
all was personally revealed to him by God; namely, the true
meaning of the word *Justitia* in the seventeenth verse of Romans 1; namely, that the word meant not the punitive justice
that awaits the offender but "the Justice which justifies and
saves us." When did this experience, the so-called "Happening in the Tower," take place? Again the historians differ: at
the latest 1518, at the earliest 1514. One thing is beyond
doubt, Luther's personal certitude about this foundation and

the force which the conviction gave to his whole action in the critical years 1518–21.

Luther would no doubt have agreed that, in the matter of justification, "he understood St. Paul better than had been the case for a thousand years." He never offered proofs that his theory was true. And how could he? How can a human intelligence discover the meaning of what is, *ex hypothesi*, a truth above the reach of reason? Catholics, from the beginning, had taken the divinely guided Church as their guide in such mysteries. Luther, too, had his more than human assistance, or thought he had. But his doctrine was not to be locked up in his own breast, for his own consolation merely. And when he came before the world, to set other men free from the tyranny whence he had so recently escaped, what could he do but assert—and, in addition, so describe the traditional system that no one would any longer believe it could be true. Luther was to prove himself—and this was already beginning in the years when he was wrestling with Romans 1:17 and other like texts—one of the most effective preachers ever known, so great a master of his own tongue, in speech and with the pen, that he is one of the creators of the language we call German. And the Lutheran conquest of Christian thought—the immediate conquest—was, in its essence, that an orator of genius persuaded the ordinary man by the thousand to throw over what every preacher he had ever heard of had always said, and to accept instead of it, merely on the word of a man who said he knew better,[9] ideas never heard of until now. The great attraction would be the unambiguous declaration that there was a divinely appointed way to be sure of one's salvation—to be sure, now, that one was going to "make" heaven.

Meanwhile Luther's new ideas caused a great stir in the little university.[10] To answer his critics in the faculty of the-

[9] And who never invokes in his support the great fact—if such it be—that the Holy Ghost personally had made this known to him. Not until the event was thirty years old did Luther, in the year before he died, first commit this story to print.

[10] There were four faculties, theology, law, medicine, and arts. In 1518 there were 22 professors altogether and a certain amount of teaching done by students also working for the higher degrees. The number of students rose rapidly after the foundation (1502), but from 1507 they fell off steadily. They rose again in the years when

ology the young professor, in September 1516 and again in September 1517, arranged that two of his pupils, as part of the exercises for their degree, should offer to defend some of the new interpretations; for example, "Man without grace is a tree than can bring forth no good fruit," "Without the faith that works through charity, even the works which appear good are sins," "Man's will, unless moved by grace, is not free," "Man, doing the best he can, sins nevertheless, for he is unable, by his own powers, either to will or to think [rightly]," "It is false to say that the will is free to choose the good or the bad. The will is not free, it is a prisoner," "Without grace the will, necessarily, only chooses what is bad," "Any love of God which is not wholly disinterested[11] is a sin." Moreover, in the disputations of 1517 there was a violent attack on the scholastic philosophy, on the theological system then reigning at Wittenberg, and a challenging comparison between Luther's ideas—presented as "the religion of grace"—and the Catholic beliefs now controverted, which appeared as "the religion of law."

His friends and his opponents, conscious that for a year and more Luther had also been airing these ideas in his sermons—courses of sermons on the Ten Commandments and on the Our Father—must have wondered how much longer he would be allowed to go on. He himself was serenely confident. "Our theology and St. Augustine are making good progress," he wrote to his friend, the prior of the Augustinians at Erfurt, May 18, 1517, "thanks be to God they prevail in the university . . . The lectures on scholastic theology are deserted and no one can be sure of an audience who does not teach our theology."

Then, in that same year, something quite unexpected happened.

The city of Wittenberg lay within the jurisdiction of the

Luther was first becoming a celebrity (1517–21), reaching the high-water mark of 552. Then, after the imperial outlawry of Luther, they fell as low as 100. Among Luther's colleagues were three men whose names are inseparable from his in Reformation history, Carlstadt, (1480–1541), Amsdorf (1483–1565), and Melanchthon (1497–1560). This brilliant humanist came to Wittenberg to teach Greek and Hebrew in 1518. Teaching theology here he wrote the first systematic account of Lutheranism, the *Loci Communes*.

[11] For example, the love of God out of gratitude for God's gifts.

Bishop of Brandenburg, whose immediate superior—metropol-itan—was the Archbishop of Magdeburg. This archbishop, in the year 1517, was a man of princely birth, Albert of Branden-burg, brother of the Elector Joachim I, who ruled the state called Brandenburg, which lay immediately to the north of Electoral Saxony and was reckoned one of the principal states of the empire. It was the ancestor state of the later kingdom of Prussia, and from Joachim the Hohenzollern kings and em-perors were descended. Archbishop Albert was at this time twenty-six years of age and had been a bishop just four years. He was still four years short of the minimum age for appoint-ment as a bishop and had needed a dispensation from the pope in order to be appointed. He had needed a dispensation also for a second anomaly, his appointment to hold also the important archiepiscopal see of Mainz—more important as a see, and also of high political importance, because the arch-bishop was one of the seven princes who elected the emperor. The Brandenburg family now had two votes in the electoral college, and as the emperor, Maximilian I, was breaking up, their influence would probably be profitable, in one way or another, within a very few years. The archbishop also held, as administrator, the see of Halberstadt.

Upon his appointment to each of these three sees he was due to pay the pope a heavy tax called annates, and for the two archiepiscopal sees an additional tax called the pallium tax. To his appointment to Mainz the objection was raised at Rome that to grant two metropolitan sees to one man was unheard of. Finally it was allowed by special dispensation, and the archbishop was asked to pay for this yet another enor-mous sum. His account with the papal treasurers for the ap-pointment to Mainz amounted, in all, to 31,000 gold ducats. Unfortunately for himself, Albert was the fourth archbishop to be appointed to Mainz in ten years—i.e., three times al-ready, in that time, 21,000 ducats had had to be raised to pay annates and pallium fees. The see was now practically bankrupt. Albert had to borrow, and the moneylenders to whom he went were the Fugger firm, of Augsburg. Their Ro-man house settled the payment to the Curia and on August 18, 1514, Albert was appointed to Mainz. The Roman officials had explained to him, when they asked the additional 10,000 ducats as an honorarium for the dispensation, that the pope—as yet ignorant of the whole affair—would allow him to re-cover this sum by means of a papal indulgence to be preached throughout his metropolitan jurisdiction; throughout a good half of Germany, that is to say. The indulgence would be preached for eight years, and of what alms were given, one half would go to the pope for the rebuilding of St. Peter's basilica in Rome, the other half to the archbishop for the use of the archdiocese of Mainz—actually to the Fugger in repayment of what they had lent to the archdiocese plus the not inconsiderable interest on this. The pope, Leo X (Giovanni de' Medici by birth), agreed to the plan on August 1, 1514, and published the bull announcing the indulgence on March 31, 1515.

As to St. Peter's: this great shrine, beneath which lay the tomb of the Apostle, had been, from the earliest centuries, a holy place to which the faithful came from every part of Christendom. Parts of the ancient church went back a thousand years. It was now in danger of collapse. Repairs were no longer possible, and Leo's predecessor, Julius II, calling in the great artists of the day, had had plans for a new church prepared and had begun to organise the finances of the great project. One way of gathering alms that seemed highly appropriate was to offer the opportunity of a plenary indulgence to whoever would contribute to the cost of this undoubtedly pious enterprise.

An indulgence, so a catechism for children in use today will tell us, is "a remission granted by the Church of the temporal punishment which often remains due to sin after the guilt has been forgiven." This admirably written answer is a perfect summary of what Luther was teaching the people of Wittenberg in his sermon on indulgences on October 31, 1516, just one year before the great controversy began. Indulgences were never said to be, or intended to be presented as, a forgiveness of sins committed, nor a permission to commit sin with an assurance that there would be no penalties to pay. Indulgences always presupposed that a man's sins had been already forgiven, that he had turned from sin and was resolved to lead a new life. This sermon is itself testimony that people were warned against misunderstanding the doctrine and use of indulgences: that they were told, for example, that to gain an indulgence gave no warrant for believing that their salvation was now assured; and, also, that only those reconciled to God through true sorrow for their sins could gain the remission of the punishment which their wrongdoing had deserved.

Indulgences are described as being "preached." Since it was

necessary, in order to gain an indulgence, that people should go to confession, and since in those days the average man rarely approached the sacraments more than once a year, it was the custom to make the granting of an indulgence an opportunity for a series of what we call today mission services. A preacher would be brought in who, day after day, would recall the great fundamental truths of religion, speak of "the four last things"—death, judgment, hell, and heaven—remind the congregation of the great mysteries of the Incarnation and of the saving passion of Christ, of the love of God for man shown in all this, exhort to prayer, to true repentance, to a real resolve to amend, and a worthy receiving of the sacraments. All would go to confession and—possibly—receive Holy Communion. They would then apply for the indulgence; and to gain this, something more was needed—the performing of some specified religious act. Nowadays—that is to say, ever since the Council of Trent removed the occasion of all the scandals—this religious act has always been the recitation of certain prayers or the performance of a fast. But in Luther's time the work specified would often be an alms to be given to some particular charity. In the case of the great indulgence of 1517, the condition was to give an alms towards the rebuilding of St. Peter's church at Rome.

In such a routine as this there is nothing to cause scandal. But how was this particular indulgence preached? And what of the procedure adopted when, individually, the faithful came to the papal official, certified him they had received the sacraments, and giving in their alms, received the indulgence and a note certifying it had been granted them? We have no knowledge of the way in which the archbishop's chief agent —the Dominican, John Tetzel—preached this indulgence. He was one of the best-known preachers of the time and had been engaged in work of this kind, on and off, for a good fifteen years. What has survived are his circular to the parish priests setting out what exactly was offered on this occasion and some notes for sermons with which he supplied them. We also possess the archbishop's instructions for Tetzel and his fellow commissaries. Tetzel, within a few months of Luther's attack, became the centre of violent controversy. All manner of stories about the way he preached were then spread around, and all manner of lies about the kind of man he was. Some of the lies, about his personal morality, Luther helped to a long existence. We have also an account of Tetzel preaching the indulgence, written many years later by a Franciscan who had since gone over to the Reformation.

What this ex-friar, now turned Reformer, had to say about Tetzel's sermons will hardly be accepted without critical examination and some support from a less partisan source. But what Tetzel's own sermon notes tell is sufficiently disturbing. He seems to have been one of that vast army of moral reformers for whom the truth of what they say hardly matters, provided it warns off their hearers from the evil they are fighting. "Tell your people," he writes to the parish priests, "that for every mortal sin a man commits he must, after making a good confession, suffer seven years in purgatory, unless he has done seven years penance. Bid them think how many mortal sins a day are committed, how many each week, each month, each year. All but infinite, then, are the pains they must undergo in the flames of purgatory. This indulgence will mean for them full remission of all the punishment due to them up to the time they gain the indulgence. And for the rest of their lives, whenever they go to confession the priest will have the power to grant them a similar indulgence; and they will receive an indulgence again in the very moment when they pass from this life to the next." After all, he says again, "if you are going to Rome, or on some other dangerous journey, you would put your hundred ducats in the bank here, and when you got to Rome present your receipt and be paid the deposit. And you would gladly pay the banker five or six or ten ducats for the convenience. You would willingly give so much to make certain of your 100 ducats and will you grudge a quarter of a florin to bring your soul that is immortal safely to the fatherland that is Paradise?"

The archbishop's instructions set out a graded list of the alms expected, varying from twenty-five golden florins from kings, queens, and bishops, to half a florin for those who earned less than mechanics and storekeepers. Those who could not pay anything would offer, instead, their prayers and fastings, "for the kingdom of heaven ought not to be more accessible to the rich than to the poor."

More seriously amiss were the declarations about indulgences to be gained which would profit the souls of those already deceased. "Can you not hear the voices of your dead father and mother pleading with you?" Tetzel bade the parish priests say to their people, " 'A tiny alms,' they are saying, 'and we shall be free from this torment. And you grudge this to us.'" The indulgence, as a favour applicable to the dead, was a very new development. The earliest known to us was granted barely forty years before this, in 1476 by Sixtus IV, and in it we find the important phrase, henceforward inseparable from such grants, *per modum suffragii*.[12] In indulgences for the living, what is wrought is done through the pope's supreme power of loosing bonds: "Whatsoever thou shalt loose on earth, I also shall loose in heaven," are the words of Christ Himself to St. Peter. But far from the popes claiming a power "to remove souls from Purgatory and to transmit them to the realms of heavenly bliss," they insist, from the first grant they ever make relative to souls in purgatory, that they are not acting as though they had power in this matter. They do no more than, as it were, add to the prayers of the living Catholic who is striving for an indulgence applicable to the dead Catholic the weight or worth of the official prayers of the Church. Indulgences, in so far as they concern the souls in purgatory, are nothing else than an especially solemn form of prayer for the dead. Luther, for example, in the sermon on indulgences already quoted, explains this as he explains the rest. "The souls in Purgatory, as the Bull expressly states," he tells the congregation, "profit by the indulgences only so far as the power of the Keys of Holy Church extends . . . *per applicationem intercessionis* [through an application of the Church's intercession]." He draws next the perfectly proper conclusion, "Hence the immediate and complete liberation of souls from Purgatory is not to be assumed."

Tetzel, however, preached the contrary: indulgences applicable to the souls of the dead were immediately effective, were gained infallibly once the specified "good work" was performed—the alms paid over—and that the living man gaining the indulgence was not in a state of grace, had not been to confession and did not mean to go to confession, made no difference to the efficiency of what he did. Here were serious errors, common at the time, and as mischievous as errors could be—even apart from the fact that, mixed up with them, was a transaction in money. A thoroughly bad-living man had only to pay over the assigned sum, and the soul on whose behalf he did this went immediately from purgatory to heaven?

This just could not be true. It only required some voice to cry this to the high heavens, and in their hearts a million

12 By the way of petition.

listeners would approve. And if this which was said in a kind of official way could not be true, perhaps other things said no less solemnly were just as little true?

The great voice was now to be heard. And in the commotion there comes into the story a personage whose action is of the very first importance, Luther's sovereign, the Elector of Saxony, Frederick III, called the Wise. He was now, in 1517, a man in the late fifties and had ruled since 1486. It was he who had founded the university. He had rebuilt the castle of Wittenberg and its church, the city hall, the Augustinian friary, and two colleges or residence halls for students: an active, "enlightened" prince, not a little touched by the new Renaissance spirit, a shrewd politician and without fear. By hereditary right he was the imperial vicar for the eastern half of the empire, an office which only came into full activity during an interregnum but which also made him a kind of superior for all the princes of this eastern part.

Frederick the Wise was a great collector of relics, and the new castle church was designed really as the setting for a permanent exhibition of his vast collection. From various popes he had secured correspondingly vast spiritual privileges for the pilgrims who venerated these relics, indulgences for those who, in the proper spiritual dispositions, made some act of respect to the relic and said certain prescribed prayers.

This great relic church was dedicated, appropriately, to All Saints, and the annual feast of All Saints, November 1, was one of the city's principal holidays. In 1517, as the feast drew near, Tetzel and his party had come close to the elector's frontier—Frederick had not invited him to preach the indulgence in his dominions. Was all Wittenberg to stream out to the neighbouring town where Tetzel was preaching the great indulgence? It has been suggested that we have here a rivalry between two spiritual crusades, each financially profitable to a personage in power. The relic church at Wittenberg was also the church of the university, where degrees were conferred, university sermons preached, and so forth. And now, on the eve of its annual feast day, Luther announced in the customary way, by a notice fastened to the door of the church, that he proposed to hold a public disputation on the subject of indulgences—the ninety-five points he was willing to argue being set out in the notice. They were also, of course, printed and distributed in the usual manner throughout the university.

With this act the whole tenor of Luther's life changed. For the student and university professor, thirty-four years of age, there were now to follow four years of the most strenuous public activity, a drama where he held the centre of the stage, with pope and emperor as his foils: a drama at which all Europe gazed. Before this new star—whose rays burned wherever they fell—even the fame of Erasmus would seem pale.

To comment here on each of the famous ninety-five statements is not possible, nor even to give a résumé of the whole which would be intelligible. But here is a selection, to show some of the leading topics and the spirit in which the paper was drawn up.[13]

There is a plain denial that the pope can remit any penalties except those which he has himself imposed, and the statement that he does not—in granting indulgences—will to do more than this. There is more than a suggestion that indulgences are unnecessary, for the dying pay all their debts by their death. Even were the magnificent promises of total pardon attainable, to realise these would be the lot of only the most perfect of mankind. The pope has no such power as what is called "the power of the Keys." And, Luther asks, who knows whether the souls in purgatory wish to be bought out of it?

All Christians who are truly contrite have already [i.e., because of this] a right to full remission of their sins and of the penalties due for committing them, without receiving any indulgence from the pope. Which indulgence is not to be scorned, however, for it is a declaration that God has remitted the penalties.

Christians ought to be taught that it is better to give alms to a poor and needy man than to use the money to obtain an indulgence. For charity makes the giver a better man, but indulgences merely free him from penalties. They should also be taught that, just as the pope needs prayers more than money, so he would rather, in giving these indulgences, that a devout prayer for him were produced than a payment of

[13] What follows is a translation and adaptation of the theses numbered 5, 13, 23, 26, 29, 36, 38, 43, 44, 48, 50, 51, 52, 58, 62, 67, 69, 70, 71, 72, 77, 79, 80, 81, 82, 86, 90, 91, 94, 95. An English translation of the theses is printed in B. L. Wolf, *Reformation Writings of Martin Luther*, Vol. 1.

money. And that if the pope knew how the preachers screw this money out of the people, he would rather see St. Peter's in ashes than rebuilt out of the skin, flesh, and bone of his flock. If he knew all, as he should, he would be glad to sell St. Peter's to find money to give to many of these poor victims of the indulgence preachers.

Even if the pope himself pledged his own soul that indulgences were effective, it would be folly to place any trust in them as a means of salvation.

These treasures of the Church whence the pope gives indulgences are not the merits of Christ and the saints, for these are continually operating, without any act of the pope, bringing to the interior-minded man grace and to the exterior-minded, the cross, death and hell. The true treasury of the Church is the most holy gospel of the glory of God and His grace.

When preachers speak about the indulgences which bring the greatest graces, what they really mean is, which bring in the most money. Bishops and parish priests are bound to receive the commissaries charged with the papal indulgences with the utmost respect. But they have the still more serious duty of using all their wits to see that the commissaries do not substitute their own fairy tales in place of what the pope directs.

Whoever speaks against the truth of these papal indulgences may he be damned and accursed. But whoever takes steps against the lust and licentiousness of speech in those who preach the papal indulgences may he be for ever blessed. For example, their saying that not St. Peter himself, if he were now pope, could grant greater graces; or that the cross with the pope's arms so prominently displayed on it[14] is equal to the cross of Christ.

Bishops and priests who allow these things to be said to their people will one day be called to account for this. The preachers' loose language in their explanation of indulgences makes it difficult, even for learned men, to save the people's respect for the popes in face of the calumnies or the shrewd questions of some of the laity. For example, they ask, why is it that the pope does not, as a most holy act of charity and a thing supremely necessary for souls—which is the most just

14 At the centres where these indulgences were preached, it was customary to set up a great cross. On this the papal arms would be displayed—a sign that the indulgence was authentic.

motive of all—himself empty purgatory, if he delivers such a host of souls for the sake of a wretched alms in aid of the rebuilding of St. Peter's: a truly trivial motive, after all? And again, why does not the pope, who today is a hundred times richer than Croesus, rebuild St. Peter's out of his own money rather than out of the misery of the poor?

To reply to these well-weighed questions of the laity by mere force, and not with the light of reason, is the way to expose both the pope and the Church to ridicule, and to make Christians discontented. If only the indulgences were preached according to the spirit and mind of the pope, all these problems would be solved very easily; or, rather, they would never arise.

Christians, therefore, ought to be exhorted that with all their strength they follow Christ Who is their head, through pain, death, and hell, and so to trust they will enter heaven through many tribulations rather than through a peaceful security.

ii Revolt and Sentence, 1517–1521

The famous Ninety-five Theses of 1517 are not, and were not in the mind of their author, any mere academic protest. They are a manifesto calling loudly to the discontented everywhere—to those reasonably discontented with the abuses and to the as yet scarcely discernible few who are discontented with the system itself. The bold, assured, not to say impudent, letter which Luther wrote to the Archbishop of Mainz, enclosing the theses, supports this. And in this preliminary to a lifetime's bitterly worded attack we must note a certain naïve disingenuousness.

Copies of the theses were sent to other universities in Germany—notably to Erfurt: they were in print within the month, and printed in German by December. With the new year, 1518, they were circulating everywhere. Tetzel's brethren sent a formal complaint to Mainz, and the archbishop sent on to Rome, as well as the ninety-five, a copy of the ninety-seven theses actually defended at Wittenberg in the previous September by Luther's pupil. Tetzel, from the University of Frankfort on the Oder, defended himself against Luther, and Luther preached at Wittenberg yet another great denunciation of the indulgence system. This in January. On February 3 the pope ordered the acting head of Luther's order to call him to account, and a command was sent that he must attend the chapter of his province that would meet at Heidelberg in April. The pope also, in March, made the Archbishop of Mainz a cardinal.

The papal directions apart, Luther must have gone to Heidelberg, for he had been for some years one of the principal officials of the order. He could expect to meet there critics as well as supporters. His principal superior, John Staupitz, was a friend on whom he could rely. And he knew that he had other support, of the most unlikely kind, and all important. His sovereign the Elector Frederick had intervened with a letter to say that Luther must not be detained at the chapter—the first of several interventions on his part, and altogether unprecedented. This is the first time for centuries that a prince has taken the step of protecting against judgment—against investigation—a man who stands close to the charge of being a heretic. Frederick the Wise is thereby one of those men who, standing at the switch points, possibly determine, by their practical, concrete decision in a particular detail, which way history shall take its course for centuries to come.

One item of the proceedings of such provincial chapters was the conferring of academic degrees. This entailed the ceremonious form of examination known as the disputation—the candidate offering to defend against all comers a number of theological theses. At Heidelberg, Luther, officially summoned there to answer charges made against the orthodoxy of his theological writings, was set to preside over this disputation; it was one of his pupils who defended, and the theses repeated the doctrine about original sin defended in 1517. Professors came in from the neighbouring university; there were some lively scenes. But the general body of Luther's brethren were for him, and the chapter was thus a kind of triumph.

A few weeks later, on May 16, in preparation for what threatened, he preached a sermon at Wittenberg on excommunication, the practical conclusion to which was that a man should be ready, for the truth's sake, to brave excommunication and, of course, should disregard it. He also prepared a detailed explanation of his criticism of indulgences and sent it, with a covering letter, to the pope. This was afterwards published (August 1518); it is known as Luther's *Resolutiones*. While he was busy on these, the general chapter of Tetzel's order met at Rome and took up the case against Luther. One of their number was the pope's personal theologian, and when the pope was shown the report on Luther which he had prepared for the chapter, orders were sent to Luther to appear at Rome within sixty days. When this reached Luther he at once appealed to the elector to protect him. Then in August the pope sent another order, this time to his own legate in Germany, that Luther was to be arrested and, if he did not recant, to be sent to Rome; and the pope wrote to the elector asking his co-operation.

This legate was one of the most remarkable men of the day, Thomas de Vio, called from his birthplace (Gaeta) Cajetan, and always known by this name. He was a Dominican friar, by fourteen years Luther's senior, who after a brilliant career in the universities of Padua, Pavia, and Rome had ruled his order for ten years as master-general. Leo X had recently (May 1, 1517) made him a cardinal, and he was now on his first mission as legate. Cajetan was a writer, and the first to produce a commentary on the *Summa Theologica* of St. Thomas Aquinas. As a philosopher and a theologian he is still reckoned an authority of the first order, and all his work is characterised by a bold originality and high intellectual courage. He was soon about to show in a very convincing way how little the years of administration had dulled his soul when, seeing from his German experiences that a new age of theology had dawned, he set himself at fifty to learn Hebrew and in the last ten years of his life produced a whole series of biblical studies done after the new Renaissance methods. Cajetan was as good as he was learned. He had laid the foundations of a real reform of his own order, and amid the worldly levity and the wickedness that surrounded Leo X his simple Dominican goodness shines out rarely.

What had brought Cajetan to Germany was the pope's anxiety at the threat of renewed Turkish aggression. At no time since the Moors crossed the Pyrenees in the eighth century was the supremacy of Christianity in Europe in such real peril as in these opening years of the sixteenth century. Not even the development of Protestantism, as a force in politics, was ever to displace this as the first anxiety of such internationally minded rulers as Charles V and his son. These were the years (1512–20) when the sultan, Selim I, made himself master of Syria and Egypt. He was master already of Asia Minor, the Crimea, Greece, and the Balkans, and his son was to conquer Hungary, to make Buda a Turkish city, and in Luther's own

lifetime to lay siege to Vienna (1529). For two thousand
miles, from Buda to Basra on the Persian Gulf—such was the
Turkish Empire. Cajetan's task was to bring the princes,
meeting at Augsburg in the summer of 1518, to unite in defence against the Turk. He brought a high distinction from
the pope for the emperor—and the cardinal's hat for Albert
of Brandenburg. Cajetan imposing the hat on this client of
the Fugger—how strange at times are the chance events of
history!

As to Luther, once again, upon the Roman summons, the
elector intervened. He brought it about that Rome changed
Cajetan's instructions. Luther would be examined in Germany, by the legate; if he refused to retract, he must be sent
to Rome. Cajetan, until a few months before this, was the
head of the order to which Tetzel belonged. Luther was anxious about his reception. But the great theologian received
him—we have Luther's word for it—in a most kindly and fatherly way, not as a judge, and with never a hint of threats.
His only wish was to put Luther right and to reconcile him
to the pope. Luther wished to argue his case, but the cardinal
refused. He put to Luther the bull of Clement VI (of 1342)
which defines the basis of the indulgence system as the infinite
treasury which the merits of Christ are. For a Catholic this
was a fact to be accepted, not a theory to be discussed. Luther,
proposing to discuss it, is in fact calling into dispute already
the essence of the papal authority. The legate gave the Augustinian a hint of what must follow if, on a later meeting,
he persisted in this attitude. And Luther left Augsburg that
same night, unmolested (October 20, 1518). It was now close
on a year since the indulgence theses were published. On November 28, Luther made his first open defiance—he wrote and
published an appeal from the judgment of Leo X to the judgment of the next general council.

In the first days of the new year, 1519, the Emperor Maximilian I died, before he had negotiated the question of his
successor. His only son had died many years before, and so
it now became the business of the electoral princes to choose
an emperor. The most obvious claimant on their votes was
the late emperor's grandson, Charles, the son of the heir
who had predeceased Maximilian, and now, by Maximilian's
death, ruler of all the Habsburg lands in Germany, perhaps
a quarter of the total area of Germany that lay within the

empire. Charles, as Duke of Burgundy, had since 1506 been the ruler of the Netherlands (which was also imperial territory) and since 1516 King of Spain and of Naples. He was now in his twentieth year. Such an accumulation of power already possessed rendered his election fearful to many a German princeling. If Charles were elected emperor, would he not attempt to turn the empire into a real unitary state, where princes would be merely an aristocracy? In what must surely have been a feeling of desperation some of them began to think of electing the one prince powerful enough to talk with Charles on equal terms, the King of France, who only four years before had won the great victory of Marignano that signalised France as the greatest military power of the Western world. But a King of France who was also the Holy Roman Emperor? Lord of two immense territories that were contiguous?

As much as any German prince, the dilemma tormented the pope. For centuries such a combination of power as either of these choices presented had been the nightmare of all the popes, not indeed for what it threatened to their own states, but from the historical recollection that it was the greatest of dangers to the freedom of religion. And Leo X, the head of the Medici family whose hold on Florence had fluctuated for a generation with the rivalry of the two great powers, had a personal anxiety thereby that was extremely acute. He would have preferred that neither Charles nor Francis were elected. His own choice—the prince whom, at any rate, he strove to persuade to enter the lists—was Frederick the Wise, Luther's own sovereign and, in these critical months since the heresiarch's appearance as such, Luther's protector.

The story of what went on in Germany during the first half of the year 1519 is as absorbing as it is intricate. But on June 27, Charles was elected—the Emperor Charles V, at a cost of nearly 900,000 florins, spent, there is no need to guess how, good money borrowed from the Fugger, and at what rate of interest!

There is, then, no reason to wonder why the case against Luther slowed down, despite the defiance of his appeal from the pope. He himself, as always, was a prodigy of work. Nearly nine hundred folio pages of print came from him in this year 1519, sermons, propaganda, controversy, works of piety. And in the height of the summer there was a great theological tourney at Leipzig before the Duke of Saxony[15] and a huge audience. The Catholic champion was a professor from the university of Ingoldstadt, John Eck. Luther had with him a colleague from Wittenberg, Andrew Bodenstein, always known as Carlstadt.[16] Eck made mincemeat of the unfortunate Carlstadt in a four-day debate on the freedom of the will, and then, on Luther's offering to debate the historicity of the papal power—an invention, said the Wittenberger, of the last four hundred years—handled him scarcely less trenchantly and secured the public admission that Luther denied any special sacredness to the decisions of general councils. Luther never again challenged the professionals.

And now they were swarming. The University of Cologne condemned his teaching in August 1519, and Louvain also, November 9. Finally, on June 15, 1520, appeared the solemn papal condemnation, the bull which begins *Exsurge Domine*.

The bull of Leo X is simple in structure and somewhat surprising in form. It begins with a statement of the pope's anxiety upon hearing that the Church in Germany is troubled with various erroneous doctrines which, condemned already in years gone by, are now reviving. Some of these errors it has been thought well to set out, "as follows . . ." And what follows is a list of forty-one propositions. Next, the pope remarks that it is evident how mischievous such ideas are, and that if they were true it would follow that the Church, whose guide is the Holy Ghost, was in error and had always been in error. Therefore, he continues, "We condemn, reprobate and utterly reject them." So far, not a word about Luther. But the bull continues, "Moreover, since the aforesaid errors, and many others, are contained in various writings of Martin Luther . . . We likewise condemn whatever he has written . . . and forbid the faithful of Christ to read [his writings], to praise, print, publish or defend them." The bishops are to make search for them and burn them. Luther is given sixty days—and his adherents with him—to recant his errors and, within a further sixty days, to certify the pope that he has done so. Should he—and they—do otherwise, "We condemn them as notorious and pertinacious heretics."

[15] The cousin of Frederick III, and to the end of his life firmly anti-Lutheran.
[16] The town where he was born.

The commission which at Rome had been at work upon the condemnation for a good four months had had before it an abundance of Luther's published works and the detailed judgment of Louvain and the official transcript of the Leipzig disputation. What it produced in the forty-one propositions of the bull was a remarkable summary of all this. Only six of the forty-one refer to indulgences, and four to purgatory, but as many as fifteen to errors about the sacraments. Of the rest, ten concern the authority of the Church, two are about good works, and there is one on free will. Eck was commissioned to take the bull to Germany and to see to its proclamation there. In many cities there were violent scenes as it was officially delivered—at Leipzig, for example, in the territory of the anti-Lutheran Duke George, and as far away from Luther's country as Mainz. It did not reach Luther until October 10. The new emperor had by now arrived in Germany, and on October 28 he was crowned at Aachen. The pope's nuncio, Aleander, pressed him to put the bull into execution; i.e., to have Luther arrested, once the time limit had expired and he had not obeyed, and to send him as a prisoner to Rome. Charles declared that this must be discussed in the coming Reichstag, or Diet, the first of his reign, which would meet at Worms on January 27, 1521.

Luther, meanwhile, and all Wittenberg with him, celebrated the last day of freedom allowed him by the bull by a riotous procession and ceremonial burning of the bull in the place where the town muck was deposited and where criminals were put to death. Into the fire they also threw the *Corpus* of Canon Law and a number of works of scholastic theology—but not St. Thomas nor Scotus, since no one was willing to make a sacrifice of so many expensive books. This was on December 10, 1520. On January 3, Leo X, by a second bull, definitively excommunicated Luther. Meanwhile the nuncio wrote to the pope that all Germany was aflame with hatred for the Curia Romana. And amid this commotion, Luther, in a kind of triumph, preaching in every great town where he halted, made his way in April to Worms: for the Diet had resolved he should be heard before any steps were taken against him.

The proceedings at Worms were brief—so far as Luther, personally, played any part. He was called in on April 17, shown a number of his books, asked whether he owned them for his work and whether he still adhered to the doctrines he had set out in them. He owned the books and asked for time to consider his answer to the second question. He was given a day, and on April 19 he made his second appearance. Standing before the emperor, the bishops, and the princes, he referred to his books as intended to attack the papacy and the teaching of the pope's adherents (*doctrinam Papistarum*) as forces which had laid waste the Christian world. As for his controversial writings, he admitted that the language used was more bitter than became a monk or a professor. But not until such evidence was brought that convinced him he was wrong, would he recant. He would then be the first to throw his books into the fire. Here his speech was interrupted. He was told that what had already been decided in councils of the Church was not matter for discussion. Would he give a plain answer: did he wish to recant or not? To which he said, "Unless I shall have been convinced by the witness of Scripture or of evident proof from reason—for I do not believe either Pope or Councils by themselves, since it is agreed that these have often made mistakes and contradicted themselves—I am overcome by the Scriptures I have quoted, my conscience is captive to God's word: I cannot, and I will not, revoke anything, for to act against conscience is neither safe nor honest."[17]

Luther before the Diet of Worms: one of the scenes on which the imagination of later times has readily, and understandably, seized. The ambassador from Venice who was an eyewitness, a very star of the Christian renaissance, Gasparo Contarini, told his government that the good will Luther enjoyed generally at Worms was beyond exaggeration and bound to issue in open acts against the bishops. Had Luther not entangled himself in manifest errors about the faith, the whole of Germany would have adored him. This, said the ambassador, was the opinion of the Duke of Bavaria—the chief of the Catholic princes after the emperor. Contarini thought that Luther was a man who would not give up his opinion, either through argument, fear, or entreaty. But, he said, at Worms he had scarcely fulfilled the expectations of him which all had held. Also, that he had powerful protectors and, despite the pope and the emperor, his books were on sale in Worms itself.

Charles V spoke out immediately. On the day following

---

[17] The famous phrase in his own tongue, with which some accounts say that Luther ended, "Here I stand. I can no other. God help me. Amen," is no longer accepted as authentic.

Luther's stand he declared to the Diet that he meant to live and die a Catholic, like all his ancestors, and to stake all "upon this course." "A single monk," said the young sovereign, "led astray by private judgment, has set himself against the faith held by all Christians for a thousand years and more, and impudently concludes that all Christians up till now have been in error." Five weeks later, May 26, the decision of the Diet was published: Luther was outlawed, as a condemned heretic; none was to give him shelter or food, nor to associate with him; wherever he might be found he was to be arrested and kept a prisoner until the emperor was able to secure him.

The condemned man was, however, by this time secure and safe. He had left Worms on April 26, after many hours spent in conference with would-be reconcilers. The evening before he set out, he had one of his rare interviews with his own elector, and Frederick told him of the plans made for his safety. Luther was, then, anything but surprised when on May 4, soon after he had entered Frederick's territory, as his company was going through the forest, four armed knights, masked, rode out of hiding and captured him. In their company he came to the famous castle of Wartburg, which dominates the town of Eisenach, where he had once gone to school. Here he remained, lost to sight, for the next ten months.

iii The Theories Go into Effect, 1522–1529

Had the earth simply opened and swallowed up Martin Luther, his disappearance could not have been more complete. In one of the outhouses of this grim and long-neglected castle —once the home of St. Elizabeth—he was to live without any companions other than his guards and the servants. He had, however, his books and, despite the loneliness, depression, and continous ill-health, he contrived to do an enormous amount of work. It was now that he translated the New Testament into German, using Erasmus' Greek version. And he wrote two long Latin tracts that were to be of the highest importance from the day they were published, On Monastic Vows and The Abolition of Private Masses. These three productions of 1521–22, together with three pamphlets published in 1520, are the foundation literature of Luther's achievement. These earlier pamphlets were, first, An Appeal to the Christian Nobles of Germany, which developed in passionate language the theme that for centuries Germany had existed to provide the popes with money; *The Babylonian Captivity of the Church*, which denounces as a popishly devised corruption of the truth the system of the seven sacraments and the idea of religious virginity; and *The Freedom of the Christian Man*, which is a simple explanation, in devotional language, of the doctrine that justification comes through faith alone—through man's confidence that, unable to do aught of himself towards his salvation, he is saved already through the saving death of Christ.

The *De Votis Monasticis*, however, is far from devotional. It is one of the more violent of Luther's diatribes, and whatever the practical problems which the state of monastic celibates in Luther's time presented, the assumptions on which he bases this criticism of the system are false and must have been known to be false to the writer. As well as the much-debated theme, "Luther the Liar," we here must make acquaintance with that other notorious topic, "Luther the Indecent." Luther scholarship is, by now, a whole-time occupation for life. And every few years or so we are reminded by some new book that Luther, dead four centuries or more, is still powerful. The rival schools are as hot with one another about "interpretations," and theories, and statements of fact, as though his ideas still swayed the world. There are certain basic questions about Luther's character which sooner or later rise up, and the writer of even the simplest account must halt his narrative and give a plain answer. Was Luther a truthful man? And I would say that he never hesitated to lie if he thought it useful. Was he a pure-minded man? I would say "Yes"; for he never wrote a line designed to excite the emotions of sex or to satisfy them, and he would undoubtedly have chastised with the maximum of severity writers of that sort. Were his ideas of marriage elevated? They were no worse than the general ideas of his age, but he spoke his mind much more freely about them, and it was a mind that ran more naturally than most to the coarsest of metaphors and similes. In this matter of coarse language, is Luther an exceptional writer? Among religious leaders, certainly; among the few who have claimed to be sent by God to restore the divine religion to its primitive state, he is uniquely coarse, nor have I ever heard of any one of these who even begins to approach him in this respect. And Germans of his own time, men no less zealous in the cause of the Reformation, were shocked by this contradiction: Bullinger, for example, saying, "Some small excuse might have been found had it been written by a swine-herd and not by a famous pastor of souls."

In general, whatever the topic, once Luther is annoyed—say, by contradiction—vulgar, filthy expressions simply pour out from him. How far does all this matter? Well, that is not a historical question, of course; but whoever wants to reach a decision must bear in mind that rural Germany, four hundred years ago, was a world whose ways of living—and what this could breed—are too unlike our own to make judgments of this sort really satisfying. One thing is certain: Luther's foulness is not amusing; even when it is a foul joke told to encourage a despondent, anxious soul, the sheer witlessness of the filth is tedious in the extreme—the vulgarity is anything rather than "radioactive."

More important is the question of truthfulness. We know from Luther's letters that he found this attack on monastic vows a hard book to write—found it hard to base on Sacred Scripture his contention that the vows were an insult to God. But it was invention, on his part, to state that the Church which had bred him taught that if a man intended to please God perfectly he must become a monk, or that the Church had two ideals of religion, a lower one for the laity and a higher one offered only to those who took vows; and it was false to say that the Church taught that the act of taking the vows operated like a second baptism, so that one who died at that moment died (because of the vows) in the state of innocence of a newly baptised child; and it was also false to say that the monks and nuns, normally, entered this life with the idea that just to do so did away with all their sins and their consequences.

To caricature the other side, and to spend oneself destroying the caricature with hot indignation and scorn, is a controversial tactic much older than Luther, and it has survived his age to flourish in our own as though it were only just devised. But, whatever the strength of the case that can be built up against the Catholic Church as it is, or against the Catholic Church because of the abuses that gather round it, historians must recognise that Luther also used, habitually and consciously, the controversial weapon just described. This is very true of his attack, not on bad monks, but on the fact and practice of good monks. And it is true of what he has to say about the Catholic teaching on those matters—e.g., grace, good works, and the like—where the difference between that teaching and his innovations was most important. The later in his life that

Luther makes his criticism, the greater the divergence from the facts tends to be—i.e., when there is such divergence. And the later Luther sometimes contradicts the more accurate critic of the earlier years of the revolt. Here is an instance. Marriage is a sin, so Catholics are taught; thus the Luther of 1540, adding that when he was a monk he shared this idea. But the Luther of 1521—already well away from Catholic belief and life—can distinguish between the popes, who do indeed forbid marriage to priests, and the heretics, who condemn marriage as sinful. Was Luther in 1540 lying? Not necessarily. Who is to say how dim a man's mind will be about his original belief after twenty years of hard debating against it? But Luther is certainly not reliable. His accuracy is not what one can take for granted.

What we have been witnessing so far (1517–22) is nothing more nor less than a duel between the German friar and the distant pope[18]—a duel which, nevertheless, because of the utter disparity between the two parties and because of its length and the continuity of the battle, is surely one of the most singular events in history. That a private individual, whose sole asset (beyond his mind and character) was his sovereign's refusal to interrupt his activities, had been able to draw into this series of engagements the majesty of the Roman See was itself a thing hardly believable, a most forceful scandal, by the fact. What plans for the future, practical plans, Luther had in his mind, plans so to change ritual and discipline that these would embody his new doctrinal discoveries and cease to be the practical exposition of what he declared to be corruptions of the Gospel, no one can say. It is possible that such problems had so far never entered his mind; that he

[18] There is not space to complete the picture by describing the great war of pamphlets and books which now broke out—a truly intensive combat in which, on the Catholic side, the University of Louvain took the lead. More, Fisher, and presently Erasmus came into it. But the most illustrious of all was More's sovereign, King Henry VIII, who answered the *Babylonian Captivity* by his *Assertio Septem Sacramentorum* (i.e., *A Defence of the Seven Sacraments*), published in 1521. This work, among other things, is a strong defence of the position that the pope is the divinely appointed head of the Church, and that it is his office, as such, to give final judgment about the meaning of Scripture. In recognition of this work the pope, Leo X, conferred on Henry the title Defender of the Faith. The English sovereigns since have continued so to style themselves.

was wholly unconscious that the revolution he had inaugurated must be completed by a reorganisation of rites and discipline; that he assumed that, all men gradually being converted to his ideas, somehow or other religion as a system would of itself be transformed. Whatever his intentions and hopes, there were others at Wittenberg burning with the desire to make such practical changes; Carlstadt, for example, and Luther's colleagues in the Leipzig disputation of 1519. While Luther, lost to the world, was busy with his fundamental literary work, they proceeded to change things very drastically. And a new spirit seemed about to influence them.

In what men called the Anabaptist movement, all the semi-religious, semi-social, apocalyptic madness of the medieval heresies was coming to life again, and two of the new prophets, arriving at Wittenberg, were hospitably received by Carlstadt and Melanchthon. The Austin Friars of Wittenberg resolved that all who chose to leave the order might do so without further ceremony, "since in Christ there are neither Jews nor Gentiles, neither monks nor layfolk. And a vow that goes contrary to the Gospel is not a vow but mere wickedness." As to the Mass, on Christmas Day, 1521, Carlstadt inaugurated a new ritual. He began with a sermon, exhorting all to communicate under both kinds; then, not wearing any of the Mass vestments, he read the Mass as far as the Gospel inclusively; he omitted everything between this point and the Canon; leaving out all the ceremonial reverences in the Canon, he followed it until he had said the words of consecration; there was no elevation of the Sacrament, but immediately Holy Communion was given, under both kinds, Carlstadt repeating to each communicant the words of consecration. "Immediately after the distribution, he went off, and almost all the people too."

Meanwhile Carlstadt was also patronising such lunacy as that study was sinful and schoolmastering also, since in the Gospel we read, "Be not called Rabbi, or master." Going round the town, he would ask all and sundry to interpret the Bible for him, explaining, again from the Bible, that it was only to the ignorant that the true meaning was revealed. With the schoolmaster and one of the Austin Friars, he led an attack on the schools and the church, from which the statues were torn down and destroyed. And Melanchthon was writing how impressed he was by the prophets, with their assertions that God held familiar conversation with them, that they could foretell the future, and the like. It was time for Luther to be allowed to reappear. On March 6, 1522, he returned. The champion against the Roman tyrant must now apply himself to the practical business of devising a new apparatus of Christian life.

It is not at all easy to build up a general picture of the gradual transformation of the religious life of Saxony in the next few years as an orderly progression. That the Mass must go because the Mass was blasphemy was one certain first principle. But since, as Melanchthon said, "the world is so much attached to the Mass that it seems impossible to wrest people from it," Luther wished that the outward appearance of the service should be as little changed as possible. In this way the common people would never become aware there was any change, said Luther, and all would be accomplished "without scandal." "There is no need to preach about this to the laity." Even the communion was to be given under one species only to those who would otherwise cease to receive the Sacrament. Forms and appearances were comparatively unimportant, and in later years Luther could say, "Thank God . . . our churches are so arranged that a layman, an Italian say or a Spaniard, who cannot understand our preaching, seeing our Mass, choir, organs, bells, etc., would surely say . . . there was no difference between it and his own."

Luther, in the sermons preached after his return to Wittenberg by which he laid the commotion caused by Carlstadt and his followers, had been clear enough that there must be an end to the saying of Mass and to the obligation of going to confession, clear also that no one must be molested who ceased to observe the prescribed days for fasting and abstinence from meat, clear also that the clergy who wished to marry could now do so freely. But despite the firm tone in which the end of the old order was thus announced, there is a steady insistence that the changes must be gradual and be brought about in a kindly and friendly way, without violence. Only then will the anti-reform party be won over to the cause.

It was not until Christmas 1524 that the elector—long hesitant because fearful of renewed rioting—gave way, and the Mass ceased to be said at Wittenberg. The new rite—a service preparatory to the congregation receiving the communion—was, as far as the Creed, identical with the Mass. Then, after a sermon, the service resumed, but at the Preface.

The Canon of the Mass was omitted, the words of consecration being said, or rather sung, by the celebrant immediately after the Preface. The elevation of the consecrated bread and wine was retained, "for the sake of the weaker brethren." Then was sung the *Pater Noster*, the celebrant communicated himself—and next the congregation, under both kinds. The Latin language continued to be used at first, but within a year Luther's German version replaced it. From what survived of the ancient rite, every expression referring to what was being done as a sacrifice was carefully cut out. This German service was imposed by the elector's authority from 1527. The ancient rite was forbidden; attendance at the new service was made obligatory. At the visitation of the parishes—carried out by the elector's authority—those suspected of "error" were brought in and questioned. If they refused to submit, they were banished. The sovereign's authority was essential to success. Unless he forbade the Mass, his theologians explained to him, all the efforts of the preachers would be in vain.

Meanwhile one monastery after another had followed the example of the Austin Friars of Wittenberg. The discontented monks streamed out, convinced by Luther's propaganda that their obligations had never been more than nominal, since, for all but the tiniest minority of mankind, to vow oneself to chastity was to vow the impossible.[19] And many nuns did the same. Luther has told the story of the flight from their convent of a band of Cistercian nuns in 1523, one of whom he was later to marry. And he wrote a pious tale about the miraculous way another nun was liberated—the miracle being that the nun in charge of the gate omitted one day to lock it. This little tract is the distant ancestor of all that vast literature, of dubious intent, of which *Maria Monk* is perhaps the best-known specimen. Some of these women went to their own homes; others came to Wittenberg, to be housed temporarily in the abandoned Augustinian monastery, which was still Luther's home. Their presence gave rise to the kind of gossip one can imagine—gossip for which there was no foundation— and to serious misgivings on the part of that sober-minded young man Melanchthon. He thought these ladies were softening Luther by their flattery. This descent of ex-monks, eager to see the prophet at whose voice their chains had fallen,

[19] This was one of the most frequently repeated of Luther's axioms, a fundamental of his case that monasticism was something opposed to the will of God.

was anything but agreeable to him. "I am going to hate the sight of these renegade monks who collect here in such numbers," he wrote; "what annoys me most is that they wish to marry at once, though they are no use for anything." And presently there were scandals about the ex-Austin Friars who had now found employment as preachers of the new evangel.

The new idea was taken up very slowly, as Luther complained, by the "stupid" subjects of the Saxon elector. And it did not, for some years, spread with any remarkable rapidity to the other states. The reason is simple enough. Until it was known that the ruler would favour the revolutionary change, the pioneers risked all the punishments meted out to heretics. Everywhere, once Luther began to print and publish, there were to be found disciples converted by his sermons and polemical tracts. But for these individuals to combine, even if only to desert the traditional church services and provide for themselves, was a highly dangerous business. It was the free cities of the empire that first went over, among them some of the greatest towns in Germany; in 1523 Frankfort on the Main and Magdeburg; in 1524 Nuremberg, Strasbourg, and Bremen. In 1524 a second prince joined the movement, Philip II, Landgrave of Hesse, a territory that had a common frontier with Electoral Saxony. He was a young man of twenty, and from the first he was a militant propagandist, who (for example) when he attended the Diet at Speier in 1526 took his preachers with him and had sermons preached in the courtyard of his residence, despite the protests of the emperor's brother, King Ferdinand, who presided at this Diet. He speedily became the Lutheran leader. Then in 1525 there came in a prize for whom Luther had long been working, a second Albert of Brandenburg, cousin of the Cardinal of Mainz. This Albert was the grand-master of a religious order whose members were soldiers, the so-called Teutonic Knights. They had been formed centuries before this time for the protection of the Far Eastern frontier of Christendom against the fierce heathen tribes beyond. That necessity had long since been provided for by the gradual conversion of all these people. The Knights remained, a sovereign order, and they ruled very extensive territories outside the borders of the empire itself. Königsberg was their chief city. Albert now abandoned his obligations as a Knight—his vows of poverty, chastity, and obedience—and declared himself Duke of Prussia, the territory of the new duchy being the lands of the order. And in 1526 he married. At the same time two of the bishops of these regions also abandoned the Catholic Church, and they too married.

The programme in these towns that went over to the new way was fairly uniform: the city authorities give permission to the Lutherans to preach, there is a certain amount of conflict, the authorities decide that the Lutherans are to continue, that there is room for only one religion if the city is to remain peaceful, the Mass is forbidden, the statues are torn down from the churches, the monasteries are abandoned (or the religious driven out), the property is confiscated to the town. Sometimes the resistance is so strong that there is a compromise. In general the Austin Friars went over; the Dominicans and the Friars Minor stood firm.

And the emperor meanwhile? The pledge of the young sovereign at Worms in 1521, that he would spend all his resources to arrest the menace of Luther, was never fulfilled. For never did the internal rivalries cease that had the first claim on his attention. During the next eight years the emperor and the King of France were to be almost continuously at war, with England the ally of Charles at one stage and of Francis I at another. But the pope, as an Italian prince, was similarly to be the ally now of one, now of the other. To the various meetings of the Diet—Nuremberg, 1524; Augsburg, 1526; Speier, 1526 and 1529—the pope sent legates, reminding the princes not of the Turks alone (Belgrade had fallen to them in 1521, Rhodes in 1522; at Mohács, in 1526, they destroyed a Christian army and became masters of Hungary) but also of the need to execute the sentence against Luther. The princes replied that this could not be done without danger of civil war, that religion's greatest need was a General Council with reform for its programme, to be held in some German city; and they sent the pope a long list of a hundred complaints. At Speier, in 1526, the very year of the pope's declaring war on Charles (as a principal of the League of Cognac) and only a few days after Mohács, the Diet declared that "while awaiting the sitting of the Council, or a national council with our own subjects, on the matters raised by the Edict of Worms, we are unanimously agreed each one so to live, govern, and carry himself as he hopes and trusts to answer for it to God and his Imperial Majesty." This vague generalisation was taken by the

Reformers as a tacit connivance with their manœuvres. When three years later the imperialists moved to revoke this declaration, the "Lutheranisers"—princes and free cities—made a formal protest that they held the revocation (which had passed by a majority) null and void. They thereby, unwittingly, brought into the vocabulary a name for themselves and for all these Reformation opponents of the Catholics, the word Protestant (April 19, 1529). In this same year the European war came to an end, with the emperor finally victorious (Treaty of Cambrai, August 1529).

iv *Essays in Compromise, 1530–1532*

With the end of the war the emperor was free once more to attend personally to affairs in Germany. Leaving Spain—for the first time since his return after the Diet which put Luther to the ban nine years before—he went to Italy, and at Bologna he was crowned emperor by the pope, February 24, 1530.[20] Then at Augsburg, in June, he met the German princes. The summons which convened this Diet had expressed the emperor's desire that every man's opinion, in the matter of religious differences, should be given a charitable hearing. The chancellor of the Elector of Saxony thereupon advised the Lutheran princes to have their case prepared in writing—the preachers themselves, he said, would hardly be given audience in the Diet. The result was the great Lutheran statement, drawn up by Melanchthon and presented in the names of seven princes and two free cities, which is called the Confession of Augsburg. It has long been regarded as one of the crucial documents of history, in the same class as Magna Carta, the Declaration of Independence, the Declaration of the Rights of Man.

This pioneer attempt to set out systematically the differences between Protestantism and Catholicism is divided into two roughly equal parts, nine pages[21] to each. In the first part it lists "The principal Articles of Faith" (21 items); in the second, "Articles in which the Abuses reformed are set out" (7 headings). Once again the present writer needs to summarise a document which, from the moment it appeared, was a cause of controversy and about which the Protestants themselves did not at the time agree, and as he summarises it he realises that,

20 He was the last emperor to be crowned by the pope.
21 Of print, of the size of this page.

by the fact, he can scarcely escape the trap that he seems to mean to interpret it and to be arguing for one side against the other. Yet he must take the risk, or the reader will have no more than a date, 1530, and the heading, *Confession of Augsburg.*

What Charles V had eternally in mind was a hope that the religious divisions would perhaps disappear once "everything . . . was rightly explained . . . on one side and the other." And to Melanchthon, nothing could have been more congenial than such a hope. Both sides would put out statements, and from a joint discussion there would issue, maybe, one true, harmonious religion in which all would be united.

The greater part of the summaries (in Part I), of "what our churches teach," are so brief that they give no clue—save perhaps to the scrutiny of professional theologians—whether the writer is Protestant or Catholic. There are, for example, five lines only on justification, three on "the Lord's Supper," three on Confession, two on Orders. The one relatively long article is that entitled "Faith and Good Works," which takes up a fourth of the whole section. It is partly a refutation of the charge that the Reformers "forbid" good works, partly an accusation that until the Reformers began, the only works of which Catholics heard anything from their priests were "*puerilia* and things not necessary," such as fasting, pilgrimages, devotion to the saints, rosaries, the monastic life. Catholics have learned from the Reformers, the Confession says, not to preach these things any longer, and they are even beginning to mention faith as a necessary concomitant of good works in the business of justification. The conclusion to this exposition of what the Protestants are teaching opens with the statement that nothing can be found in it which differs from Scripture, from the Catholic Church, and from the Roman Church, in so far as it is known from writers. "Which being the case it is a harsh judgment to call us heretics."

The real difference between "us" and the Catholic opponents—it is said—is in the attitude taken to what the Confession calls "abuses." There is a reference to the tumults which have accompanied the attempts to reform the abuses—the cause of which disorders had been the natural reaction in the Protestant mind to the calumnies spread by the Catholics. The emperor will now hear the truth about the changes made. The points to be explained and defended refer to the giving of Holy Communion under both kinds, clerical marriage, the

Mass, confession, abstinence from foods, traditions, monastic vows, the authority of the Church. In all these matters the Confession says what has been done and gives reasons to justify the change.

Inevitably this second section is controversial; it is, of course, intended as a base for discussion. It may be imagined that the opponents would find the opening words of the third paragraph startling, "Our churches are falsely accused of having abolished the Mass. We have retained it, celebrate it with the utmost reverence, and with almost all the old ceremonial save that a few hymns in German have been added as a way to teach the people." Then follows a reasoned argument against what Melanchthon holds to be the Catholic teaching about the Mass as a sacrifice, and the statement that the Mass is no more than "a communicating of the sacrament" to such as wish to receive it. There is one Mass every day, in each Protestant church, for this purpose. A good half of this second part of the Confession is given to the two points of monastic vows and church authority. In the concluding paragraph the author explains that the need to be brief has caused many things to be omitted which are subjects of general complaint; indulgences, for example. He repeats that his one concern has been that the emperor shall understand that the Protestants, whether in doctrine or in ritual, have accepted nothing that is contrary to Scripture or the Catholic Church, "for it is notorious that we have taken the most diligent pains to prevent new and impious doctrines from creeping into our churches."

The Confession was handed to the emperor on June 25, 1530, and read to the Diet. On the recommendation of the papal legate—Cardinal Campeggio, lately busy in London as judge in the matrimonial suit of Henry VIII—the emperor handed the document to a commission of theologians. Melanchthon had a conference with Campeggio while this examination was proceeding. But on August 3, Charles V, after studying the report of the Catholic theologians—since called the *Confutation of the Confession of Augsburg*—accepted its judgment of the meaning and value of the statement of the Protestant princes. The report admitted that many things called for improvement in the Church, and the emperor pledged himself to do all he could to bring this about. He also said that, seeing that there was so much agreement between Protestants and Catholics, he hoped they would return to the bosom of the Church. If they did so, there was nothing that they might not look for from him. But otherwise, he would have no choice but to act as became the [official] guardian and protector of the Church. There were further discussions that went on for some weeks.

But when the Diet closed, September 22, unity was, of course, no nearer and the decision was dead against the Protestants. They were given until the following April to consider whether they would profess "the same faith as the pope, the emperor, all the princes and the whole Christian world" on these matters where a difference had been shown to exist. And the emperor would consider what his policy must be. Meanwhile, in the dominions of these Protestants there must be no further propaganda, no pro-Lutheran books printed or sold, and no more pressure used to force anyone to go over to their religion, no interference to prevent "those who follow the old religion" from doing this, no interference with monks whether in their church services, their hearing confessions, their administering the Holy Eucharist in the old way. This was law from the date of its publication, November 19, 1530.

The famous Confession was not put together as a comprehensive statement of belief. It was a state document, the act of the Lutheran princes, and its purpose was to clear them, before the Diet, from the charge that they were heretics and from the consequences of the charge, to vindicate their claim that the new religion should be tolerated. Only in later years —thirty years and more after the events of 1530—did it begin to be given that theological quality which is the basis of its popular fame. It cannot be denied that, *as written*, it was an attempt—and how naïvely executed!—to throw dust in the eyes of the emperor, and that Luther (for example) who had no share in drafting the document, understood this well. Some of the main contentions, or doctrines, of the new school were passed over in silence; others were stated so ambiguously that they might equally well stand for views directly contradictory.[22] As it did not deceive the Catholics, so it displeased mightily a number of the Reformers, who considered that so much had been conceded that the cause came near to being betrayed.

To the *Confutatio* produced by the Catholic scholars at

[22] "It was not entirely sincere. . . . Its statements both positive and negative, are intentionally incomplete in many important passages. . . ." Harnack, quoted in Grisar, *Luther*, vol. III, p. 332.

Augsburg, Melanchthon, in due course, replied with an *Apologia*, in which, to the accompaniment of such words as liar, blasphemer, hypocrite, donkey, etc., etc., he repeated all his nonsense about Catholic doctrine as though the *Confutatio* had not proved what a caricature this was. One of his feats had been to cite St. Augustine, in the Confession, as a witness to the truth of Luther's views on justification, while in these very weeks he was writing to one who was to be his colleague at Augsburg that St. Augustine's teaching on this matter must be ignored since it was contrary to St. Paul and to Luther. And to Campeggio, the legate, he was writing, "We reverence the authority of the Pope of Rome and the whole hierarchy, and only beg he may not cast us off . . . For no other reason are we hated as we are in Germany than because we defend and uphold the dogmas of the Roman Church with such constancy." Campeggio, need it be said, was in no danger of believing Philip Melanchthon. When the legate advised Charles V, on the day following the presentation of the Confession, to have it examined by professionals, he said quite simply to the emperor that to discuss it would be pure waste of time; that in doing this he would be playing into the enemy's hands, whose hope it was to prolong matters, with the wish never to end them and to lead the emperor into a labyrinth of talk from which he would never emerge.

Campeggio, indeed, was willing that dispensations should be granted for the use of the chalice in Holy Communion and for the marriage of the clergy. Had he known how Luther reacted to Melanchthon's simple joy in sending this news he would scarcely have been surprised. "My reply," the patriarch wrote back to Augsburg, "is, to use Amsdorf's way of speaking, that I s—— on the dispensation of the Legate and his master; we can find dispensations for ourselves." "Do I beg of you," he wrote at the same time to his close friend George Spalatin, "speak privily to [our people at Augsburg] as Amsdorf would, 'The Pope and the Legate can —— my ——.'" The correspondence of these commissioners of Luther's party leaves no doubt that the Confession of Augsburg was the manoeuvre of men who felt themselves desperately caught. Luther consoled Melanchthon, fearful and anxious about this rôle and about the future, by writing quite simply, "Once we have escaped from the peril and have made sure of peace, it will be an easy matter to amend our deceits and our fall, because

God's mercy is watching over us."[23] To the congregation at Wittenberg, on his return, Luther told the story that the Papists had been forced to admit that on every point the Lutheran doctrine was the same as their own.

Luther had to soothe his leading supporter. To Philip of Hesse he wrote when all was over, "I trust that your Highness will not take offence that we offered to accept certain things, such as fasting, festivals, meats, and chants, for we knew well that they could not accept any such offer, and it serves to raise our repute still further and enables me in my booklet to paint their disrepute still more forcibly. It would indeed have been a mistake on our part, had the offer been accepted." This throws some light on Luther's picture of the debates at Augsburg where he contrasts with "the Papists," interested in repression alone, "the humility, patience and pleading" of his own party—all thrown away, of course, "upon these obstinate men."

The difference in tone between the Diet's decree against Luther in 1521 and its vague ultimatum to the princes in 1530 is as obvious as it is remarkable: in 1521 even Luther's protector only appeared in the shadow. Within a few months of the decision of 1530, however, the princes had organised. They made it clear that any attempt of the emperor to enforce the threats would be resisted. At a conference held at Schmalkalden, in Thuringia, they announced their purpose, February 27, 1531. "Whereas it is altogether likely that those who have the pure Word of God preached in their territory, and thereby have abolished many abuses, are to be prevented by force from continuing this service so pleasing to God," the twenty signatories pledged themselves that "whenever any one of us is attacked on account of the Word of God . . ." all would immediately come to his assistance. The signatories were, for Electoral Saxony, the dukes John and John Frederick (father and son); for Brunswick, the four dukes, Philip, Otto, Ernest, and Francis; for Hesse, Philip II; for Anhalt, the prince Wolfgang; for Mansfeld, the counts Gebhard and Albert; and representatives of the following twelve free cities: in north Germany, Lübeck, Bremen, and Magdeburg; in central Ger-

---

[23] Luther had another story about the Diet. A troop of devils, disguised as monks, set out for Augsburg. But as they were being ferried over the Rhine they disappeared into thin air. Melanchthon agreed that this was a portent of some terrible evil.

many, Nuremberg; in south Germany, Reutlingen, Ulm, Biberach, Memmingen, Isny, and Lindau; the Swiss city of Constance, and the Alsatian city of Strasbourg. The material resources these allies disposed of were contemptible, no doubt, in comparison with those of the emperor. But before Charles V could use his power he must first revolutionise the constitution of the empire or create a new spirit in the Catholic princes. None would really aid him in an armed expedition where victory would mean the disappearance of so many princely liberties. And many would take the side of the League. The fatal April 15 of 1531, the last day given the Protestants before the threats of the Augsburg Diet could be enforced, came and went, and nothing happened. In December the chiefs of the League tightened their organisation. In April 1532 they gave it a constitution. Other princes and cities joined them. Then came the news that the Turks were once more moving up the valley of the Danube. And the emperor and the League came to terms—the formal understanding that we know as the *Interim* of Nuremberg, July 23, 1532.

In the pact it is explicitly stated that between the emperor and the parties named there has been a quarrel about religion which no negotiation, at any of the Diets, has been able to heal. All endeavours to come to an understanding have been fruitless. And now a Turkish invasion is threatening. Unless there is peace within the empire the Turks cannot be fought off. So the emperor has mercifully consented to a common, public peace between himself and all the states of the empire, to last until the General Council of the Church meets or until the states are again convoked and decide otherwise, the condition being that until one or other of those events "no one shall make war on any other for reason of religion or for any other reason . . . but treat one another with true friendship and Christian charity." And the emperor has ordered that all judicial processes for matter of religion begun, or in preparation, on his part against the Elector of Saxony and his associates are to be abrogated and suspended until such General Council or meeting of the Diet. The Elector of Saxony and the others have, on their part, promised faithfully to observe the peace and not to use it to take advantage of any man, and that they will faithfully give their aid in the war against the Turks. The pact was signed by the princes who had signed the original pact of Schmalkalden (with the exception of Philip of Hesse and Otto of Brunswick-Lüneburg) and by the

Margrave of Brandenburg; the original cities also signed it and another twelve with them, the most important of which was Hamburg.

The treaty marks a turning point in this history. It is a truce where the side who are, in law, rebels are treated by authority as enjoying equal rights. There is latent in it a recognition that the new thing—the Protestant state, and so Protestantism—has come to stay.

v *Zwingli*

Melanchthon's *Confession* was only one of three such statements presented to the emperor at the Diet of Augsburg. By the year 1530 there were other bodies whom we may also call Protestants, who did not derive from Luther, and who now responded to the imperial invitation that all should speak their mind. One of these *Apologiae* came in the name of the free cities of Strasbourg, Constance, Memmingen, and Lindau. The other, presented on July 8, 1530, was the *Fidei ratio*, or *System of Belief*, of Ulrich Zwingli, of Zürich, a Reformer equal in stature to Luther and to Calvin, and whose untimely death on the battlefield of Kappel, only fifteen months after the *Fidei ratio*, brought to an end, in mid-term, a singularly personal theological development. Zwingli was Luther's junior by seven weeks only. When he fell at Kappel he was near the end of his forty-seventh year. He came from peasant stock, one of a family of ten, from the high mountain country east of Zürich. The family was not poor. Zwingli's father was the mayor of the village and his father's brother was the parish priest.

With Zwingli we make contact with a world very differently organised, politically and socially, from that which bred Luther, and with a Reformation that is not dependent on princes. The Switzerland into which he was born in 1484 was indeed a country of peasants. But politically it was a matter of thirteen mutually independent cantons bound together in a loose federation. Long ago, by dint of furious fighting, the Swiss had made good their claims to be independent of the emperor and of all other lands too. Whatever the democracies —i.e., the well-to-do middle-class merchants, lawyers, tradesmen—decided was settled definitively, as by a power that was sovereign.

For two generations now the main importance of the Swiss

cantons to the Western world had been that they produced
the finest infantry in Europe and that the cantons were ready
to hire these to the highest bidder. War, in this sense, was
almost the national industry. The traditional enemy was the
family of Habsburg, now the holders—*in perpetuum*, it would
seem—of the dignity of Holy Roman Emperor. But in the
days when Zwingli was growing to manhood the cantons
swung to the emperor's side as well as to France, as political
hopes and the security of pay moved them. Zürich, the city of
which Zwingli would be for twelve years the very life, had a
quasi-alliance, for the supply of soldiers, with the Holy See,
and this was to have its effect on Rome's attitude to Zwingli's
first activities as a Reformer. It was, then, a very military
world in which he grew up, the first generation of the almost
continuous wars between France and Spain and the emperor
that had begun when the French invaded Italy in 1494 and,
with two brief intervals, went on until the Treaty of Cambrai
in 1529. In all the great battles of that time—Agnadello,
Novara, Marignano, Pavia—the Swiss soldiers had their famous
part. And Zwingli knew the wars from personal experience,
for he went with the troops as a chaplain and was present at
the bloody fights of Novara and Marignano.

Zwingli's whole formal education was humanist, the home
of his uncle the priest, schools at Basel and at Berne, and the
universities first of Vienna and next of Basel—and when one
says Basel it is immediately of Froben that one thinks and of
Erasmus, whose books Froben printed and for whom Basel
was, for so many years, home. It is of course at Basel that
Erasmus lies buried.

Zwingli was in his twenty-third year when he became a
priest (1506). What determined this we do not know—except
the fact that the Church was still the obvious career for a
scholarly young man without means, and that he had grown
up among scholars devoted to the idea of reforming religious
life through a re-education of the Christian people. That
Zwingli, who had never spent an hour in a class of theology,
who had all the Erasmian prejudice against the theology of
the schools, and had had no training or testing of any kind,
took up the new way of life without misgiving was not so surprising in the year 1506. He was most zealous, and his country
parish, Glarus, was soon the scene of great activity, and
especially of great preaching. To Glarus he took his books,
and what with the classics, the Bible, and whatever he could

get of Erasmus, Zwingli's education continued at a great pace. He was an excellent Latinist, had a good technical knowledge of music and a good singing voice—two qualities not necessarily found together.

Zwingli remained at Glarus for ten years. He was a passionate patriot who took an active interest in all the public questions of his time. More and more he showed himself a leading opponent of the traditional policy of foreign alliances and the hiring of mercenaries. This made enemies for him among the wealthy *bourgeoisie*, and when in 1516 he was offered a preaching post at Einsiedeln—a great centre of pilgrimages—he did not refuse. Two years later came the chance of still greater opportunities—to be, in fact, parish priest and preacher of the great collegiate church at Zürich, the Grossmünster, which was the centre of the town's religious life. There were objections to his appointment, but in the end they were overcome. By the end of 1518 Zwingli's sermons were filling the great church. Luther had now got to the first crisis of his career as a Reformer, his meeting at Augsburg with Cajetan. So far his name has not occurred in any document we can connect with Zwingli or with Zürich.

Zürich was a town of about seven thousand people. The city with the canton was, to all intents and purposes, an independent republic within the Swiss Confederation and entirely in the hands of its wealthier citizens. Ecclesiastically it formed a single parish in the diocese of Constance. There were three houses of friars in the town—Dominicans, Franciscans, and Augustinians—and an abbey of nuns.

What was there new about these first famous sermons of Zwingli, the text of which has not come down to us? First, he preached every day; and next, the sermons were a continuous explanation, chapter by chapter, of the whole of the New Testament, which went on for years. And into this spoken commentary Zwingli seemingly brought the whole of life: the public policy of the town, the ills of religion no less than the sins of the citizens. Zwingli was already, in mind, bitterly anti-papal, in part for political reasons, the question of the military alliance and the feeling that Leo X, by going over to the victor of Marignano, had played the traitor to the Swiss. The news of Luther's open declaration at Leipzig in July 1519 that the papacy was but a man-made office, without any divine authority at all, seems, however, to have brought to a head a complication of *malaises* from which Zwingli had been suffering for a good three years; and also to have stimulated him as a practical example. Luther, he now said, was "the Elias of our times"—Elias, the prophet carried off to heaven in a fiery chariot at the end of his ministry, and whose reappearance on earth (for he must return in order to die) will be one of the signs foretelling the end of the world.

But the real crux of his own life, for Zwingli, had come three years before this, in 1516, the year of Leo X's concordat with France, the year of Erasmus' Greek Testament, and the year also of a spiritual consequence of Zwingli's study of this. The passionate enthusiasm of the Swiss humanist for the Netherlander, at this time, it is hardly possible to exaggerate. The language of one of his letters of 1516 to Erasmus is all but fantastic in its devotion. The reason appears to be that Erasmus, unknown to himself, had become to the younger man an angel of light and the means of deliverance from a very plague of immorality that had taken hold of him. In the *Enchiridion*, and elsewhere too, Erasmus lays great stress on Bible-reading habits as a preservative against sin—especially against this particular sin; indeed, he seems to suggest that to be such a preservative is an almost inevitable effect of such study. Zwingli read now, in the original words, St. Paul's first epistle to the Corinthians and, a priest of ten years' standing, he was seized with the impulse to make a resolution "to have no relations with a woman, since Paul has said that it is a good thing to have no contact with them." And for the rest of the time that he spent at Glarus, and for his first year at Einsiedeln, he was able to keep his pledge. Then, Zwingli's own words, "I succumbed, and like the dog returned to his vomit, as the apostle Peter says." It had never been a matter of affection, apparently, but just what the unfortunate man describes.

When Zwingli wrote his account of it all at Einsiedeln in 1518, as an answer to charges made at Zürich when he sought the post at the Grossmünster, he had been in this wretched state of relapse for a year or so. And he had given up all hope of recovery. For in this letter he first defends himself (relatively) by saying he has rigorously left alone women who are married, and virgins. And with these he will never have aught to do. But more than this, knowing his weakness, he now refuses to promise. In later years he was to marry. His wife was a younger woman, of good family, a widow with three children. The marriage was apparently a happy one.

One of the greatest unsolved Reformation problems is the

relation of Zwingli's theology to that of Luther. How far is
Zwingli Luther's pupil? There are likenesses, there are differences—major differences—in more than one fundamental of belief. The most notorious of these differences is in their teaching about the Eucharist. Luther, to the end of his life, believed
that Christ is really present in what the communicant receives
at the hand of the minister, and not only in the soul of the
communicant as he receives. For Zwingli, what the communicant receives is bread and wine and no more than bread and
wine. The Eucharist was divinely instituted, he teaches, to be
a joyous commemoration of Christ's coming and a public act
of thanksgiving for the benefits which that has brought to
man. The differences, the implications latent in the two men's
views, and the controversies they aroused cannot, obviously,
be dealt with here. They were the occasion of bitter exchanges
between the two Reformers, and when in 1529 Philip II of
Hesse actually brought them together in his castle of Marburg
(October 1529) they were scarcely polite in their theological
argumentation.

Zwingli's sermons provoked opposition. His open talk
about the pope, and his wide correspondence with like-
minded friends in other parts of Switzerland, were known to
all. Already in May 1520—a month or so before the bull of
Leo X against Luther—it was being said in Switzerland that
Zwingli and Luther should be burned in the same fire. In
that year he surrendered to the pope the pension which for
some years had been paid him for services rendered the Holy
See at Zürich.

The first open breach with the Catholic Church came at
the beginning of Lent, 1522. On Ash Wednesday, as an act of
defiance some prominent citizens had a meat meal and Zwingli
was present. They made no secret of the affair, and in a sermon, which he took care to print, Zwingli defended them. In
the controversy which followed there was a declaration from
the city authorities in favour of sermons being based on Scripture only, "to the exclusion of Scotus and Thomas and such
like," and a confirmation of this from the canons of the Grossmünster. Zwingli addressed to the bishop, who had sent a
remonstrance to the rulers of Zürich, a polemical tract "cor-
recting," phrase by phrase, the theology of his protest and
illustrating the criticism by challenging various Catholic doctrines. In November he publicly "put off" his priestly character and accepted the council's appointment as official

preacher to the city; and the new year, 1523, opened with the first of three public disputations in which the Catholic life of Zürich was brought to an end.

For the first, January 29, Zwingli wrote the sixty-seven theses which are the earliest outline of his version of the religion of Christ. Against him there argued John Faber, the bishop's vicar-general, later to be a famous Bishop of Vienna, who now wrote to a friend in Mainz, "A new Luther has arisen in Zürich." The council, at the end of this tourney, announced that since no one had been able to overthrow Zwingli by the testimony of Scripture, he was to continue as a preacher. Also, all other preachers were to preach nothing but what was so confirmed. The bishop's protest against this fell on deaf ears, nor did he venture to do more than threaten those who disobeyed with the indignation of the emperor.

The clergy in Zürich now began to find wives, and even among the nuns. In August, Zwingli openly attacked the Mass, going through the rite phrase by phrase and stigmatising its assertions as blasphemy. Orders were issued by the Council for the reform of the Grossmünster, the number of its priests and clergy to be reduced (there were fifty-four in all) and their incomes used for "Christian and useful purposes." There were to be daily lectures in Hebrew, Greek, and Latin, "as is necessary for the right understanding of Holy Scripture." And invitations were now sent out for the second disputation.

It would, of course, be a mistake to assume that all Switzerland (or even all Zürich) admired Zwingli and his friends as much as they admired one another. From the District of Obwalden, for example, came the following reply to the invitation (October 25, 1523): "We are always glad to be at your service, but we have no specially well-learned people, only pious and reverend priests who expound to us the holy Gospels and other holy Scriptures, such as were expounded to our forefathers and as the holy Popes and the Council have commanded us. This will we follow and believe to our lives' end, and sooner suffer death therefor, until Pope and Council command us the contrary. Further, we have no intention, so far as it rests with us, of changing what of old time has been so regularly resolved, in common with the whole of Christendom, by consent of Spiritualty and Temporalty. Moreover, we are not disposed to believe that our Lord God has bestowed so much grace on Zwingli, more than on the dear Saints and Doctors, all of whom suffered death and martyrdom for the

Faith's sake: and we have not been specially informed that he leads a spiritual life above all others, but rather that he is more given to disturbance than to peace and quiet. Wherefore we will not send any one to him, nor to the likes of him. For we do not believe in him: and, [in proof] that this is so, our mind is that if we had hold of him and could contrive to make our own reckoning with him, we should so reward him that he would never do any more. No more, save to commend you to God."

The end came on April 12, 1525, the Wednesday of Holy Week, when Mass was said for the last time in the Grossmünster. The feast of the institution of the Holy Eucharist on the next day was the occasion of introducing the new ritual. Zwingli describes it: "As soon as the sermon is over, unleavened bread and wine shall first be placed upon a table on the floor of the nave, and then the ordinance and action of Christ, in accordance with His institution of this memorial, shall be recited openly and intelligibly, in German, as hereafter follows. Then the bread shall be carried round by the appointed ministers on large wooden trenchers from one seat to the next, and each shall break off a bit or a mouthful with his hand and eat it. Then they shall go round with the wine likewise; and no one shall move from his place. When that is done, in open and clear words praise and thanksgiving shall be offered to God in an audible and distinct voice: and then the whole multitude of the congregation shall say 'Amen' at the end."

In the account given to Charles V at Augsburg we are told, "While the sacrament of the Lord's body and blood is eaten and drunk another of the ministers reads from the pulpit from the gospel of St. John, beginning at the 13th chapter . . . For we eat and drink the sacrament of the Supper sitting down and silently listening to the word of the Lord."

Zwingli is sometimes loosely described as an incipient rationalist, as one whose immediately radical changes in ritual, for example, came of meditations that went beyond any differences in the interpretation of a book believed to be divine. But this Swiss was as wholehearted a believer and a "Bible-man" as was ever Luther or Calvin. He was by temperament and by early training more of a humanist than Luther, and he had an instinct for systematisation, as his book, The False Religion and the True, would show.

The changes in Zürich had hardly been brought about when

the Catholic cantons and the Reformed began to organise in leagues. War came in 1531, and in the battle of Kappel, a few miles to the south of Zürich, the Catholics were victorious (October 11). Zwingli's body was among the slain. The ensuing peace of Kappel checked the militant party at Zürich; and perhaps also the character of Zwingli's successor as *antistes*, the mild and fatherly Henry Bullinger, who was in later years to play such a part in the lives of the English Reformers.

Luther made no secret of his joy at the news of Zwingli's end. "It is well that Zwingli, Carlstadt and Pellican lie dead on the battlefield,"[24] he is recorded as saying, "for otherwise we could not have kept the Landgrave [Philip II of Hesse], Strasbourg and others of our neighbours [i.e., faithful to the Lutheran doctrine]. Oh, what a triumph this is, that they have perished. How well God knows his business." Relief? Partly the ready abuse of a passionate hater of contradiction? "It pains me," he had written some years before, "that Zwingli and his followers take offence at my saying 'What I write must be true.'" Erasmus, for his own reasons, was no less relieved by the news. He had been morally driven out of Basel when the Mass was abolished there, and it was from his retreat at Freiburg-im-Breisgau that he wrote, "We are free from great fear by the death of the two preachers, Zwingli and Oecolampadius,[25] whose fate has wrought an incredible change in the mind of many. This is the wonderful hand of God on high . . . if Bellona had favoured them, it would have been all over with us."

By this year 1531, of the cantons called "town cantons," Berne had been reformed since 1528, Basel since 1529, and the new religion was established in Appenzell, Glarus, and Schaffhausen; of the "forest cantons," Constance also had been reformed in 1527. The French-speaking districts in the south had also been "invaded," by an enthusiastic refugee from France, Guillaume Farel. He failed at Lausanne, but won over Neuchâtel in 1530. In Geneva the last days of the Catholic régime were approaching. Farel made his first attempt there in 1532.

---

[24] It was at first falsely reported that the two last-named had also been killed.

[25] The Reformer of Basel (1482–1531). He died of grief at the news of the disaster at Kappel.

vi *The Anabaptists*

Into every chapter of the history of the Reformation there comes, sooner or later, a reference to "the Anabaptists." And always they are a people against whom every man's hand is turned. The name—a name coined by their deriding enemies (like the nineteenth-century "Dunker"), which means a re-baptiser—is applied to a variety of groups, in no way linked by any organisation or common authority, and often with very little common belief beyond the principle that, in religion, there is no authority except the individual conscience.

The religious ideas stigmatised as Anabaptist are often of very ancient lineage and antedate the Reformation by centuries. They are simply a reappearance of the long-ago condemned doctrines of the Beghards or Beguines, heretics crying out in the wilderness of a material age that the true religion has nothing to do with such material things as rites and authority, organisation and laws, people to whom the text "God is Spirit" was an authorisation and a command to live only as the urges impelled them which they conceived came from the Spirit.

That such ideas, if generally accepted and put into practice, spelled the end of law and order was as evident to the mass of men in the early Middle Ages as it is to us. Sectaries of this sort were pitilessly slain—nor did the contrast between these mischievous doctrines and any inoffensive, even mild and kindly, character of the believers cause feelings of remorse or regret in the repressor. Let it once be believed in any society that a particular group is really threatening to overthrow the distribution of property, to introduce a new conception of right and wrong, to prohibit and to crush all ways of life but its own, and the society will react savagely.

"Anabaptists," appearing in an age of social stability and high living, which is not concerned with more than the appearances of religion, with religion as a social decency, would make the figure of eccentrics merely and cause smiles or jeers in the measure they moved away from the general way of life. In other times to hold on to such beliefs was a sign, not of intellectual eccentricity, but of moral perversity—the thinkers (it was held) must know that their ideas were bad things, and although they *could* abandon them they preferred to cling to them. This in the face of repeated demonstrations by au-

thority that the ideas were bad things, and of commands that
they be abandoned. The refusal was "resistance to the known
truth"; it was "obstinacy in sin," and if it issued in final im-
penitence as the flames consumed the last of the sectary, that
was the logical order and what might be expected. Nor did
the rulers wait, before acting, until the propaganda for the
ideas had produced a respectable number of adherents—or
even until the social and political implications of the belief
were brought into the light of day, or for evidence that the
accused had grasped these implications.

Under the surface of orthodoxy universally supreme, "Anabaptist" ideas seethed in more than one place through all the
Middle Ages, it would seem. The sudden appearance of such
a propagandist as Luther, calling to all Germany in a voice of
great power that the Christian religion means, first of all, that
man is free in his belief from any such authority as pope,
bishop, priest have usurped—how did this sound in the ears
of this oppressed underground world of eccentrics? Some of
them, appearing fully grown as from another planet, soon
made their way into the Lutheran camp. We have seen how
"the Prophets of Zwickau" disturbed Melanchthon and captured Carlstadt. Then Carlstadt and Müntzer of Zwickau
passed into southern Germany, preaching their own version
of the good tidings; and presently, in southern Germany there
broke out in 1524 the great rising of the peasants.

These peasants were not all Anabaptists or Protestants, nor
was the movement primarily a religious business at all. The
peasants rose, as in every other generation, in a desperate hope
to escape their horrible lot. What they ask is the abolition of
serfdom, the right to fish and to hunt, no more forced labour,
no more tithes, relief from the intolerable strain that the man
on whom they depend economically is also their political lord,
and their judge when they are accused of wrongdoing. They
also ask—some of them, for the rising was widespread and not
at all co-ordinated in its beginnings—that they have the right
to elect their own priests. What next happened was that all
over southern Germany bands of peasants—to which the
criminal elements soon joined themselves—wandered about
burning castles and monasteries, killing, looting and destroying. Neither Lutherans nor Anabaptists had caused the rising. The incendiary language in which preachers of all sorts
spoke of "freedom now attained" helped, no doubt. Luther,
to whom a statement of the peasants' demands was sent, re-

plied in his usual thoughtless, declamatory way, heaping blame on the lords. It was their opposition to him—"to the preaching of the Gospel"—which had brought about this war. "It is not the peasants who have risen against you, it is God Himself." And at the same time he lectured the peasants on the need to be patient and to remember that "he who takes up the sword will perish by the sword." The tide turned once the princes formed a military alliance. In the one battle that took place, Frankenhausen, the peasants were annihilated. Müntzer was taken, tortured and beheaded.

The peasants were slain by the thousand everywhere in reprisal, and Luther, now converted for ever from his sentimental confidence in the common man, urged on the princes in a murderous little tract, "Kill them, strangle them; what else is to be done to the mad dog who leaps at you? Strike, throttle, stab, secretly or openly . . . there is nothing more poisonous, more hurtful, more devilish, than a rebel." And years later he complacently praised himself, "It was I who slew all the peasants in the insurrection, for it was I who commanded them to be slaughtered; their blood is on my head . . . But I throw the responsibility on our Lord God Who instructed me to give this order"—the Anabaptists having no monopoly of inspiration and the duty of executing it. It is supposed that something like 100,000 of the peasants were killed in these few months of 1524–25.

The association of certain radical preachers with the peasants, the appearance of "Anabaptist" doctrines among the demands the peasants put forward, served the controversialists well, of course. And the Peasants' War did much to convince the princes that these social claims—equality of all men, sinfulness of possessing as though goods were really one's own, sinfulness of oaths, of wars, coming millennium when the little flock of the elect should rule on earth the re-established Kingdom of God—were no mere utopian fantasies but signs of a revolution already preparing. From this time the Anabaptists—i.e., all who professed such ideas—were everywhere inevitably put to death. In 1534 refugees from the proscription in the northern Netherlands made themselves masters of the little city of Münster in Westphalia, driving out the prince-bishop, a typical ecclesiastical baron of the time. Under the rule of the Dutchman, Jan of Leyden, they now set up the apocalyptic kingdom of their dreams. It was a terrible tyranny, where the ordinary people starved and the elect lived like

princes, with Jan of Leyden as king, at the summit, and his
sixteen wives. Executions were the order of the day—among
them one of Jan's sultanas—and then came the recapture of
the city by the princes, massacres, and the execution of Jan
by such torture as a red Indian could not have excelled. From
this time forward, anything that smacked of eccentricity in
the Protestant's religious practice was enough to endanger
the oddity's life.

The Low Countries, especially the north, and southern Germany and Moravia were the chief centres where these people
developed. They made their way into England in the time
of Henry VIII, who had a score of them burned on one day
in 1535, and of Edward VI, who burned a Dutchman in 1551
and whose government was preparing for a general attack on
native Anabaptists in Essex and Kent when the king died in
1553. It has often been thought that the great majority of
those put to death as heretics in the next five years, by his
Catholic sister Mary, from these regions were Anabaptists.
Elizabeth, too, is on record for the burning of two Dutch
Anabaptists in 1575, "in great horror," says the contemporary
account, "with roaring and crying." On the continent things
were much worse, and in the Low Countries as many as 617
of the 877 put to death as heretics by Charles V and Philip II
are said to have been Anabaptists.

The persecution did not by any means stamp out the sect.
They lived down the prejudices caused by the association with
their movement of such moral monsters as Jan of Leyden.
They were the means of preserving what, in the nature of
things, would seem to be the aim and the first justification of
Luther, Calvin, and of all the other successful Reformers who
were their deadliest foes: the principle, that is to say, that
men have the right to form their own religious groups, to join
a group or not to join, to leave it when they choose; that
these groups are equal in their rights and subject to no authority but what they themselves choose; that the groups are
free to choose the way they shall worship; that every individual
is free to choose what he shall believe. Whatever the theologians may need to say—or the philosophers—about the value of
these principles, they have had a great history (thanks, first,
to the Anabaptists) in the last three hundred years, nor is
that history at an end.

CHAPTER FIVE

The English Reformation
1527—1553

i *The Relevance of the Royal Divorce*

With the *Interim* of Nuremberg (1532) the most interesting
stage of the Reformation in Germany closes. The long—unfore-
seeable and unexpected—development that had begun when
Luther's sovereign intervened to protect the nascent heresiarch from the first endeavours of the pope to suppress him,
has issued in a compromise which, by the fact, is a victory
for Luther: Catholics must endure the certitude that Lutheranism has come to stay, that in certain parts of the Christian
world the religion of the pope is to count for less than nothing; that before the Catholics, for the future, and in their
midst, there will stand this citadel of anti-Catholicism,
whence at any moment a war against Catholicism may issue.
The numerous biographies of Luther have, all of them, this
in common: that they deal with the last half of the Reformer's
public life in very much less than half the space which they
give to the earlier years, say between 1517 and 1532. This
agreement is a measure of the accomplishment which the
Interim marks.

The era of fundamental revolt and of basic refoundation
is, in fact, over. The effort henceforward goes to consolidate
the gain, to perfect the organisation, to defend it, to maintain unity within the victorious ranks. And none of these important activities is spectacular. The ordinary man's interest
now shifts to the England of Henry VIII, where changes have
lately been in progress more exciting to the imagination than
even the great days of 1517–21 in Germany: a king of mature
years has been maintaining that his wife of half a lifetime has
never really been his wife, and has appealed to the pope to

confirm the truth of his contention; there has been a trial of the marriage suit at London, with two cardinals, commissioned by the pope, sitting as judges; there has been the dramatic climax that as judgment was seemingly about to be given in favour of the king, legal sleight of hand snatched the prize from his very grasp. And now the very year of the *Interim* sees, on the part of this anti-Lutheran champion of Holy Church,[1] the opening moves of a cold, determined scheme to destroy the papal authority within his kingdom. Here is something more than theologians debating in universities; or, in turn, rousing by their sermons and pamphlets an already discontented, ill-instructed Catholic people to throw over ancient rites and rules and the authority which has promulgated them.

At first sight the English affair is the oft-experienced crisis of one of the kings of Europe defying a particular act of the pope's authority and about to bring to bear such pressure on the pope that the objectionable papal policy will be reversed. But on this occasion the nature of what is in dispute—i.e., the jurisdiction of the pope, as divinely commissioned head of the Church, in the matter of the sacrament of Matrimony—and the fact that this particular papal-royal duel is to be fought at a time when whole provinces of Christendom are already in open, successful revolt against the very idea of the papacy: these two circumstances do much to make the contest between King Henry VIII and Pope Clement VII the most important thing of its kind that history has known. Its effects, indeed, endure to this day, and, it has been reasonably argued, they are one main cause of the weakness which so baffles the Western world as it confronts the new menaces of Communism and the East.

Let that be as it may, there is no phase of the Reformation more worthy of study than the Reformation in England; for this small country, the southern two thirds of an island off the coast of Europe, with a population not one fifth that of France, not one half that of Spain, poor in natural resources and backward in many respects, awkward and ignorant indeed by comparison with Italy or the Low Countries, is destined to a unique good fortune in the leadership of the world. What is unique is that the peculiar political ideals which gave birth

[1] Cf. *supra*, p. 119, n. 18.

to the English state, and which are its life, have also come
to be the ideals of other "kingless commonwealths" lying beyond seas and oceans of whose very existence the thinkers
who created these ideals did not so much as dream. The ultimate effects of the Reformation in England have thereby been
world-wide; it is through its effect in England that the Reformation still survives as a world force.

When in the year 1527 the English king began the long
series of official acts which collectively are called his divorce
suit[2] the "state-of-the-Church" problem was, so far as we can
tell, far less acute in England than anywhere in continental
Europe, save Spain. For example, gross scandals among high
ecclesiastics were, by comparison, unknown. There was, however, the usual story of an untrained, ignorant clergy; of the
chasm between these and the trained theologians and canonists who ruled them; there were present, on all sides, the three
great abuses of the benefice system—namely, absenteeism,
pluralities, and expectatives. There was the usual, largely
justified, grumbling discontent of the laity at the clergy's
professional insufficiency (not to say incompetence), at clerical privileges fiercely defended, and at the general spirit of
the Canon Law which, in so far as it touched the layman,
ruled him as if he were not an adult human being but a child.
There was the special, accidental, and most important fact
that for twelve years now the king's chief minister, and regarded as the real ruler of the kingdom, was the Archbishop
of York, Thomas Wolsey, cardinal and (by special grant)
legate *a latere* for life. Never before, nor since, has any subject of the English crown possessed such power, nor any English statesman enjoyed such enormous wealth. Wolsey is such
a phenomenon and he bred such general hatred in his lifetime that his career demands more than a passing mention
in any account of the Reformation in England.

[2] Divorce in the modern sense of the word (i.e., such a dissolution
of a true marriage that it leaves the parties free to contract a new
marriage) was not what Henry VIII ever had in mind. From the traditional belief that a marriage between baptised persons is absolutely
indissoluble once it is consummated, the king never wavered all his
life. What he sought from the pope was a judicial declaration that
his marriage to Catherine had never been a marriage, could never
have been a marriage, because of her close relation to him; viz., that
she had been the wife of his deceased brother, Arthur.

He was now fifty-two, a portly figure of a man whom alas, and in the age of Holbein, only inferior artists painted; a strong man (from what we can learn of his features), somewhat wooden, wholly insensitive, and as vulgar in mind as the pictures make him seem. He was not himself a scholar, and by training neither a theologian nor a canonist. He was, and had been since the days when he managed the finances of his college,[3] an excellent man of affairs, with the first of all recommendations for a career as such, that he liked work. Wolsey had been lord chancellor since 1515; that is to say, he was the speaker of the House of Lords whenever Parliament was sitting, and the chief of the king's judges, presiding in the king's Court of Chancery and the Court of Star Chamber and in lesser courts also. More than this, he was the king's principal minister, and of such capacity and in such favour with the king that to him all the rest were, in fact, subordinate; and Wolsey really came to rule the council as though the other members were schoolboys. The whole affairs of the kingdom—justice, finance, diplomacy, home affairs, foreign affairs—passed through Wolsey's hands. And to him, as legate *a latere*, the pope had virtually delegated for life the full papal power in all that concerned the administration of ecclesiastical matters. In the shadow of this magnificent delegation the ancient primatial authority of the Archbishop of Canterbury wilted and all but died. Only by permission of the legate did bishops now move and have their episcopal being. And his legacy (as the cardinal called what we might style, more clumsily, his legateship) was, of all his appointments, that in which he took most pride and the office which he regarded as the foundation of his great position. It was a marvellous opportunity, had the man been another Ximenes. But he was utterly secular and dishonesty itself, albeit splendidly robed; how splendidly we can all read in the biography by a gentleman of his household, George Cavendish, where we move in Wolsey's very company and stare incredibly at the scale of the splendour, at the array, the state, the pomp—and the power behind them. From Cavendish we can turn to the modern scholars and see the other side: the accountancy figures; the detail of the public action, in the law courts, in Parliament, in the king's council, in the vast correspondence with the king's ambassadors, in the great diplomatic journeys abroad,

[3] Magdalen College, Oxford.

in the mistakes; Thomas Wolsey, England itself, to all appearances.

It was of course the king who was England. By his royal breath he had made Wolsey, who but for the king would have rusted away his talents in petty clerical politics. And the king withdrawing the favour that, to all men of state, in these times, was life, Wolsey fell back into his first nothingness—amid universal rejoicing. The nobles had, from the beginning, hated this too powerful upstart; the bishops resented this unusually authorised superior who had so diminished their rôle; the moneyed men hated the minister who had fleeced them for years with unusual taxes and unnecessary wars; all hated him for his personal arrogance and for the fear with which his ruthlessness had filled their hearts for now so many years. But that these Catholics began to hate the Catholic religion because this tyrant happened to be a cardinal or because, at the king's request, the pope had so lavishly equipped the tyrant with spiritual authority, or that existing hates had been fanned by these considerations, of this we have no evidence. But Wolsey's career did present the spectacle of civil and ecclesiastical authority, at the highest level, joined in a single personage—and this may have had its influence on the king's mind when Henry VIII turned to reorganise the Church in England.

Wolsey offered the all but unique example of moral turpitude in the ranks of the English episcopate, and of a real indifference to the spiritual duties of his office. One of his children he placed as a nun in the famous abbey of Shaftesbury, a royal foundation and one of the rare convents of women possessed of great wealth. And the career of his son, bred to the clerical profession in the worst sense of this term, can be traced through the state papers for nearly twenty years after Wolsey's fall from power. The cardinal was also the solitary pluralist among the bishops—and on what a scale! In the last stage of his success he was spiritual ruler of the whole of the north of England save Cumberland, a part of Westmorland, and Lancashire south of the Ribble. For years he had also held the administration of the two sees whose bishops were absentee Italians, Worcester and Salisbury; and since 1528 he had the administration of Winchester also. As an administrator he was, thereby, spiritual lord of a territory that ran from London Bridge to the borders of Devon, and from the Dorset coast to where the city of Birmingham now stands.

And in no one of these territories which he ruled did Wolsey
ever spend so much as a day as its bishop. As is known, it
was actually on the eve of his taking possession of his cathedral
at York that the long arm of the king hauled him back to
London and the Tower, to answer a charge of treason. It was
on that last journey that the cardinal died, at Leicester Abbey, November 29, 1530. When they came to prepare the
corpse for burial, they found that under the splendid robes
the penitent was wearing a shirt of hair—brother, in his last
months, to the Carthusians, to Fisher and to More.

England was not a country greatly troubled by heresy in
the Middle Ages. There were no Cathari in the thirteenth century, no Beghards or Fraticelli to disturb the even round in
the fourteenth. Then came Wycliffe, a theological heretic, a
scholastic of scholastics, indeed, and for thirty years after his
death in 1384 the association of those who took up his heresies
was, sporadically, a cause of serious trouble to the government. Lollardy did not disappear with the suppression of the
rising of 1415 and the burning of the one layman of any social
and political importance who was a Lollard, Sir John Old-
castle. But it was, from then on, what it is found in the early
years of Henry VIII, the faith of a mere handful of people—
poor folk for the most part, peasants and artisans—scattered
through the villages of the Chiltern Hills, the little cloth
towns of the Essex-Suffolk border, and the villages along the
Kent-Sussex line. To which it must be added that there were
Lollards—well-to-do Lollards, and educated—among the London merchants.

All through the fifteenth century there were, at intervals,
raids on these Lollard centres, arrests, abjurations, and occa-
sionally the death at the stake of a stalwart who refused to
submit or who, having once recanted, had relapsed into
heresy. In Henry VIII's reign there was such a raid, by the
Archbishop of Canterbury's authority, in the Kent villages referred to, in 1511; there was another in Buckinghamshire in
1521, and one in the Essex towns and in London in 1528.
These heretics were something of an informal secret society,
very simply organised if at all, but in constant touch, the one
group with another. They had no clergy, nor special rites, for
they believed neither to be part of God's way. They clung
to their manuscript copies of the Lollard translation of the
Gospels and to certain little treatises of devotion. They never

married outside their own body, were bitterly anti-Church, and cursed heartily the system in which they were compelled to make outward profession or be discovered for what they were. Though certain of the new sixteenth-century sects would appeal to them, from a similarity of views about doctrine and about the unimportance of rites—the sects so loosely spoken of as Anabaptists, for example—the Lollards were in no way a force in what was now about to happen in England.

Much more pertinent were the activities of a handful of clerical graduates of the university of Cambridge in the twelve years between Luther's first Wittenberg defiance and the fall of Wolsey. At Cambridge, from about the year 1520, there was a group of students in theology, members of various colleges, who were sympathetically interested in Luther's theories. They read his books and met to discuss them at the White Horse Inn, a tavern of easy access from the backs of the particular colleges where most of them dwelt. There seems to have been no secret about their meetings, however, for the inn was presently "Germany," or "Little Germany," to all the university. From this little group of Cambridge men rather than from any other one source, the whole of the English Reformation, as the execution of a theological ideal, was to develop. Among these graduates, "obscure men" indeed in the 1520's, were William Tyndale, Robert Barnes, Thomas Bilney, John Frith, John Lambert, and Rowland Taylor, all of whom were to be burnt at the stake; and the following Protestant bishops, Cranmer, Latimer, Ridley, Foxe, Shaxton, Coverdale, Matthew Parker, and Richard Cox.

Inevitably, as the years passed, these groups came into conflict with authority. Already in 1521, as part of the publication in England of Leo X's condemnation of Luther, there had been a great ceremonial burning of his books outside St. Paul's Cathedral in London, with all the bishops present, Wolsey presiding and John Fisher, Bishop of Rochester, preaching the sermon. In 1525, on Christmas Eve, Dr. Robert Barnes, a friar of the order to which Luther belonged, and prior of their monastery at Cambridge, preached a sermon in which he called for the abolition of the special observances of such feasts as Christmas. He was denounced for heresy and sent to Wolsey for judgment. And a few weeks later, having given up his theories, he figured as one of the principals in a second ceremonial burning of Lutheran books at St. Paul's, barefoot, clad in his shirt, and carrying on his shoulders the wood with which, as a heretic, he had deserved to be burned.

Prior Barnes had in prospect a long and varied history before, in 1540, he came to his terrible end at the stake, sent there by no cardinal or pope, but by the new head of his church, King Henry VIII! Meanwhile, during the weeks when his friends laboured to save him in 1526, something more important than his sermon was preparing—the first printed New Testament in the English tongue. William Tyndale, whose work this was, has the immensely important place in the history of his country that he was the first influence in the formation of the English Protestant mind. He is so important that one is tempted to exaggerate and to say that he is the foundation on which all the rest has been built. Tyndale was, at this time, a priest, perhaps thirty years of age, born in the English west country, and educated both at Oxford and at Cambridge. And he had been, from early years, an enthusiastic opponent of the existing church system, which, so he considered, necessarily bred the scandals that, on all hands, so shocked the devout. When he left Cambridge to become the domestic chaplain of a knight in his own part of the country, William Tyndale developed a talent for preaching, and soon he was denounced as a heretic to the vicar-general of the absentee bishop.[4] Tyndale got away in time, however, and made his way to London.

It is interesting that Tyndale was essentially a scholar, a master of the ancient classical languages, and, by choice, a dweller in the world of manuscripts and books. He was, however, that fortunate scholar who possesses, as we say, "the common touch." And when his technical scholarship began to work upon such raw material as the inspired Scriptures and the mysteries of religion, Tyndale took fire with the passion to make the fruit of his meditations available to the humblest of mankind. Tyndale was, again, one of those revolutionaries who have had to do their work from a distant exile. In London a wealthy, semi-heretical merchant provided an income, and in Germany—whither Tyndale fled in 1524—for a time in Luther's own town of Wittenberg, Tyndale's views developed, in the closest possible relation to the new theology. Tyndale's influence was through two things, principally.

---

[4] From 1498 to 1535 the see of Worcester was used by Henry VII and Henry VIII as a means of rewarding the Italian canonists who served as their agents at the Roman Curia.

First of all, he translated the New Testament—and a little of the Old—into the English of his own time, and he supplied the translation with notes; the translation is, of course, one of the masterpieces of English writing and the notes, explaining the New Testament in the sense of the new doctrines, conveyed to the reader that these new doctrines were the real meaning of the New Testament. In the second place, Tyndale wrote pamphlets, marvellous pamphlets, written in that simple English of which so few have had the secret; pamphlets which described the abuses that disfigured the life of the Church, the real abuses, and others too; abuses which (so Tyndale argued) were the proof that the Church as it now existed was a merely human institution, a barrier between man and the truth of God. All this in such militant language that it would really bring the reader to his feet with the resolve, "At all costs, this must be abolished."

Tyndale is a pioneer in English history, the first publicity man. The bishops and the king rightly regarded him as the gravest menace of the time to the established order of things. We know nowadays, from the studies of scholars, that quite a lot of Tyndale is nothing more or less than a word-for-word translation of Luther. In the pamphlets of Tyndale which so many of the English were reading, in those notes with which he had equipped his translation of the New Testament, the English reader was really reading Martin Luther. And in Tyndale's pamphlets the key doctrine of the Reformation is set out in all its plainness: that the one thing necessary for man in order to save his soul, the one essential act on man's part, is not repentance, is not charity, but confidence in God; not confidence that God will save a man if the man does his best, but confidence that God has already saved him, independently of anything a man has done or will do. Tyndale is the first populariser of Luther's doctrines in England.

Tyndale's *New Testament*, printed in two formats, appeared in 1526. It was presently smuggled into England, and by November of that year the Archbishop of Canterbury was ordering search to be made for it and the destruction of all copies found. In 1528 the translator's first major pamphlet appeared, *The Obedience of a Christian Man*, and in 1530 his second, *The Practice of Prelates*. And along with the copies of these, got into England at great hazard and circulated by stealth through the agency of a kind of society of true believers, other anti-clerical and anti-Catholic tracts began to come in, the work of other clerical expatriates, William Roy, for example, and Jerome Barlow, both one-time Franciscan Friars of the Observance.

It was not only the bishops who took action against this new propaganda literature. On May 24, 1530, at a great gathering of prelates and officers of state in Westminster Hall, with the king presiding, 252 passages taken from the writings of Tyndale and others were published and condemned as "corrupt doctrine." It was forbidden to possess these works, and owners of such books were ordered to surrender them for destruction. In this lengthy list of heretical statements the reader can see, more readily than elsewhere, what an extraordinary medley of anti-clerical, anti-Catholic, anti-social, and anti-intellectual ideas were already flooding over the normally passive English mind.[5]

Here are a few extracts from the catalogue: Faith only doth justify us; saints in heaven cannot help us thither; the commandments be given us not to do them, but to know our damnation and call for mercy to God; beware of good intents, they are damned of God; every man is a priest; purgatory is of the pope's invention; the children of faith be under no law; whoever first ordained universities . . . he was a star that fell from heaven to earth; universities are the gate to hell; God bindeth us to that which is impossible; keeping of virginity and chastity of religion is a devilish thing; Christ ordained that there should be no sin but unbelief and infidelities; St. Thomas [Aquinas] savoureth nothing of the Spirit of God; the New Testament of Christ will not suffer any law of compulsion, but only of counsel and exhortation; we have as great right and as much right to heaven as Christ; bodily labour is commanded to all persons; the good Christian shall not defend himself by justice in no manner; he that is rich . . . may not use or spend his goods as he will; no man is under the secular power, but they that be out of the Christian estate, and out of God's kingdom; Christian men among themselves have nought to do with the sword nor with the law, for that is to them neither needful nor profitable; men of war are not allowed by the Gospel; matrimony is as gold, the spiritual estates are as dung; thou canst not perish or be damned what-

[5] The list is printed in Vol. II of the present writer's *The Reformation in England*, pp. 331–46.

soever thing thou shalt outwardly either do or else leave un-
done; we owe nothing to any man saving only love.

Had those subjects of the king, now menaced with pains
and penalties, only known it, the most remarkable thing about
his great gesture of May 1530 was that some of the bishops
were beginning to wonder whether, secretly, it was not the
king who was making possible the importation and circula-
tion of the proscribed books. King Henry VIII had, indeed,
at this moment, urgent reasons of his own for wishing to embarrass the spiritual authority, and even the highest of all.
We need, before the story proceeds any further, to say something about a major complication peculiar to the early history
of the Reformation in England; namely, the king's divorce
suit. By this year, 1530, the king had suffered his first great
defeat in this affair, at the hands of the timorous, shrinking
pope. The deadlock had set in that was to endure for another
three years or so. Henry had just begun the "war of nerves."

The Reformation in England has often been described as
the achievement of politicians. It was not, in its essence, so it
is said, a matter of religious belief at all. And, again, that the
whole affair really arose out of the king's passion for a lady
who was not his wife, and out of her determination that she
should become his wife. Or, a related explanation of the facts,
that it all came from the king's understandable and very reasonable anxiety to have a son lawfully begotten, recognisably
his heir, and thereby a guarantee to all, that the forty years
of domestic peace, of security and prosperity, that the Tudor
house had given England, would not, on the king's death, suffer any fatal interruption. To the patriot king, facing anxiously
the certitude that his queen had borne and lost the last of
her children, that the present heir was his ten-year-old daughter, that there were still alive men in whose veins ran the
blood of the old royal family, and that something like a renewal of the Wars of the Roses was not impossible; to Henry,
meditating all this, and still no more than thirty-five years of
age, there came the thought that his queen's failure to rear
any of the sons born to them was the manifest sign of divine
displeasure—displeasure at the mock marriage which, in all
good faith, he had contracted with the one woman in the
world who could not possibly be his wife, his dead brother's
widow. Such unions are incest. The Scripture said as much.

The pope who had given leave for the marriage had gone beyond all possibility of papal jurisdiction. His successor must rectify the great error. The unconscious incest of seventeen years must end, now it was recognised as such, and God's judgment given. The king, free to marry, would choose again, and a younger wife would bring him the needed son. Nor would choice be difficult. The younger lady was there, and Henry was already passionately in love with her, Anne Boleyn.

Many questions arise, as we study this affair, to which we shall never know the answers. At what date did the king fall in love with Anne and know that his affection was returned? Was he, at this date, already worrying about the succession? Had the idea already occurred to him that the queen and he were not married, could not possibly be married, given the declarations in the Book of Leviticus? Or did he first fall for Anne and meet the lady's flat refusal—prompted by the recollection of her elder sister's fate, ruined by Henry, then cast off and married to one of the rank and file of his gentlemen in attendance? Did Anne take the line, marriage or nothing, and, to support her incredible suggestion of what was seemingly impossible, put the Bible into Henry's hands? And, if so, who was it that introduced Anne to the texts in Leviticus?

What is certain is the passion for Anne and the determination to wrest from the Holy See a declaration that the marriage in possession had been, from the beginning, null and void. And what is important, for the story of the Reformation, is the effect of the king's failure upon his "temper"; whence the interest of the historian of the Reformation in England in all the incidents of the long half-legal, half-diplomatic duel between king and pope, the acts and sayings that now brought out in Henry the very totality of masculine rage and ruthlessness and craft vis-à-vis the See of Rome, all its works and pomps. Not Luther himself, it is certain, was more dominated by this hatred than was, henceforward, the English king.

The first public act in the divorce suit was the king's citation (in May 1527) to answer, in the court of the cardinal legate, a charge that for eighteen years now he had been living in sin with the woman who had once been his brother's wife. To this charge the king's lawyers replied that Catherine was his wife and that the marriage was good by virtue of the dispensation granted by Pope Julius II in 1503. And at this point, on May 31, this collusive lawsuit—for it was an arranged affair between Henry and Wolsey—abruptly ended.

In these weeks while, in the utmost secrecy, the royal canonists had been thus experimenting with the case, the news had arrived that on May 6 the troops of Charles V had stormed Rome and had put the city to the sack, and that the pope—Clement VII—was now their prisoner. Wolsey, when he presently crossed to France in order to settle various problems arising out of the treaty lately negotiated (April 30), would have additional matters of the highest importance to discuss—a scheme, for example, to secure his own nomination as a kind of vice-pope during Clement VII's captivity.

And during his stay in France the new matter of the desired divorce never left Wolsey's mind for a moment. He sent, for example, to the English ambassadors at the court of Charles V, so that they might not be uneasy at rumours about Henry wishing to be rid of his Spanish wife—the aunt, of course, of the King of Spain—a lying tale about the recent matrimonial trial. He said it had taken place merely to put an end to doubts about the legitimacy of the princess Mary raised by the French diplomatists lately negotiating the treaty of April 30. And—lest Charles V should find out the lie by direct reference to France—Wolsey forbade the ambassadors to mention it to him or to anyone else. He also wrote home that he would contrive so to open the matter to the King of France—to whom Henry had, by treaty just pledged his daughter and heir, Mary, as a future wife, or daughter-in-law—that there would be no fear of any sudden revocation of the treaty. Finally, towards the end of his lengthy visit, the cardinal did Henry the great service of amending the incredibly foolish instructions with which the king had equipped one of his secretaries, Dr. William Knight, sent (by the king) to introduce "the great matter" to Rome itself. And from Knight's papers the cardinal learned, for the first time, that Henry not only wanted to be free of Catherine, but proposed to put in her place Anne Boleyn, daughter of the newest of Henry's peers, Lord Rochford, and a niece of the Duke of Norfolk, Wolsey's greatest enemy.

With Knight's mission to Rome the protagonists really get to grips. In the following December (1527) Wolsey laid his plan before the king's resident agent at the papal court, Sir Gregory Casale—the story of the king's anxieties arising out of his biblical meditations, and of the uncertainties about flaws in the dispensation granted by Pope Julius. The agent was to seek a commission for Wolsey to judge the case, with the special clause that no appeal could be allowed from the sentence he gave. Knight came home, in January 1528, with a judge's commission certainly for Wolsey, but with nothing of that extraordinary character which the cardinal knew he would need. A few weeks later, therefore, in February, he sent out another messenger, two of them rather, his own choice this time, and no fumblers; they were Edward Foxe and Stephen Gardiner, two of his own trained secretaries. Their instructions were more explicit, and Gardiner's rough, brow-beating manner was soon given full scope. Wolsey, in his own letters to the pope, set the tone for his lieutenant, threatening Clement—from the first letter—with schism, if the king failed to get his way.

How Pope Clement VII succumbed to this campaign is what every one knows. He was a clever man, and young for a pope (no more than fifty); in no way vicious or vindictive; scrupulous, even, in matters of justice; but a lamentably weak man, a marvel always of indecision and vacillation, and still visibly suffering from the terrible events of the last few months, acutely conscious that the threats of the English king were serious; a man whose nature it was to allow events to drift, in the crazy hope that something or other would happen to reverse the direction of the current. If only Catherine would die, if only God would change the king's mind, if only the king would just marry Anne out of hand! The pope actually said these things. Gardiner scolded, pleaded, threatened, and finally won from this wreck of a man the appointment as judges of the two cardinals whom Wolsey asked for, himself and Lorenzo Campeggio, one of the great lawyers of the day, who had been legate to Germany in 1524 and who was to advise Charles V at Augsburg in 1530. Campeggio had already visited England, as legate, in 1518, and he was under a serious obligation to Henry VIII, who had conferred upon him the wealthy see of Salisbury. The pope had granted the judges the most ample powers, and (privately) he had sent (June 23, 1528) a written promise to Henry VIII that he would entertain no appeal against their decision. Also, he had given to Campeggio a document which conceded the fullness of what Wolsey and Henry had demanded—the famous decretal bull. This—it would seem—so set out the law and narrowed the legal issue that, commanding the judges to take this as their guide, it was just not possible for them to give a sentence against the king. But Clement VII did not *send* this bull to England. He gave it to the personal care of Campeggio, whom he instructed that the bull was not to be used. It was indeed a "blind," to be read by Campeggio to Henry and to Wolsey, but never for a moment to be let out of his hands, and, once shown to them, it was to be destroyed. Wolsey, in begging for this bull, had said he did not want it in order to use it, but merely that the sight of it would convince his royal master that he was all powerful with the pope. And the pope had taken Wolsey at his word.

It was October (1528) before Campeggio arrived in London. For Wolsey, meanwhile, the ordinary problems of a semi-despot's grand vizier had, of course, never ceased. Since February 1528 there had been added the complication of a war with Charles V which, as the cardinal admitted, not a man in England wanted but himself. In practice this meant a quarrel with the Low Countries, the chief market for English goods and produce, and the inevitable sequel, in England, of unemployment, general distress, and sporadic rioting. Nowhere was there more discontent than in London. Soon arrangements had to be made for the renewal of trade with the Netherlands. England was henceforth only nominally in the war. And her ally, the King of France, Henry's one and only "friend" in the matter of the divorce, was not pleased. What were England's prospects when France and Spain should come to make a peace? And what were the prospects of the cardinal, whose pride and vanity had led him so to blunder? And then, in the months between Clement VII's commissioning Campeggio and the legate's arrival, the fatal "sweating sickness" had descended on England, and people had died like flies: eighteen of the household of the Archbishop of Canterbury, for example, in four days; a good half of the small circle of the king's boon companions; one in four of the population of London. Henry, "in a jelly of fear," had spent the summer fleeing before the plague, from manor to manor, earnest to receive the sacraments very frequently, and indicting to Anne (who had gone down with the disease at her home) those love letters which still survive, one of the most curious items in all the vast collections of the Vatican.

Campeggio soon found that he was face to face with problems that were insoluble. The king seemed unalterably fixed in the idea that the pope could do nothing else but make possible the marriage with Anne. He was ready with arguments on all the theological points, and he had Clement VII's written promises. He made no secret that he was prepared to argue that popes who granted dispensations for affinity in the first degree went beyond all possibility of human powers. And when Wolsey spoke of the certitude that Henry VIII, if thwarted, would really break with the papacy, Campeggio evidently felt that he said no more than the truth. Nor did the experienced Italian canonist make any more headway with the queen. Catherine utterly refused the pope's suggestion that she become a nun and, making no reply to the case which the king would put, resign herself ("for the peace of the Church") to lose by default. She stood to it that she was the king's lawful wife, their daughter was his lawful heir. And to the legate the queen made a solemn declaration that, when she married Henry, she was still a virgin. Campeggio believed she spoke the truth. If she did so, then Henry also knew that of which she spoke; and what, then, of the case based on Leviticus, the case that depended wholly on the fact that Catherine's first marriage had been consummated? Or rather, what of his sincerity in putting it forward? But Campeggio knew that in a legal process the queen's own word, unsupported, proved nothing.

And then, before Campeggio had been in London a month, Catherine made a move that dislocated all the arrangements of Henry and Wolsey. There was in existence, in Spain, as they had known since January last, a second dispensing document (a brief) signed by the same pope who had signed the bull, and this was said to lack all those phrases on which the argument of invalidity had been based. Neither Henry nor Wolsey had seen the text of this brief, nor did they know that Catherine even knew the brief existed. But the emperor had taken care, months ago, that she should have an attested copy, and now, in the first days of November, she produced it. Gone immediately were the English king's desires that Campeggio should move more speedily. Something must be done first to destroy the force of the new discovery. Catherine was told that only the original would serve at the trial, and compelled to write to Spain to ask for it. And a new embassy was sent to Rome to beg the pope to order the emperor to send the original to London! So simple, naïve even, can great potentates be who have never before been in real conflict with their equals. They added to their demand at Rome that the pope should order the legates, on receipt of the brief, to pronounce it spurious.

Meanwhile, on November 8, the king went into the City of London and made a great declaration to the notables of court and the citizens about his motives, lamenting that God's law compelled him to separate from the best of women, and threatening death to whoever stood in the way of his plan. Anne was now back at court, living in the palace, more magnificently housed than the queen, and with a larger train of attendants.

The mission to Rome of 1529, led once again by Stephen Gardiner, was unsuccessful. For one thing, the pope was seriously ill for weeks at a time, more than once thought to be dying. Campeggio's despatches, moreover, had surely taught Clement VII that the situation in London was too desperate for trifling. There were no more of those generous if ambiguous promises. Instead, Gardiner was now plainly told that there were limits to the pope's powers and that the queen's side must be heard, if she put in an appeal. When Henry VIII learned that the emperor was going to demand that, in the interest of justice, the trial be removed from London, where counsel, witnesses, judges, and defendant were all at the petitioner's mercy, and be judged at Rome by the pope himself, he suddenly changed his tactics. The trial in London could not begin too soon. The question of the brief was to be ignored, and Gardiner was now charged to prevent its being sent out of Spain. The legates in London would try the case with the bull alone before the court. The king's leave to Wolsey and to Campeggio to hold the court was given under the great seal of the realm, and on May 31, 1529, the solemnities began. Gardiner was recalled to manage the king's case.

The trial was a succession of dramatic surprises. At the second session the queen appeared, to read personally a formal objection against the judges as not impartial. At the third session this was overruled. Whereupon Catherine appealed from the cardinals to the pope, and then, throwing herself at the king's feet, challenged him to deny that she had been a most faithful wife and that she was a virgin when he married her. To this last he made no answer. The case proceeded with the queen taking no part, with the evidence and arguments for Henry's contention uncontested. Campeggio grew more and more anxious. Only one sentence was going to be possible, his letters say this explicitly. And then he saw the way out;

and on the day when Henry expected him to give sentence—
and when he himself had felt doomed to do so—he coolly,
blandly explained that the annual legal holiday for Roman
courts had now begun and that the court was adjourned until
October 1. This was on July 23, 1529.

Abroad, the Franco-Spanish war was over; in another fortnight the Treaty of Cambrai would be signed. While, before
the legates, the king's canonists performed their solemn liturgies, the King of France had lost his last army in Italy (June
21). Charles V was master of the continent, and the pope had
already made his peace with him (June 29). Wolsey, as minister, was finished. Also, although this news had not yet
reached England, on July 16 the pope had moved the case
into his own court at Rome.

ii *King Henry VIII, 1530–1547*

What has all this distraction about "the private life of
Henry VIII" (which was so very public a private life) to do
with the history of the Reformation? With new theologies
about grace and salvation and about the Eucharist? Nothing,
of course. But the English king will now carry out all that he
has been threatening against the pope and against the papacy.
"It will be all over with the authority of the Apostolic See in
this country, if the divorce does not go through," Campeggio
had written to Clement VII. The king will now begin to say
that the pope's authority is not a thing intended and set up by
God; that it is, on the contrary, nothing more than a vast
clerical fraud—a foreign clerical fraud. He will become as bitterly anti-papal as Luther himself and, in the course of the
revolution that ensues, he will find the apostles of the new
Lutheran theologies (which he continues to abhor), the
brethren of the White Horse Inn reunions, useful agents, and
he will give them one opportunity after another. They will, for
example, be useful to the king, as preachers and propagan-
dists, when he proceeds to extract from all his subjects a
sworn declaration that they too repudiate the papacy, and
that, in place of the pope, they acknowledge, as the God-
designed supreme head of Christ's Church in this country,
King Henry VIII himself.

When, concomitantly with the king's pronouncement
about the papacy, his subjects are put to death for their refusal to make the acknowledgement required, we have, recog-

nisably, reached a turning point in history; and what is in progress is, unmistakably, a revolutionary change in a nation's religion, a change consciously intended by the governing authority that wills it.

It took Henry VIII something like six years to reach this point, to progress from the arrest of Wolsey for a praemunire to the execution of More for denial of the royal supremacy. The road which the king chose was one of the strictest legality. It was by means of a handful of new statutes that he brought about "a series of changes more profound and wide-reaching than any which had yet been accomplished in the annals of English legislation . . . the greatest revolution in English History." The famous Reformation Parliament of King Henry VIII was, thereby, "the most important parliament in English History." It was summoned within a fortnight of Campeggio's adjournment of the trial, and it sat for the unprecedented length of seven years nearly.

The Parliament met on November 3, 1529. Wolsey had been dismissed from the chancellorship on October 16. In his place, speaking in Henry's presence the king's intentions and wishes, the Lords and Commons heard Sir Thomas More. They heard this new lord chancellor—who, most surprisingly, was a layman—announce that no section of the nation more urgently needed reforming than the clergy, and that the matter was open for Parliament to try what it could do. What Lords and Commons would have liked even more than this was to revenge themselves on Wolsey; but when Parliament prepared to do this, by a monstrously lengthy bill of attainder, the king intervened. He had other plans; the cardinal had already (in October) appeared in the king's criminal court, charged with having exercised, as legate of the pope, a foreign jurisdiction within the realm. To which he had made no defence, offered no excuse, but very humbly had acknowledged his guilt and thrown himself on the king's mercy. And Henry showed himself merciful indeed. There was neither imprisonment nor fine exacted. All that happened was that Wolsey lost everything save his place as Archbishop of York, and that he was ordered to betake himself to his diocese.

The act of confession and surrender which the king had wrested from Wolsey was, however, in itself and in its all but immediate consequences, an event of the very first importance. Never had the Canon Law, with its fundamental idea that religion is subject to no earthly superior, been so perfectly embodied in the person of a single Englishman as in this moment when, by Wolsey's act, it acknowledged the king's law for its master. The plea of guilty was spectacular testimony, also, to the fear which the anger of Henry VIII could inspire. The mightiest subject that had ever been, allowed himself to be ruined without a word, buying pardon for a crime that was mere legal technicality—and in which the king had throughout been his accomplice—by a great act of treason to the spiritual jurisdiction whose officer he was, and to which the very king had admitted himself subject.

Soon, very soon, the king would "discover" that there had been other—clerical—accomplices in the legate's crime; and the experience of what threats had been able to win from the legate would serve in the business of turning their guilt also to profit.

Meanwhile, it was with the great surrender freshly accomplished before their very eyes that the Parliament of December 1529 fell upon some of those clerical abuses which had been the theme of a thousand angry, private debates for many a long year: the ancient right to take the best beast, or piece of furniture, or clothing of a deceased parishioner was restricted; the fees payable to the bishop for probate of wills were now fixed by law, and severe penalties provided for prelates and their officials who tried to get more; the clerical pluralist was henceforth liable to punishment in the king's courts, and the absentee parish priest also, and the cleric who took to trade in land or in house property. More ominously than even this invasion of the sacred domain of the Canon Law was the enactment that made it a penal offence to evade this last act by obtaining licences from the pope, whether to hold more than one benefice or to be absent from one's benefice.

The parliamentary session of 1529 was brief—as were all sessions in the sixteenth century. It took only four weeks (November 3 to December 5) for Commons and Lords to deal with these important bills, and others too, of course; to debate, amend, debate anew, and pass them. Whatever the freedom of speech, there was little time for very much of it.[6]

And the moral of what happened in this Parliament, in this its first session, is surely that the influential laity are willing

---

[6] "To speak of parliament doing anything is hardly more than metaphorical: things are done rather in parliament than by it." Pickthorn, Henry VIII, p. 236.

to move against the clergy, that the king is ready to support them, that the clergy can be compelled by this alliance to an unwonted submissiveness. The clergy, in 1529, were defeated —this reservation has its importance—not on any matter of Christian belief, but in what touched their own good name as shepherds of souls, in a matter where they had themselves enjoyed an ample leisure to improve things as they had enjoyed the power, and where for centuries they had never done more than pass resolutions.

In all this parliamentary activity about the clergy and their ways, there was nothing that brought the king's great desire closer to his grasp. The friendly French ambassador described him, in January 1530, as so utterly perplexed that he did not know what to do next. And nine months later Henry was still helplessly threshing round and talking wildly, and all but ready to abandon the great design. Fifteen-thirty was a bad year for the king. The moves in the "war of nerves" against the pope, whose purpose was to fend off the evil day when Clement must consent to listen to the defendant's answer to the plaintiff's case, were, so far, failures: the embassy to the pope (then at Bologna for the coronation of Charles V) in the spring, the patriotic petition of the English notables in the summer, and the scarcely rewarding canvass of the French and Italian universities. The pope was, of course, as slow-moving as ever, but (because of the emperor's victories?) he now found courage to act a little more decently. His replies to England would soon begin to be stiff with such a fundamental principle as that the marriage in possession has rights and entails obligations.

But not all the pressure of the emperor, of which the legend has so much to say, could so prevail over the fact that the pope believed in Henry VIII's threats as to induce Clement to take up the appeal lodged by the defendant in the case, and set it on the way to trial and judgment. For four years (July 1529–September 1533) this appeal would lie in the pigeonholes at Rome awaiting a hearing—all the endeavours of Charles V notwithstanding. And when it was finally drawn thence and examined, this, again, was not due to any action of the defendant's imperial nephew, nor to any kind of consideration of the queen's interests: it was an act to which the pope was driven by the challenge of Henry's marriage with Anne and the challenge of his archbishop's judicial decision declaring invalid because anti-scriptural a papal dispensation of a matrimonial impediment.

When Henry married Anne, in January 1533, with his nullity suit still pending, he passed from acts that are threats to acts that are open denials of the pope's right to rule, in such matters, the whole Church of Christ. It is now not possible for Henry to go back, nor for the pope to ignore what has been done. But the king's position cannot be reconciled with the idea of the Church that has filled the English mind for all but a thousand years. Only in a religion basically transformed, that has experienced a revolution, can the king's act vis-à-vis Anne Boleyn be given a semblance of legality, of ecclesiastical respectability. Henry does not shrink from the only solution open to him. And what he devises he successfully imposes upon his people with the minimum of friction; upon the reluctant as upon the indifferent. And he does this primarily through a management of the Parliament so skilful that, given that the king had no precedents to guide him, no tradition on which to rely, we must acknowledge it sets Henry VIII very high among English practitioners of the craft of government.

The task before the king called for something of this rare kind if it were ever to be achieved; that is to say, if king and Parliament were ever to be accepted as the supreme authority in the religious life of the country—the first revolution, which was, in effect, the gate through which the continental revolution in religion was to enter, not England, but the institutional life of England. For in England the Reformation, in every sense, depended on the initiative of the crown. Nor is it easy to see how, in a great state, it could have been otherwise. There was no place, in a great state, for the German way: the connivance of the ruler of a state no larger than Yorkshire with the semi-popular iconoclastic demonstrations led by a theological demagogue, with the gradual destruction of one religious system and the installation of another, the quasi-unanimity of opinion in the little towns consenting to it all. Had Windsor, not London, been Henry's capital, and had his domain not extended beyond the counties in the Thames valley, he too—supposing Windsor to have bred a Luther—might have been content (or compelled?) to follow a general uprising that he could scarcely repress, even had he wished. But in England, until the government gave the sign, no mobs moved—except in protest against the government for favouring the novelties.

Behind all the changes we are now to consider of the years 1529–34, there can be discerned the working of a powerful and logical mind, which clearly sees the steps to be taken and the order in which they must be taken; here was the source of the general strategy (the successive acts of Parliament, the acts of the Convocation and of the courts) and of the special tactics which reduced the opposition of various groups and of individuals powerfully placed. The "logical mind" was, actually, a joint affair. The keen-witted, all-observing king played a leading part in the deliberation, as he played the only part in the ultimate decisions; the king, who has never been more truly described than in his own saying, "If I thought my cap knew what I was thinking, I would throw it into the fire"; a man as pitiless as his father before him, or his daughter in the years to come, whenever another human being stood in the way of a scheme thought to be vital. Henry is a man eminently capable of action, as the critical weeks show that follow the trial in 1529. It is the king who then decides to call a Parliament and who chooses who shall take Wolsey's place. It is he who decides how the cardinal shall be dealt with, and that the Commons shall be let loose upon the clergy. In these weeks the king shows himself a master of the political arts. But, unlike Henry VII or Elizabeth I, Henry had a prodigal side to his character and no natural liking for the routine of work; and when the fit to hunt (for example) seized him, secretaries might need to pursue him for days before they could secure the all-important signature for documents of state.

What was lacking in the king was found in the new servant who, in the years 1530–35, came gradually to dominate the national scene, Wolsey's one-time factotum, Thomas Cromwell.

Wolsey had been no more than a butcher's son, from the insignificant town of Ipswich. Cromwell was the son, it appears, of a blacksmith. He was born at Putney, on the Surrey shore of the Thames, in 1483, the same year as Luther and Zwingli. He had had to climb by the hard way; by an unusual, personal conquest of the hostile world. In thirty years or so of adolescence and maturity he had been everything in turn: soldier of fortune in the Italian wars, trader and cloth merchant, abroad and at home, moneylender, attorney, real estate man; and then, in the last ten years, the general manager of the private finances of the cardinal legate. When Wolsey, on the eve of his fall, had won from the pope the dissolution of a score of small monasteries, their little wealth to go to his own two foundations, the new colleges at Oxford and at Ipswich, it was Cromwell who saw to the detailed execution of the scheme. When Wolsey fell from power Cromwell was, again, the inevitable intermediary—through whom creditors were paid, debts due collected, and the high interested parties satisfied to whom the royal beneficence had allotted a share of the cardinal's offices, and jurisdictions, and possessions.

When did Cromwell make his first significant contact with the king? Was it towards the end of the disastrous year 1530? There was, in Henry's entourage at this moment, a highly intelligent and singularly truthful man, of really innocent life, who knew the king well, who was, indeed, his near kinsman, and who was horrified at the wickedness Henry had in hand and at what its consequences for the country must be. This was Reginald Pole, now in his thirty-first year, and marked out for high office in the Church.[7] From Pole we have quite a circumstantial story about this very matter of the beginning of Cromwell's first association with the king.

According to Pole—and whatever the value of his testimony, it is all that we have—Cromwell, in an audience with the king, told him that the divorce suit had gone awry chiefly through the incompetence of his advisors. No success was possible along the line they had taken—the plan of wresting a favourable decision from the pope by one means or another. There was only one way—Henry must be declared free to marry by the whole body of the clergy of his realm; and to bring this about the king must first secure that they repudiate the pope's claim to be the final judge, throughout the Catholic world, in all religious matters. They must acknowledge that it is not the pope but the English king who is head of the Church of Christ in England. And Cromwell also promised to make Henry the richest prince in Christendom.

Whether Pole's memory was accurate or his information

[7] Henry's mother, Elizabeth of York, and Pole's mother were first cousins; the two men's grandfathers, on this maternal side, were brothers, King Edward IV and George, Duke of Clarence. And Henry's father, King Henry VII, and Pole's father were likewise first cousins, their mothers being half sisters, daughters of Margaret Beauchamp by successive husbands.

trustworthy, whether it was in Cromwell's brain or no that the grand strategy of the next few years thus originated, Cromwell undoubtedly organised the detailed execution of it. Everywhere the impress of his man-of-affairs mentality and his habits of business routine is manifest. And Cromwell, from his continental wanderings, from his familiarity with the Italy of Julius II and Leo X, had brought back a mind as little spiritual as his countenance. Though in a moment of stress he could be discovered reading, with tears in his eyes, the Little Office of the Blessed Virgin Mary, he could also carry about a manuscript Machiavelli and offer to lend it to Pole in an amiable effort to set the young royalty on a surer path to ultimate fortune. Yet if with Cromwell morality suffered occlusion when matters of state rose above the horizon, he never became the complete monster. He seemingly spoke from the heart when, on More's final refusal to follow the king in 1534, he "sware a great oath, that he had liever that his own son (which is of truth a goodly young gentleman, and shall I trust come to much worship) had lost his head, than that I should thus have refused the oath."[8]

In the August of the king's bad year, 1530, the royal hand set the lawyers to work against eight of the bishops, and the first preparations were made for their prosecution on the charge of being Wolsey's abettors in the crime to which he had confessed. By October the plan had been changed. In December the king—or the king and Cromwell?—was ready, and the whole body of the clergy, from the Archbishop of Canterbury down to the most junior parish priest, were indicted as the legate's accomplices[9]—all liable, if the case were proved, to lose all they had and to be imprisoned for life. What lay behind this grotesquely extravagant indictment was soon revealed. The bishops were told that the king was willing to compound with the clergy for the penalties, and when Parliament met, January 1531, they made the king a great offer. But he demanded £100,000—two and a half times what

[8] Sir Thomas More to Margaret Roper, from the Tower, 1534, about April 17. Rogers, *Correspondence of Sir Thomas More* (1947), p. 506.

[9] Dr. J. J. Scarisbrick has recently shown (*Cambridge Historical Journal*, July 1955), that the crime alleged against the clergy was their exercise of the Canon Law jurisdiction.

they offered[10]—and he brushed aside the tribute to him as the defender of orthodoxy in which they proposed to enshrine this "free gift." The clergy must acknowledge their guilt, and the "gift" as connected with the king's generous pardon for it; and when they set out to recast the text, they were then told that they must insert a recognition of the king as "the only supreme lord, and even supreme head, of the Church in England." After days spent in devising alternatives, which the king rejected, the clause was finally passed, with a limiting phrase, "in so far as is lawful according to the law of Christ" (February 1531).

If the whole body of the clergy could be penalised for their routine business with the criminal, Wolsey, why not all the laymen too? The laymen certainly thought such a danger was possible, and they raised such a clamour that to them also an explicit pardon was granted and embodied in a statute—but without any demand for such a "free gift" as the clergy had had to vote (March 29). In May there were protests about the new idea of a royal ecclesiastical supremacy from the clergy of the north and from seven dioceses of the province of Canterbury, from London among the rest. In that same month, too, the king sent some of his chief advisors to Catherine to urge her to withdraw her appeal. But she stood by her rights and would not be bullied. In July the king, without any kind of speech, left her for ever and sent her a command to leave Windsor, where they had last made an appearance of living together. Pole, too, about this time parted from the king, and on the friendliest of terms, despite his hostility to the divorce and the memorandum in which he had set down his views. Henry and Anne were now living together. Soon there would be rumours of a pregnancy.[11] There was, in October, a further—and vain—attempt to force a surrender from Catherine. Once again she addressed the pope, begging that the case might come to trial, and telling the story of her expulsion and Anne's installation in her place. All of which brought from Clement VII, on January 25, 1532, a strongly worded rebuke to the king, but no more.

By the time the news of this reached Henry, he was busy once again with the management of Parliament. The clerical

[10] About this time, £100,000 was the amount of the annual ordinary revenue of the country.

[11] See Lingard, *History of England*, V, pp. 1, 2, and the sources he quotes.

surrender of the previous year was to be made to produce further surrenders. In the first place, there was discussed at length, and finally passed, a bill that forbade for the future all payments to the pope, by new bishops, of the customary tax, called annates, the tax which had sent Albert of Brandenburg to the Fugger. Should the pope, in reprisal, refuse to issue the bulls appointing the bishop and authorising his consecration, the refusal was to be ignored and the consecration was to take place notwithstanding, the bishop to be considered as the lawful bishop just as truly as though the pope had appointed him in the traditional way. The statute laid down in detail the new procedure of election, confirmation, and consecration, and provided appropriate heavy penalties for ecclesiastics who violated it or who came to an arrangement with Rome to evade it. In the Lords every bishop and abbot present voted against the bill. In the Commons there was also much opposition, chiefly to a clause which left it to the king to say when, if ever, the act should go into force. This First Annates Act was, in fact, another move in the business of terrifying the pope. Unless he surrendered his right to the annates, one extremely important part of his jurisdiction as pope would, in England, come to an end. Everything was now ready, in fact, for the inauguration of an episcopate that would be wholly royal and altogether independent of the Apostolic See.[12]

While this bill was still before Parliament, the Commons were also considering a lengthy petition to the king for protection against the clergy. This touched on something more fundamental even than the pope's rights over the appointment of bishops. With a wealth of examples to illustrate how evil the thing was of which they complained, the Commons pointed out to the king that in his realm there was, in active operation, a second governmental system, over which he had no control: his people were the subjects of a second set of rulers (the bishops), with their own system of laws (the Canon Law), made in assemblies in which no layman had either voice or vote (the synods), with officials to arrest the accused, courts to try him, prisons to confine those convicted, and even with a power over men's lives (the heresy cases).

This petition, we know now, had originated with the king; the joint work of himself and Thomas Cromwell, sent to be introduced in the House of Commons for debate (and acceptance).

[12] As had already been devised in Scandinavia, see p. 207.

On March 18, having been duly debated, it was presented to the king by the speaker, and the king handed it to the bishops. Convocation took sixteen days to study it and to frame an answer—a lengthy, detailed denial of the various charges made, and a strong defence of the right of the Church to make laws which all members of the Church are bound in conscience to obey. When the king passed this on to the Commons (April 30) he made no secret where his sympathies lay. "We think their answer will smally please you, for it seementh to us very slender," he said. There were ten days of comings and goings between the Commons and the prelates, a second draft, which was rejected, and even a third. Then on May 10 the king showed his hand. He sent to Convocation a short declaration in three articles, and the bishops and clergy ceased to resist. They pledged themselves never to make any new laws without the king's permission, and they consented that the whole body of the church law should be revised by a commission which the king should name, with power to abolish whatever laws it thought fit. This is the action known as *The Submission of the Clergy*. Without any reference at all to the title of supreme head voted in February 1531, it placed the whole life of the Church at the mercy of the king. Unlike the Annates Act, it was absolute. The date was May 16, 1532. On the next day, Sir Thomas More, who had throughout this business been the chief advisor of the minority[13] who in Convocation opposed the king, resigned his office of lord chancellor.

One unlooked-for incident of this menacing session had been a protest on February 24 from the Archbishop of Canterbury, William Warham, that he regarded as null and void all laws passed by this Parliament which derogated from the rights of the Roman see. Warham, eighty-four years of age, was the last survivor of the great lawyers who had formed the council of the king's father, King Henry VII, and had served for twelve years as lord chancellor, and he had made it clear that he was not prepared, in disobedience to the papal mandate, to try the marriage suit in his own court of Canterbury. He had said this explicitly. The king was preparing to punish him with a prosecution for praemunire when suddenly, as the old man was making ready his defence (or defiance), death claimed him, August 23, 1532. The way was open for the king to choose an archbishop wholly to his liking, and Henry's

[13] The most active of these was Gardiner, Bishop of Winchester since 1531.

choice fell upon a priest who until lately had never left the scholarly precincts of Cambridge, Dr. Thomas Cranmer. He was also a one-time habitué of the gatherings at the White Horse Inn, and with this appointment the Reformation—in the usual sense of the word—makes its first entry into English public life.

Cranmer, at this time, was serving as ambassador at the court of Charles V.[14] It was several weeks before his recall reached him (November 18). The various formalities, of election and so forth, were gone through, and in January 1533 the record was sent off to Rome with the king's petition for his appointment. Protests against the appointment, from the emperor's ambassador in London, followed almost as soon as the news got out, warnings to the Holy See that it was notorious that the elect was a Lutheran. It was while these various messengers were racing across Europe that the king, on January 25, went through a form of marriage with Anne, in such secrecy that, neither then nor later, was it even known who the priest was who blessed it. The fact was that Anne was pregnant, and the child—the long-desired heir—must come into the world as the child of the King and Queen of England. At Rome there was no opposition to Cranmer's appointment (January 23). The bulls arrived in March and on the thirtieth he was consecrated.[15]

Four days before this there had been a great debate in Convocation on the related questions, (i) whether it lay within the papal power to grant such a dispensation as that which authorised Henry to marry his brother's widow, (ii) whether Catherine's marriage with Arthur had been proved to have been consummated. As to i, the bishops and prelates voted the negative, by 59 votes to 16, and the affirmative as to ii, by 38 to 6. The new archiepiscopal judge of the case would be fully instructed as to law and to fact. Moreover, by virtue of a new statute, debated in these same months of February and March, while he awaited his bulls, all matrimonial cases, for the future, were to be judged with final judgment in the courts of the English bishops, the appeal to Rome

[14] While in Germany he had married a niece of one of the leading Reformers, Andreas Osiander—a marriage that could not be a marriage by any law then obtaining. Even Luther's marriage, in Luther's own state, was so dubiously regarded by lawyers that, at the end of his life, he was anxious about the fate of his property.

[15] Cranmer's age should be mentioned. He was born in 1489.

being abolished and heavy penalties provided for whoever attempted any such appeal.

This Statute of Appeals became law on April 7. On the eleventh Cranmer issued a respectful monition, "as prostrate at the feet of your majesty," dictated to him by the king, summoning—or rather "beseeching"—Henry to submit to judgment the matter of his marriage to Catherine. The next day, Easter Eve, Anne made her first appearance at court as the queen, and her coronation was announced for June 1. On May 8 the trial before Cranmer began. Sentence was given on the twenty-third—that the marriage with Catherine had never been a marriage, and Henry was solemnly ordered to separate from her. Sending the judgment to the king, the archbishop also desired "to know your pleasure concerning the second matrimony . . . for the time of the coronation is so near at hand that the matter requires good expedition." On May 28, after another judicial enquiry, Cranmer pronounced the marriage with Anne good and lawful, and on Whitsunday, June 1, he crowned her queen in Westminster Abbey. All that now remained to complete the triumph was the appearance of the heir. But Anne's child, born on September 7, was a girl, the future Queen Elizabeth, no less.

The pope had not waited for this last news to act—it was, of course, a detail without significance in the duel. On July 11 the proceedings of Cranmer's court were quashed, and those who had taken part in them were excommunicated. The king, too, was excommunicated, with effect from the end of September. And, at long last, the pope made up his mind to try the case he had called into his courts now four years ago. While this was going through the appropriate stages at Rome, the king organised a great scheme of anti-papal propaganda, on the related themes that the papal primacy over the Church was a man-made fiction, with no foundation in God's law, and that to repudiate the fiction as such must be instinctive with patriotic Englishmen. Sermons were ordered to be preached to drive home to all that in England the pope had no more rights than, say, the Archbishop of Naples; pamphlets, part argumentation, part mere rhetoric and abuse, were put out—one of them written by the king himself; scholars were set to excavate arguments from the works of Wycliffe, the classic English heretic whose disciples Henry until now had persecuted even to the stake. It was in the midst of the greatest turmoil England had ever known, and with a dreadful deed of blood in preparation which would cow the critics, that the Parliament resumed its sittings on January 15, 1534.

The deed of blood was the condemnation by attainder (i.e., by an act of Parliament, without any trial) and the execution at Tyburn of "the Nun of Kent" and four priests condemned as her accomplices. "We now enter on a period which is happily unique in the annals of England, a period of terror. It lasts from [1534 to 1540]."[16]

The Parliament, in the ten weeks of its spring session, 1534, passed, as well as many other laws, the following five acts:

i. The Heresy Act, which removed from the list of doctrines contrary to the Christian faith the denial that the pope is the divinely instituted head of the Church; what the king's subjects were about to be commanded to do in the laws that follow, was, up to this moment, a capital crime, for which, less than two years before, a man had been burned at the stake. The act also provided that the bishops should ignore accusations of heresy unless made by two persons of substance, and that they should try the heretics in open court. The penalty of death at the stake, to be inflicted by the sheriff, was retained.

ii. The Ecclesiastical Appointments Act laid down that, for the future, the pope was to be totally ignored in the appointment and consecration of bishops; chapters were to elect within twelve days the man designated by the king, and the archbishop was to confirm the election and consecrate the elect. Heavy penalties were provided for recalcitrant chapters or prelates and for those who took notice of any Roman reprisals for their obedience to the statue.

iii. The pledge given by the clergy in May 1532 never to make laws without the king's consent, and to enforce only those parts of the existing church law which the king allowed, was now worked into the form of a statute which expressly forbade the clergy to do these things, under heavy penalties; and, as well as this, the statute completed the revolution of the Appeals Act of the previous session by declaring explicitly that no appeals of any kind should be made to the courts of the pope, now baldly referred to as "the Bishop of Rome," and by making the king's Court of Chancery the final court of appeal for all ecclesiastical cases.

[16] H. A. L. Fisher, *History of England from the Accession of Henry VII to the Death of Henry VIII* (1910), p. 328. For "The Nun of Kent" cf. p. 177, *infra.*

iv. England being a country subject to no earthly power but its own king—a fourth statute declares—and whatever other laws have there been admitted deriving their force solely from the king's allowance of such laws, it follows that it is within the king's power (within the power of king, Lords, and Commons "in this your most High Court of Parliament") to authorise dispensations from those laws. Moreover, the king "is supreme head of the Church of England, as the prelates and clergy of your realm . . . have recognised,"[17] with full power over all church law. And so the statute proceeds to abolish the tax called Peter pence, to forbid any future application to the pope for dispensations in any matter of church law (permission to eat meat in Lent, for example, or to marry a relative), and to enact that the Archbishop of Canterbury shall, for the future, have power to grant all these dispensations. He is not given absolute power to refuse them. Petitioners whom he has refused have a remedy in the king's Court of Chancery, where the archbishop can be compelled by a writ to appear and justify his refusal. If, despite the order of the court, he persists in the refusal, he is to be punished as the king chooses, and the dispensation is to be issued by royal commissioners.

v. The act which, so the king told the Parliament, was "the first and most advantageous" of all of these, was that now known as the First Succession Act. It did two things never done before: it settled with legal clarity the descent of the crown upon the reigning king's death, and it imposed an oath to be taken individually, by every one of the king's adult subjects, of both sexes. By this oath they swore they would observe, maintain, and defend "the whole contents of" this act. The penalty provided for refusing the oath was the loss of all property, and imprisonment for as long as the king chose. As to the "contents" of the statute, in the preamble there is a statement that the Bishop of Rome has been able, for lack of such statutes as this, to invest whom he pleased with "other men's kingdoms"; then the statute enacts that "by authority of this present parliament" the marriage between Henry and Catherine is "adjudged to be against the laws of Almighty God . . . [and] utterly void . . . any licence, dispensation . . . to the contrary . . . notwithstanding"; the marriage between

---

[17] The reference is to the vote of February 11, 1531. That the clergy then made their acknowledgement under a qualifying clause is suppressed.

Henry and Anne is "undoubtful, true, sincere, and perfect" according to Cranmer's "just judgment" (of May 1533); the grounds of this decision, as well as this marriage, are "good and consonant to the law of Almighty God, without error or default"; moreover, with regard to the general question of the possibility of marrying persons closely related by blood or through marriage, the statute, enumerating fourteen such relationships, declares that "no man," whatever his rank or place, has power to dispense with the divine prohibition of such marriages; the statute now makes it an offence to attempt such marriages, any that have taken place are to be regarded as no marriages and the children of them are illegitimate, "any foreign laws . . . dispensations . . . to the contrary notwithstanding"; the children of the marriage of Henry and Anne are declared the king's lawful issue, and the order in which the crown shall descend to them is set out; next comes a direction that the statute is to be brought to the notice of the whole country by proclamation on May 1, 1534 (it is now March); the penalties for "any exterior act or deed" meant to "prejudice" or "disturb" the king's marriage to Anne is the penalty for high treason; the penalty for slandering the marriage by words is loss of all goods and imprisonment at the king's pleasure; arrangements are made for the government should the heir be a minor when he succeeds; the statute concludes with the clauses enacting the oath. Very strangely the statute does not provide any text of the oath which it imposes.

These acts received the royal assent on March 30; all the members of both houses were immediately sworn as the Succession Act directed; and the Parliament went into recess. And on March 31, Convocation, before it adjourned—that is to say, the Lower House—answered in the negative by 34 to 4 (with one member doubtful) the question, "Whether the Roman Pontiff has any greater jurisdiction bestowed on him by God in the Holy Scriptures in this realm of England, than any other foreign bishop?" No doubt it was at the order of the king that this vote was taken, as was the like vote in the Convocation of the province of York, the members of which denied the papal authority unanimously.

Meanwhile, on March 23, the pope had delivered his judgment in the king's suit for a declaration that his marriage to Catherine was no marriage. The marriage was declared a truly valid marriage, and Henry was told of his duty to restore Catherine to her rightful place in his life. The news of this seems to have reached London on April 3—Good Friday, in this year 1534.

All this lawmaking of the spring of 1534 had been done in an atmosphere heavy with threats of death. One of the new laws, which took some weeks to put through all its stages, was that decreeing the punishment of treason to the woman known as the Nun of Kent, or the Holy Maid of Kent, and four priests, her companions. The Holy Maid was one Elizabeth Barton, twenty-eight years of age, and a Benedictine nun who, for some eight or nine years now, had been seeing visions, hearing divine warnings, and uttering prophecies—of late years they were prophecies of what would befall the king if he did not return to his wife and send Anne away. That the Holy Maid was very highly thought of for all these marvels, and for her pious life, by such personages as Archbishop Warham and Bishop Fisher is as certain as, to us, it is certain that the poor woman's "experiences" had nothing whatever about them of a supernatural character. She was, in fact, as a learned Bollandist has written, *"une malheureuse hystérique, souvent en proie à de violents accés de son mal."* Thousands believed in her unquestioningly.

As the king's plans for the religious revolution developed, the nun promised to be a first-class hindrance, and one of Cranmer's duties, round about the time of the birth of Anne Boleyn's daughter, was to get from this poor woman, by "spiritual" wheedling and coaxing, an admission that she knew her visions and so forth had not come from God. This done, Cromwell busied himself preparing a list of important opponents of the new régime who had ever made any contacts with the nun. If they could be associated with her "guilt," they could conveniently be eliminated when her time came. Into the bill of attainder, which appeared in the Lords on February 21, 1534, the names of More and Fisher were introduced. Both, on hearing this, wrote to protest their innocence. More was allowed to explain himself to the council after the third reading of the bill. This was granted at the urgent petition of the lord chancellor, the king being made aware that to refuse him a hearing might provoke a parliamentary crisis. More's name was now (March 6–12) taken out of the bill. Fisher escaped the major accusation, but as one guilty of misprision he had to pay a heavy fine to the king. On Monday, April 20, the nun and the four priests were put to death at Tyburn, and that same day "most part of the city was sworn," in accordance with the Succession Act.

By April 20 More, and Fisher also, had finally lost their liberty. They had refused the oath—More the first layman outside the Parliament to be asked to take it—on April 13, and were now in the Tower. A visitation was in progress of the reformed Franciscans called Observants—the order to which Ximenes had belonged—great favourites of Henry's father and of Henry's wife, the order whose church at Greenwich was the court church. An Augustinian and a Dominican were employed to persuade them of the lawfulness of the oath, but in vain; and on June 14 two cartloads of friars, from Greenwich and from Richmond, made their way to the Tower. There was also resistance from the London house of the Carthusian monks, upon whom two of the king's clerical legists, one of them a bishop, were set to work.

The administration of the new oath was, indeed, the great business of all these months between the two parliamentary sessions of 1534. With the handful of exceptions noted, the whole country agreed to take it. Even to Catherine and to her daughter Mary the oath was offered and, short of physical violence, everything was done to force them to swear—but in vain. What this population, one half of them poor, illiterate peasants, made of the phrase which expressed the matter to which their sacred obligation referred—"the whole contents of the Act"; how far popular lectures were organised to point out the full implications of this generality; these are matters where, if we must guess, we can only guess in one way. What of the clergy? Among the educated minority there would be some who, Reformers at heart, really meant what they swore; there would be legal careerists, well able to reconcile with conscience whatever the interest of their career called on them to do in fulfilment of a newly enacted legal obligation; and there would be those who knew they were swearing falsely and, through fear, consciously perjured themselves. And, like the parochial clergy, the religious orders took the oath en masse. Prelates, secular and regular, had the special distinction that they each signed a joint declaration of their repudiation of the traditional faith—namely, a declaration that "the Bishop of Rome has not, in Scripture, any greater jurisdiction in this kingdom of England, than any other foreign bishop." The actual document survives, to this day a startling witness, in its stark simplicity, of their wholesale, cowardly apostasy.[18]

For a great proportion of this gigantic national operation, the principal means was Cranmer, who as Archbishop of Canterbury conducted (personally and by commissioners) a visitation of the best part of the south of England in these summer months, seeing to it everywhere that the priests and the people took the new oath. And somewhere about this time Cranmer did something else, which we can perhaps regard as his first official act to advance those Lutheran ideas to which, alone of the bishops, he had given assent. This act was the archbishop's prohibition of all preaching, for the next twelve months, on the principal topics in controversy these sixteen years between Catholics and Lutherans. There were to be no sermons, either in criticism of or in defence of, the doctrine that justification is by faith alone, that there is a purgatory, that praying to the saints is lawful, and paying reverence to their images, and going on pilgrimage; nor is anything to be said about the question whether priests can marry. For an archbishop to forbid Catholics to defend their traditional beliefs, on the points most notoriously attacked for years, was a harm which no "protection" afforded by a prohibition of heretical sermons could offset.

There is one thing more, in this rough-and-ready tableau of the immediate effects of the revolutionary acts of 1534: we are not, it seems, to conclude that because those who braved the king's anger were so utterly insignificant in number Henry VIII had on his side any passive good will of the majority. The despatches of the envoy of Charles V tell a tale of revolt simmering in every county of the realm, of great lords coming to him by stealth with prayers that the emperor will send an army to put things right—it is not quite fifty years since King Henry's own father landed in Wales and, with a handful of foreign mercenaries as a nucleus, overthrew the last royal tyrant. More convincing, however, than the wishful thinking that was to be, for generations now, the chief occupation of the lay leaders of the opposition, are the notes, in Cromwell's innumerable memoranda, of active preparations for defence against invasion, "beacons, fortresses, munitions, ships." And presently—in another twelve months—there will be diplomatic missions to Germany, to discuss an alliance with Luther's own sovereign.

[18] A reproduction of the first page of this document forms the frontispiece of my book, *The Reformation in England*, Vol. I (1950).

Parliament met again on November 3. In the six weeks of this short session it passed acts of attainder against More and Fisher, and three statutes that completed the laws passed in the spring. The Supremacy Act made it English law that the king and all his successors were to be taken as "the only supreme head in earth of the Church of England, called *Ecclesia Anglicana*,"[19] with all the "jurisdictions" belonging to that dignity, with "full power and authority," among other things, "to reform . . . correct . . . and amend . . . all . . . heresies, abuses . . . whatsoever . . . which by any manner, spiritual authority or jurisdiction ought or may lawfully be reformed . . . corrected . . . or amended[;] . . . any . . . foreign law, foreign authority . . . to the contrary . . . notwithstanding." The act is merely declaratory; that is to say, it says nothing of penalties for denials that the king possesses this power over religion.

A second Act of Succession supplies the official text of the oath imposed by the former act, and already sworn by so many thousands of the king's subjects. It declares that this oath is the one sworn by Parliament at the end of the last session and is the one then meant to be taken by all. As to those who refuse the oath, the commissioners' certificate of refusal, sent in to the King's Bench, suffices as an indictment.

The third statute, the Treasons Act, makes it high treason, and punishable as such, to "maliciously wish, will, or desire, by words or writing . . . to deprive the king or his heirs apparent of their dignity, title or name"—to wish, for example, and to express this in speech, to deprive the king of his title of supreme head of the Church as defined in the Supremacy Act.

With the new year, 1535, the king can proceed, by means of the Supremacy Act and the Treasons Act, to deal out to the recusants of 1534 punishments far more spectacular than life imprisonment and beggary. Half a score of executions will —from the rank and character of those put to death—show the nation, and indeed all Christendom, that the king will stop at nothing in the promotion of his new designs.

As King Henry VIII kept the Christmas of 1534 he might well have done so in the spirit of a man who has just won a

[19] The famous limitation of 1531—"in so far as, by the law of Christ, this is allowed"—is suppressed.

great war, and with unexpected ease. What remained now was to take over the administration of the conquered territories. In the first weeks of the new year the titles of the defeated enemy were attached, and in two commissions, issued as Supreme Head of the Church of Christ in England, the king ordered Cromwell to undertake a general visitation of all the ecclesiastical establishments of the country and their personnel, from Westminster Abbey and St. Paul's Cathedral to the humblest village church, and to make a detailed survey of all their property.

In February there came an order to the bishops to surrender to the king their authority and the documents by virtue of which they had exercised their authority and had received consecration. In return for these papal bulls each bishop received a licence from the king as Supreme Head, permitting him to ordain those found suitable, to appoint parish priests, to make visitations of his diocese, to punish evil livers, and so forth. The bishop is piously admonished that episcopal carelessness is the root of all evils, and is told that he is granted these powers for just so long as the king's good will pleases. From the bishops there had, moreover, been exacted a repudiation of the pope so carefully detailed that it is just not possible that they could have any doubt whatever as to what they were doing. "I firmly affirm," they say, "and openly declare and will declare . . . that [the Roman papacy] is a thing invented by men . . . The Bishop of Rome is not 'the pope,' is not 'the Supreme Pontiff' . . . but simply the Bishop of Rome, my brother . . ." And they began most energetically, under the eye of Cromwell, to organise the preaching of this repudiation throughout their jurisdictions.

In April the king struck down the first of the little band who had stood firm for what all had, until lately, believed to be the divinely ordered constitution of the Church. Four priests were tried (April 29), charged with treason for having replied to the commissioners who, in the Tower, interrogated them, "The king our sovereign lord is not Supreme Head on earth of the Church of England." Three were Carthusian monks, one a Bridgettine of Syon. They were found guilty, condemned, and on May 4 hanged (in their religious dress), drawn, and quartered at Tyburn before a huge crowd and a silent band of courtiers, headed by the Duke of Norfolk (the lord treasurer, Queen Anne's uncle) and the king's young illegitimate son, the Duke of Richmond.[20] According to one account, Henry also looked on, one of a party of nobles who came masked. Three days later the commissioners made their final attempt to trap the Bishop of Rochester into speech against the supremacy. While his answers were being studied the news arrived that the new pope, Paul III,[21] had, on May 22, made him a cardinal. On June 12 three more of the Carthusian monks were brought to trial and condemned. The bishop was tried on June 17. The monks were butchered at Tyburn on June 19 and the bishop beheaded, June 22, on Tower Hill. The charge in all four cases was the same, a spoken denial that the king is the Supreme Head on earth of the Church of England.

Four days after the bishop's execution the commissioners were named for the trial of More. This took place on July 1. In all More's various examinations before the council, who brought the king's command that he should declare his mind about the supremacy, the one-time lord chancellor would say no more than, "I will not meddle with such matters." To entrap such an intelligence, and so experienced a lawyer, into admissions that were a breach of the law was beyond the capacity of the king's legal hacks. "He kept wholly silent," says one part of the long indictment on which he was tried. Cromwell reminded him of the king's passionate anger when thwarted. And More repeated that with no man ever had he discussed these topics; "I am (quoth I) the king's true faithful subject and daily bedesman, and pray for His Highness, and all his, and all the realm. I do nobody no harm, I say none harm, I think none harm, but wish everybody good. And if this be not enough to keep a man alive, in good faith I long not to live." He was, of course, condemned, and then—before sentence was passed—he delivered his mind freely and powerfully on the unlawfulness of the new supremacy. On July 6 he was beheaded. To the crowd around the scaffold he said no more than to beg them "to pray for him, and to bear witness with him that he should now there suffer death, in and

[20] There was a fifth victim, the vicar of Isleworth (the parish in which Syon monastery is situated), John Haile by name, guilty on his own confession of saying plainly that the king's marriage with Anne was mere living in sin, that his life was "more foul and stinking than a sow, wallowing and defiling herself in any filthy place," and that "Three parts of England is against the king."

[21] Clement VII died September 25, 1534. Paul III was elected on the following October 13.

for the faith of the Holy Catholic Church." And he also said "that he died the King's good servant, but God's first."

Cromwell's memoranda about preparations for national defence[22] carry with them the unspoken truth, ever before administrators, that no national activity is so costly as war. And even without what new burdens might thus, in 1534, be reasonably anticipated, the national finances were already in a very bad way by that time, the annual, ordinary revenue down to about £100,000. What had long been needed, as well as a better financial system, was the discovery of new sources of permanent revenue. And somewhere about the time when Cromwell began to organise the revolution in the relations of State and Church, and in the relations between English Catholics and their supreme spiritual lord, the pope, the thought of the endowments of the Church came forcibly across his attention as the king's chief financial counsellor. What if the king could possess himself of all those properties, a gross income of perhaps £300,000 every year? An income from which the necessary outgoings could, by an economical administration, be trimmed down very considerably from the present rates—if bishops (for example) were put on a fixed annual salary, archbishops with something more, deans (if retained) with something less, and so forth?

This all-embracing reform Cromwell presumably thought beyond the possibility of his power. But in addition to the act of 1534 which, for the benefit of the revenue, revived the abolished annates tax (and extended what had applied only to sees to every benefice in the country), an act which also laid an annual income tax of 10 per cent on all clerical revenues, he began to make ready for the dissolution of the monastic communities and the confiscation of their property to the use of the king. And this was determined on before a single commissioner of the king's vicar-general had detected a single incontinent monk, before any of those scabrous reports and their sniggering covering letters—the work of "men upon whose word it is impossible to depend"—had been written. "Money was the main motive that started the vicar-general's engines, and that was what mattered most to his master."[23]

[22] See p. 179, *supra*.
[23] The phrases quoted are from Fisher, *op. cit.*, p. 203 and Pickthorn, *op. cit.*, p. 270.

The king's commission to Cromwell to make these visitations, as vicar-general of the Supreme Head, is dated January 21, 1535. It was not until July, until after the executions, that the work began; and the commissioners (who usually worked in couples, though sometimes singly) were busy for the next six or seven months, with the eight hundred or so religious houses of England and Wales and their eight or nine thousand monks, Canons Regular, and nuns for their prey. The reports on the way the religious lived came through all that time, but long before this information was completed the king and his minister had before them the great financial inventory of the whole ecclesiastical system, prepared under the commission of January 30, 1535. They could now know to a penny how much each abbey was worth as a going concern, from such lordly houses as Westminster with a revenue of £2,409, or Christ Church, Canterbury with £2,374, to the thirty-two convents of nuns, now about to be suppressed, no one of which had more than £25 annual income.

Cromwell had been through all this before. As Wolsey's man of affairs he had seen to the dissolution and the selling up of the properties of the 29 abbeys which Pope Clement VII allowed Wolsey to suppress in 1524–28 in the interests of the colleges he was founding at Ipswich and at Oxford. That was just over seven years ago. And surveying the enormous task that now faced him, Cromwell first set the machine which he had designed to the comparatively simple business of making away with the abbeys of less than £200 annual revenue and with less than 12 inmates each. There were 318 such houses, of which 103 were convents of women. The sum of their revenues amounted to perhaps £20,000, something like one seventh of the total monastic revenues. The number of religious living in these poor and insignificant homes has been calculated at 1,500.

The only use to which, in the campaign against the monastic institutions, the king and his minister ever put the damning evidence which the report on morals must have been (had it been believed) was a reference in the preamble to the Act for the Dissolution of the Lesser Monasteries; viz., that "manifest sin, vicious, carnal and abominable living is daily used and committed among the little and small abbeys." And then, very pointedly, the authors of the act, with reports before them which, if true, proved what they were next about to say to be a most cynical piece of lying, note the contrast offered by "divers great and solemn monasteries of this realm, wherein (thanks be to God) religion is right well kept and observed"—every one of which monasteries would also, between the winter of 1537 and April 10, 1540, be destroyed, nonetheless, by this same Supreme Head.

The statute called the Dissolution of the Lesser Monasteries Act enacted that the whole property of these 318 monasteries belonged to the king, and it placed no restriction of any kind on his use of the property, although the rights of the creditors of the monasteries were secured. To the 318 superiors there was a pledge of a yearly pension suited to their present condition. Of the rest, the priests could choose between transfer to another house of the order and the chance of employment as parochial clergy. The others, if professed before the age of twenty-five, were sent home; otherwise they were transferred to other abbeys. How the House of Commons would have received the bill if left to itself, we do not know; but it seems to be the fact that the king came in to deliver the project personally (March 11, 1536) and that he made a great speech about it to them. The measure was no sooner law than, once again, the machinery of royal commissioners was set up for the work of expulsion, destruction, and sale; the bells and the lead stripped from the roofs were melted down and kept for the king's use; the jewels and church plate sent up to London; the moveables sold off. The management of the estates passed under the control of a new and most efficient organ of centralized administration, the Court for the Augmentations of the King's Revenue, created by an act of this same parliamentary session.

The effect of the Act of Suppression was far from uniform —Lincolnshire, where 34 out of 46 abbeys disappeared; East Anglia, which lost 28 out of 40; and the more settled half of Yorkshire, where out of 44 houses 25 were destroyed, suffered most. But everywhere it was a spectacular announcement that a redistribution of property had begun that was to be more far-reaching in its effect than any such event since the Norman Conquest, redistribution on such a scale as England was not to see again until this twentieth century. Changes of this sort, four hundred years ago, could not but mean ruin to scores of thousands of the poorest of the peasantry, the breakup of the small communities which were their world, and a future that was truly beggary. It is not surprising that it was Lincolnshire and eastern Yorkshire which, in the autumn of this year 1536, suddenly burst open with that Pilgrimage of Grace, the rising which, for a moment, seemed about to cast the despoiling king from his throne.

Meanwhile, on April 14, 1536, the Reformation Parliament, as we call it, was dissolved. It had been summoned nearly seven years before, in the weeks that immediately followed the unexpected public collapse of the king's greatest effort to get Anne for his wife with the blessing of the Church. Its end all but coincided with the tragic end of Anne herself —beheaded for alleged adultery, May 19, and, on the eve of her execution, declared by Cranmer, sitting once again as supreme matrimonial judge, never to have been Henry's wife. The next Parliament would face the nice problem of enabling (and compelling) all who, in obedience to threats, had freely sworn some months ago that Anne was, "according to God's law," Henry's only true wife to swear now that she had never been anything of the kind. That Parliament met within three weeks of Anne's bloody end, but not before a Queen Jane had been enthroned in Anne's place—for whose marriage to the king Cranmer had expedited a dispensation on the very day of Anne's execution, to whom the king was betrothed on the morrow of that event, and to whom he was married ten days later (May 30). What had really finished Anne was that Henry had come to dislike her—and to fancy someone else (several someone elses, but finally Jane Seymour)—and that the death of his real wife, Catherine, on January 7, 1536, had left him free (could he but be rid of Anne) to make a marriage whose validity no man, anywhere, would doubt. It was Queen Jane Seymour who gave Henry his son, the future King Edward VI, born October 12, 1537.

And now, while Parliament with laws and oaths was once again screening the royal indescribable, something much more important in its nature was happening at his command, in the field of his spiritual supremacy.

In all the years that had passed since the king's great drive against heresy (of May 1530)[24] there had been hardly any change in the official attitude towards the new Reformation theology. For three years a crypto-Lutheran had been Archbishop of Canterbury. Another five priests of this same quality (two of them previously convicted of heresy) had since been promoted to various sees. Cromwell, the architect of the

[24] See p. 153, *supra.*

new régime, vicar-general of the Supreme Head on earth, after Christ, of the Church of England, had never been hostile to the Lutheran doctrines. Nevertheless, the only novelty, so far, had been the archbishop's order forbidding preachers to attack the Lutheran doctrine of justification by only faith, and clerical marriage. This was in the summer of 1534.

Towards the end of the following year, however, five months or so after the execution of More, political necessity —the "international situation"—led, accidentally enough, but inevitably, to the beginnings of a wholly new development and of changes that were to be permanent. The new pope, Paul III, a singularly able man, seemed dangerously in earnest about the plan for a General Council. To wreck this plan by diplomatic means (or to thwart the council should it assemble) called for anti-papal allies. The "Gallicanism" of the French king would hardly be at Henry's service—so fresh in the mind of the French king was the memory of the indignities which the late entente had brought him, and so revolting the fact of the executions. The English king was driven to the depths of condescension, to negotiate with the Lutheran princes of Germany, now allied in the League of Schmalkalden.

The king's envoys were Edward Foxe, Gardiner's old colleague in the management of the king's divorce, and now Bishop of Hereford, and Lutheran-minded; Nicholas Heath, a priest and a legist, who would one day be lord chancellor and the last Catholic Archbishop of York; and, thirdly, Robert Barnes, the one-time prior of the Augustinians at Cambridge and imprisoned by Wolsey for heresy, who had later fled the country, and to whom the king had now given a safe conduct, finding a man personally known to Luther and Melanchthon a most useful diplomatic agent in Germany. The long-drawn-out discussions at Wittenberg (November 1535–June 1536) ended in little more than words of good will. The Lutherans would not accept the English king's theology about the impediments to marriage, and Henry refused to pledge himself to the Confession of Augsburg. Nor would he agree to the Lutheran contention that Masses where none but the celebrant communicated should be abolished and that the marriage of priests and of one-time monks or nuns was lawful.

Nevertheless, these discussions influenced what has been called "the first confession of faith" of the Church of England, as a king-governed institution—the Ten Articles ac-

cepted by the Convocation on July 12, 1536. These profess
to make clear, to the supposedly bewildered, ordinary man,
what parts of religious practice are no more than man-devised
rules for good order. He is told that there are three sacraments,
Baptism, Penance, and the Holy Eucharist—and that in this
last, Christ is really and bodily present. But the Mass is not
so much as mentioned. What justification means is set out
in words that are a translation of Melanchthon. There is a
purgatory, it is said, and the souls therein may be helped by
the prayers of the faithful, but not by indulgences, nor by
the offering of Masses. Saints are lawfully honoured; they may
be prayed to that, in turn, they may pray for us to God. Their
images are lawful, but only as reminders of these personages
and their holy lives. The images themselves are not to be venerated by ceremonies. Ceremonies such as holy water, blessed
ashes, blessed bread, and so forth, are also lawful, provided
it is understood that they are no more than concrete reminders of the perfection we should strive after, and that they do
nothing towards the remission of our sins.

These points had been in debate among the bishops, by
the king's command, for some months already. The scenes in
the Convocation were a trial of strength between the two parties. The Lutheran-minded were disappointed that the Wittenberg influence had not achieved more, and it needed the
personal intervention of the king before they consented to
what, for them, was a miserable compromise.

Whoever actually wrote the Articles, it was as the king's
own handiwork that they were put to Convocation and published. And more important, by far, for the future than
whether their content was "reformist" or "conservative" was
the revolutionary fact that they were imposed by the king
and accepted because he imposed them. Yet once again the
royal supremacy is something more than the extension of the
royal power of police to the life of the cleric. It is a power
that claims to distinguish between what is divine and what is
human in religion.

The king's next activity as head of the Church followed
within the month—an order for the visitation of the whole
Church in England, commissioners touring the country to enquire into the lives of all the parish clergy and how they did
their duty. In a code of Injunctions, Cromwell, as the king's
vicar-general, gave the clergy a new rule of life. One novelty
was that, Sunday by Sunday for the next three months, they

were all to preach that the authority exercised by the pope was a blasphemous and tyrannical sham, and that by God's appointment it was the king who was, under Christ, the head of the Church in England. And twice every quarter for the rest of their lives, they were to preach this same sermon, every parish priest in every one of the eight thousand parish churches of the kingdom.

These last agents of the head of the Church had barely got to work when their grave proceedings—and the actual dissolution of the abbeys—were suddenly interrupted by a popular insurrection in Lincolnshire. It subsided as speedily as it had arisen, on the approach of the king's troops and promises that grievances would be considered; but there had been ten thousand men in movement, and Lincoln itself had been in their power for a week (October 6–13). While that appearance of insurgent victory still held, a much more formidable rising began in Yorkshire, at the cloth town of Beverley (October 8). Within a week York, the second city of the kingdom, had opened its gates to a host of twenty thousand, many of them mounted, led by Robert Aske, a gentleman of the county and a lawyer. As the news spread, there were other risings, in Yorkshire and in Durham; the great lords of the north were organising, Percys and Nevilles; the port of Hull was taken, and the castle of Pontefract, which was a main key to the king's control of the north. By October 23, only five miles separated "the flower of the north," at Doncaster— thirty or forty thousand men, well mounted, well provided —from the royal army not one tenth their number.

It was the Duke of Norfolk, the king's commander-in-chief, who saved the day for the king. Aske, a singularly simple-minded man for a lawyer, had never intended more than a demonstration that would encourage the king to shed his evil, heretical advisors and would ease (what Henry was presumed to desiderate) a return to the good old days. Norfolk's arrival at Doncaster was the signal for dissensions between such leaders as Aske, leading a "pilgrimage" to petition the king, and tough warriors like Sir Thomas Percy. Aske prevailed. There was no attack. Norfolk was allowed to speak. And from this moment the Pilgrimage of Grace was doomed. Negotiations were opened with the king, and—this objective attained —the great host dispersed (October 30).

In a great conference at Pontefract, two hundred represent-

atives of the Pilgrims, peers, knights, gentry, and commons
met in order to prepare a reasoned statement of their demands. This has survived, and it shows the Pilgrimage unique
among insurrections. There is hardly any phase of national
life that was not considered in these debates. The Pilgrims
ask for the punishment of the heretical bishops (Cranmer and
five others named) and speak bitterly of the cowardice of the
others who have allowed, without protest, the sacrilegious
plunder of the abbeys. They ask for the punishment of the
three wicked ministers of the king, Cromwell, Audley, and
Rich (the recently promoted chancellor of the Court of the
Augmentations). They demand the suppression of the heretical books now allowed to circulate, and again give names.
They ask that the monasteries be preserved, as centres of religious life and for their social value, and that the authors
of the notorious reports be punished for their extortions and
"their abominable acts." They ask for recognition of the pope
as supreme head of the Church, "as before." Every man, Aske
was to explain after his arrest, "was glad to set foward" for
the repeal of the Act of Supremacy. And one of the reasons
why the Pilgrims called for repeal of the new Treasons Act
was that it had stifled the opinions of the learned divines
defending the papal supremacy.

The rest of this tale is soon told. Norfolk made a show of
accepting all this for report to the king, though all this time he
had the king's instructions merely to let the Pilgrims talk
themselves into a false security. There were long delays, intrigues with the court, and rumours of intrigues, disappointments, and new sporadic demonstrations (January 1537) that
served as the pretext for royal severities. And then repression
manu militari, and through the king's courts. In all, 216 were
put to death, it is thought; among whom were Aske, of course,
and some of the lords and knights, half a dozen abbots, 38
monks of various orders, and 16 parish priests. The last, Robert Aske, was hanged at York, July 12, 1537. Another three
years and Cromwell, too, would be going to execution.

While the king was directing the liquidation of the Pilgrimage, his bishops and theologians were busy—at his command—
with the preparation of a very lengthy statement of belief
that was, at the same time, a kind of *vade mecum* to the
spiritual life. It appeared in September 1537, *The Institution
of a Christian Man.* At the last moment the king had declined

to put his name to it, and since it came to the public as the work of the bishops, as the *Bishops' Book* it has always been known. Except for its return to the old belief that there are seven sacraments, this work is still more friendly to the new German theologies than were the Articles of 1536. In the summer of 1538 there came the official visit of the German theologians that was first spoken of at the time of Foxe's and Barnes' mission to Wittenberg in 1535. Their discussions with Cranmer and others of the bishops led to a certain measure of agreement, but the king remained inflexible in his attachment to the belief that private Masses are pleasing to God, that the sacrament of the Holy Eucharist is truly received when received under the sole form of bread, and that it is unlawful for the clergy to marry. The only memorials of these weeks of debate are a never-sanctioned agreement, set out in thirteen articles, and the argumentative correspondence between the king and the German divines.

Just before they left England, Cromwell, in the king's name, imposed a second series of Injunctions on the clergy, September 30, 1538. The chief of the new regulations are instructions to purify the cult of the saints and of images and relics from superstition, instructions cast in such language as to suggest that almost nowhere is it safe to allow the ordinary man the luxury of so dangerous a devotion. And where these devotions are an occasion of superstition, the Injunctions command the utter destruction of shrines, statues, pictures, and relics. The royal government gave the best evidence of what these Injunctions meant by tearing down, in this summer, shrines which had for centuries been centres of international pilgrimage, of Our Lady at Walsingham in Norfolk, for example, and of St. Thomas at Canterbury. From this last shrine whole waggonloads of gold and silver, jewels, precious hangings were carted away to the king's treasury, while the relics of the saint were burned. The most magnificent jewel then known, the great ruby of France, given to the shrine by the French king who was the saint's contemporary, Henry VIII took for himself and, set in a ring, it thenceforth graced his sacrilegious hand.

Besides loosing this war against one important element of popular religion, the Injunctions of 1538 inaugurated a new era for the ordinary Englishman when they commanded each parish priest to provide, by Easter 1539, "one book of the whole Bible of the largest volume, in English," to be "set up in some convenient place within the said church . . . whereas your parishioners may most commodiously resort to the same and read it." The priests were ordered not to discourage any one, "privily or apertly," from reading this Bible or from listening to others read it. On the contrary, they were to explain that this was the "very lively word of God," which Christians must believe if they are to be saved. The translation of this first authorised Bible was in part the forbidden version of Tyndale, in part that of Miles Coverdale, a one-time Austin Friar. It contained all those prologues by Tyndale, and annotations, which were, in so large a part, Luther's own work. In 1539 a new, splendid edition was prepared, the famous Great Bible, and this was seven times reprinted in two years.

Shrines looted, images profaned, relics burned, in an age when for the first time clerics were being allowed to say freely that the whole cultus of the saints was a superstition and a grievous sin—what else but a most lively propaganda for Reformation ideals were the Injunctions of the anti-Lutheran king and the events of the years 1537–39? What else was the destruction, now consummated, not of monasteries alone, but of monasticism? For in these same years all those "great and solemn monasteries," which, so the act of 1536 implied, there was no reason to touch, fell into the king's hands, through surrenders induced by terror: Benedictines, Cistercians, Canons Regular, to the number of 184 autonomous houses, with their 62 dependent priories and 57 cells; the 18 "greater" convents of nuns; the 179 friaries, Dominican, Franciscan, Austin Friars, Carmelites; the 43 English commanderies of the Knights of St. John of Jerusalem; and the 47 lesser monasteries exempted by the king from the suppression in 1536. In all, a matter of 590 establishments, with a total annual revenue of well over £100,000, were given over to the king in the years 1537–40, and the king's title to them secured by a special act of Parliament. When, in 1539, yet another delegation from Wittenberg arrived in London, the English sympathisers with the new ways may well have felt that the final triumph was at hand.

Actually, in the spring of that year, the king was to give the clearest of signs that, in some of the matters regarded as fundamental by the Germans, he remained as hostile to their ideas as when he had written his book against their leader. After a great theological tourney in the House of Lords between the bishops of the opposing factions, the statute known as the Six Articles Act was enacted: not easily, indeed, but only (as more than once already) with the personal intervention of the king, who "confounded them all (i.e., the pro-Lutheran bishops) with God's learning"; as one of the lay lords wrote. By this act, which came into force on June 28, 1539, the king's forty-eighth birthday, all who henceforward denied Transubstantiation were liable to be burnt as heretics and to lose all their property as traitors; those who taught that, in order to receive the sacrament of the Holy Eucharist, communion under both species was necessary, or that private Masses were contrary to God's law, or that actual confession of sins to a priest was not necessary to the sacrament of Penance, priests who married, and men or women who violated their solemn vows of chastity—all these were to be hanged as felons. Special courts were to be set up to try offences against the act.

The king, in bringing this about, revoked nothing of all that he had done. There was no "Catholic reaction" in this statute. He did no more than show, by a penal law of great ferocity, that his old determination not to go forward, in the Reformers' sense, was as strong as ever. Cranmer, we are told, sent his wife back to Germany; Latimer and Shaxton were forced to resign their sees and kept under lock and key for the next few months. And in a great raid in London, five hundred arrests were made. All, presumably, recanted, for all were pardoned. In 1541 there was a second raid in London, and more than two hundred were arrested. A handful of these were sent to prison, and the rest discharged on giving bail. The act was rarely put into force, indeed, and in 1544 its procedure was notably mitigated.

When old Lord Darcy appeared before the council to answer for his actions during the Pilgrimage of Grace, with a boldness as rare in that sycophantic time as it is refreshing, he blamed Cromwell to his face as "the chief causer of all this rebellion." His own doom clear to him, he made a kind of forecast about Lord Cromwell: "I trust that ere thou die . . . yet shall there one head remain that shall strike off thy head." And so it came to pass. Less than twelve months after the passing of the Six Articles Act, Cromwell was in the Tower. On July 28, 1540, destroyed by his own invention of attainder without any hearing, he was beheaded. The alleged offences were heresy and treason. He was guilty of neither. But his policy had com-

mitted Henry VIII to a war he did not want, against the
emperor, and as the ally of the Duke of Cleves whom Charles
was about to crush; and had also committed the king to the
duke's sister, Anne, whom he had married in the previous
January. Henry's unquotable language about her person may be
read in the interrogatories that preceded Cromwell's destruction, he whom the king held responsible for the marriage being
the first repository of the royal anguish, and preserved from
death just a few days more in order to swear to the confidences,
and so provide the evidence to prove non-consummation and
a way out for Henry, now *aetatis suae* fifty. With Cromwell's
death something like anarchy descended, not on the administration, but on the highest levels of directive policy. He did
so much harm to the Catholic Church that to the earliest
Protestant historians it was reputed to him as purest Reformation orthodoxy. Foxe's Book of Martyrs has a wonderful account of the execution, complete with profession of faith.
Cromwell's actual last words were that he died a Catholic.

King Henry VIII's version of the Christian religion, it seems
safe to say, satisfied almost none of his subjects. The bishops,
left to themselves and with all pressure removed, would have
divided straightway into two groups, of which the one would
have knelt at the feet of the pope and begged for reconciliation, while the other would have translated into act all the
theories and suggestions and recommendations of Luther and
Melanchthon. The six and a half years which remained to the
king at the death of Cromwell are filled with the antagonistic
intrigues of these two groups.

As to the king, he is, as always, greatly influenced in his
attitude towards the two parties by the relations that obtain
between his two European rivals, the Emperor-King of Spain
and the King of France—the potential executors of the excommunication decreed by Pope Paul III in 1538. That Henry's
views about the Lutheran theologies changed at all in these
last years of his life is more than doubtful. When the long-
promised revision of the *Bishops' Book* at last appeared in
1543, it was not the Lutheranisers who gained comfort from
the changes. And the act of Parliament which imposed the
King's Book—as this was generally called—renewed all the old
condemnation of Tyndale's works and of his biblical translations, and forbade the general public to read even the Bible
that was authorised. Lutherans were sent to the stake, under

the Six Articles Act, in 1543 and again in 1546, in which year there was a great official burning of heretical books, when the Bible of Tyndale and of Coverdale once more helped to feed the fires. And when Henry died, January 28, 1547, he left behind him a will whose provisions are a most striking testimony of his belief in the doctrine that souls in purgatory can be helped through the offering of the Mass. On the other hand, the education of his two younger children, Elizabeth (aged thirteen and a half at his death) and Edward (just four years younger), had been left entirely in the hands of Lutheranisers, of Protestants—if by the time we come to 1547 it is possible to use that term without unhistorical implications.

In those last, curious six years of Henry's reign, the two leading personages in public life were bishops, Cranmer and Stephen Gardiner. None of the laymen in the council rise above mediocrity, whether as diplomats or as administrators—nor is any one of them given the chance to show himself the third Wolsey or the second Cromwell. The only noteworthy figures among them are the two soldiers, Edward Seymour, Earl of Hertford, brother of Henry's third queen, uncle therefore of the heir to the throne, and John Dudley, Viscount Lisle. Cranmer is outside politics, but influential always by reason of the king's unfailing personal affection for him. Gardiner is the indispensable diplomat, the trained and experienced advisor on foreign affairs—and the author of the classic defence of the royal supremacy as part of the Christian faith, the book *De Vera Obedientia*, published in 1535. At the time of King Henry's death he is a man of fifty, Cranmer is fifty-eight, and the two soldiers are between forty and forty-four. The king was in his fifty-sixth year.

iii *Cranmer, 1547–1553*

The closing scenes of the life of King Henry VIII are familiar to us from the very textbooks: the sudden collapse of the king, who had been seriously ill for some weeks, on January 27, 1547; Cranmer sent for and arriving to find his master speechless and obviously near the end; in the gallery outside the sickroom Paget, the secretary, walking up and down with Hertford, the two perfecting their many arrangements, with mutual promises—among the things arranged is to keep the death a secret until they have made sure of the other men of state. The king's will set up, for the protection of the child of nine who was to succeed, a great council of co-equal regents, of which these two were members. The rest were summoned once Henry was dead—January 28—and all swore an oath faithfully to execute the will. The little king was brought to London and proclaimed, and then, within the month, the will was thrown aside, Hertford named as Protector and the rest as his council.[25]

Socially and politically the reign thus inaugurated was one long disaster. The men in power were, almost without exception, mere adventurers, avid to loot the state and especially what remained of the wealth of the Church. To a man they professed a religious interest in the desires of their ecclesiastical colleagues to change the doctrine and rites of the Church. But not even those with whom this profession was sincere, were disinterested. It is a fact generally accepted that the Reformation of King Edward VI's reign was brought about by an alliance between politicians utterly worldly, devoid of morality, and Reformers so bigoted as to play blindly into their hands. Not for the first time it might be seen how hatred could make clerical zeal strangely indulgent to the sins of the mighty, of the men whose power alone procured for hatred its opportunity to destroy. When the day of reckoning came and the new religious structure was cast down as easily as it had been built, and when the lay lords had reverted, their clerical allies, now held in durance, made no secret that the lords' profession of zeal had been mere profanity and mockery of God.

There were now no more of those complicated manœuvres which had marked the last ten years of King Henry's reign. The course was set for the complete "Protestantising" of that church where the king was supreme head, and from that course, for the six and a half years of King Edward VI's reign, the government never swerved. Cranmer, at last, came into his own. What he now achieved has lasted to this day.

Edward VI was crowned with the Mass, as Henry VIII was buried with the Mass. Cranmer was the celebrant at the coronation, Gardiner at the funeral. It was his last public official act for many a year. The Lent of 1547 was remarkably ushered in by two of his colleagues, Barlow and Ridley,[26]

[25] And the nobles had themselves promoted socially, e.g., Hertford became Duke of Somerset, and Dudley, Earl of Warwick.

[26] Ridley was made Bishop of Rochester a few months later.

preaching vigorously, at Paul's Cross, against the very idea of Lent—the long season of penitential exercises in preparation for the feast of Easter and the general communion day. They also denounced the veneration of images as idolatry. Soon mobs began to destroy the images, and when Gardiner protested against scenes of this sort that had taken place in his own diocese, at Portsmouth, he fell into bad odour. When he refused to co-operate with Cranmer in the preparation of a book of homilies for the use of the unlettered mass of the clergy, his case was still worse. These homilies—the *First Book of Homilies*, they came to be called—appeared on July 31, a weighty volume, ordered to be read to the people, Sunday by Sunday, at Mass by the priest. Since what they taught contradicted the doctrine of the book in possession, the *King's Book* of 1543, which was authorised by a law that forbade all other statements of doctrine, Gardiner had a good excuse for refusing to use the *Homilies*. He was however, after a lively correspondence with Cranmer and with the Protector, thrown into prison, to remain there (save for a brief interval of six months) as long as Edward VI reigned—the ablest man in public life, the only possible leader, of any weight, against the "Protestanising" party.

The *Homilies*, twelve in number, were the work of several writers, the chief of whom was the archbishop himself. On all the points in controversy these thirty years between the Reformers and the Church in which they were bred, the *Homilies* set out the Reformation solution. Here, in clear and unmistakable language, all the foundation doctrines of Protestantism are taught: that the Bible is the only source of true knowledge of God, Who makes its meaning clear to the true believer as he piously reads it; that by Adam's sin the very nature of man has been corrupted, and irremediably so; that the salvation of mankind avails only to the man who confidently believes that, by virtue of the death of Christ, he personally is saved—justification is through faith alone; that there are two sacraments only, Baptism and the Supper of the Lord, and that these do not bring about justification—Baptism is not even mentioned in the homily, *Of the Salvation of all mankind*; that a man's good works are without effect, relative, that is to say, to his salvation—they are no more than evidence of the reality of his faith, and a duty because commanded of God; that every action of the natural man, no matter how good it is in itself, is a sin in the sight of God and deserving of eternal punishment in hell; and that, for those who have not the faith that saves, hell is the inevitable destiny. Additional homilies on such matters as fasting, almsdeeds, prayer, the mysteries of the passion and resurrection of Christ and of the Eucharist are promised for a later edition of the work. Meanwhile, in the present series there is much scornful, fiercely written denunciation of the pious practices traditional for centuries among Catholics, and of doctrines also.

The *Homilies*, and the new duty of reading them to their parishioners, were brought to the knowledge of the clergy through a royal visitation of the Church. The Injunctions which the visitors brought with them had much to say, yet once again, of the *superstitious* use of images, and again ordered the priest to remove such images as were occasions of superstition. This distinction—a distinction without a difference, it may be thought, to the leading Reformers—was soon to disappear. On February 21, 1548, the king's council would order that all images be taken out of the churches. Meanwhile, as though foreseeing this, a clean sweep was made of the churches in London; the frescoes were covered over with a heavy coat of white, the walls adorned with selected texts from Scripture.

Parliament met on November 4, 1547. The first statute enacted dealt with the mass of unseemly, profane literature and talk reviling and mocking the doctrine of the Holy Eucharist. Such revilers, after May 1, 1548, were liable to fine and imprisonment at the king's pleasure. The statute also provided that, for the future, Holy Communion should be administered "under both the kinds, that is to say, of bread and wine." A second act of this Parliament, the act dissolving the chantries, brought about the ruin of innumerable schools of the kind we today call high schools. A chantry was, basically, an endowment to keep a priest whose duty it was to say Mass for the soul of the man whose will had provided the endowment. Very often, indeed, it was also a stated duty of the priest to keep a school. Nearly two hundred high schools, it has been calculated, were abolished or brought very low by this dissolution of the chantries—there were something like two thousand chantry priests in all. The various institutions called King Edward VI Grammar Schools are not so much the foundation of a royal pioneer of free education, but rather they are schools of an earlier date which managed to escape the confiscation of his reign. The Privy Council records give as the reason for the

Chantries Act of 1547 the realm's urgent need of money. The preamble to the statute says nothing of this, but speaks of the belief that the souls of Christians deceased can be aided through the sacrifice of the Mass as superstitious and as a "hindrance" to "the very true and perfect salvation through Jesus Christ." And it also speaks of the great service it will be to the nation to use the chantry endowments to build new schools and to improve the universities.

In an earlier Chantries Act, passed in the last years of King Henry's reign, an act for the king's life only, Parliament had given him all the colleges of the country, and there was a moment when Oxford and Cambridge seemed about to suffer the fate of the abbeys. The act of 1547, which expressly exempted the colleges of the two university towns, did well to speak of "augmenting" these institutions. After nearly twenty years of general upheaval they were in a parlous state—"wells that had almost dried up," one Reformer declared, preaching before the little king. Nine tenths of the student body had disappeared, he also said, and England was likely to become "more barbarous than Scythia." There were, indeed, two years in this reign when at Oxford not a single degree was conferred. Thousands of books had been destroyed in the various royal visitations, as thousands had been destroyed when the abbeys came down. The university library had disappeared. At Cambridge, from about 1538, the university, hard-driven for money, began to sell its books, and what had once been the library was used as a lecture room. The testimony to this decay, from the indignant Reformation divines, is general.

The statute which prescribed the new rules about Holy Communion did not provide a new ritual. The authors of the change did not, however, mean that the priests should carry it out by simply adding an additional Latin sentence to the existing rite as they took the chalice to the communicants. They prepared, and in March 1548 there was published, by the king's command, the most revolutionary novelty so far seen: directions, called *The Order of Communion*, for a separate service, not in Latin, but in English, to be added to the Mass on communion days. The *Order* was an adaptation of a Lutheran rite devised by the recently converted Archbishop of Cologne, and its opening directions delivered a powerful blow against another sacrament, Penance. For the communicants were told that, if they were in a state of sin, they need not confess to a priest before receiving communion; the general absolution pronounced in the communion rite was sufficient. Nor must those who preferred to go to confession consider these others less good Christians than themselves.

Still greater changes were in preparation during the remainder of this year 1548. When Parliament reassembled, it was presented with a work that must have seemed the Reformation itself. The whole collection of the Catholic liturgical service books was abolished—the missal, the graduale, the breviary, the processional, and the rest. In their place was a single volume, and in the English tongue, called *The Book of the Common Prayer and administration of the Sacraments and other Rites and Ceremonies of the Church: after the use of the Church of England*. It was sanctioned by Parliament, after some stormy debates, January 21, 1549, and ordered to be used from the following Whitsunday, June 9. The history of the composition of this book is not known. We have drafts of various parts in Cranmer's hand, and we know that there was a conference of bishops and learned divines who worked on the project in the summer of 1548. And that is all. Cranmer is universally credited with the authorship of the singularly graceful prayers.

In this Book of Common Prayer—the Prayer Book is a handier way to refer to it—Cranmer attacked a problem which had occupied many minds (Catholic minds) for a generation now, the problem of how to simplify and shorten the official daily service of the Church, called the Divine Office. Cranmer's solution must be pronounced rarely successful. It was achieved, of course, only at a price—the wonderful hymns of the breviary, for example, disappeared entirely, and, the language of the book being English, there disappeared also a great heritage of plain song, music that had developed from the rhythms natural to the Latin language. The great achievement, however, stands; namely, that the English henceforth possessed a daily service of public prayer, of great beauty, in their own tongue, and of practical length. The Morning Prayer of this book would come to be the standard daily service—and for centuries the standard Sunday service—in place of the Mass: not of the *Latin* Mass, but of the Mass.

This Prayer Book imposed by law in 1549 contains, however, a service called Mass, "The Supper of the Lord and the Holy Communion, commonly called the Mass." Since the government which imposed the book referred to the Mass as the "old superstitious service" and could remonstrate with the heir to the throne, the Lady Mary, who clung to that "old service," that the Mass was the product of "the corruption of time," something nourished by "barbarousness and ignorance," and since Cranmer had for the theology of which the Mass was the expression as passionate a hatred as though it were a living enemy, it can hardly be that, in his beautiful English, he intended no more than merely to translate the Mass and thereby endow it with a career of further usefulness in the Church where he was now such a power. The ambiguity in the title quoted is willed. It is part of the policy which we have seen operating at the behest of Luther, and which was explained to Martin Bucer, when he was Cranmer's guest in the interval between the passing of the act and the book's coming into use: "Concessions" have had to be made, which, however, "are only to be retained for a time, lest the people, not having yet learned Christ, should be deterred by too extensive innovations from embracing his religion." And a Reformer who was English, and soon to be very famous, John Hooper, complained that the new Communion Service was what could be made to seem like the Mass by a celebrant of the anti-Protestant party. The text of this service has been studied exhaustively, debated endlessly. What no one denies is that its source is partly Catholic, partly Lutheran, and that whatever, in the Catholic source, indicates or implies a belief that what is going on is a sacrifice to God (in the ordinary—not figurative—sense of these last three words) of the Body and Blood of Christ, truly present on the altar, has been sedulously cut out. There were no keener judges alive of what was or was not the Mass than the continental theologians whose lives were one long crusade against the Mass. Neither Bullinger nor Calvin had any fault to find with the new service on this score—that it was still the Mass.[27]

In the west of England, at the village of Sampford Courtenay in Devonshire, the first introduction of the new rite, on the Feast of Pentecost, 1549, was the occasion of a riot; and this rapidly became a rebellion. Liturgical progress was rudely interrupted by a demand that the whole policy of the last sixteen years—since the marriage of Henry and Anne Boleyn —be reversed. The spring of this year had seen county after county sputtering with riot, and in Oxfordshire a miniature

27 This same Parliament also passed an act declaring utterly void all laws or canons forbidding marriage to ecclesiastical or spiritual persons as such, and making void all penalties provided by such laws.

rebellion, with the suppression of which Lord Grey was already engaged when the west country now took fire. Rebels from Cornwall, and the Devon men, whose aim was a march on London, combined to besiege Exeter; and Russell, the experienced soldier whom the nervous Protector sent down from London, had to stand by for more than a month until sufficient troops—German mercenaries, in part—were found for him. On the local levies he could place no reliance; they were of the same mind as the rebels.

Before Russell moved, another rising, of still greater strength, had broken out on the other side of the kingdom, in Norfolk (July 7). Its leader was a well-to-do tanner, Robert Kett. While Russell advanced to relieve the siege of Exeter, fighting bloodily from Honiton west, Kett defeated the royal troops and took Norwich (August 1). Another four weeks, and all was over in the west. Russell, after much desperate fighting, had been completely victorious, and the usual tale of executions by martial law followed. To Norfolk, after the first defeat, the Protector had sent Warwick, and in a bloody battle outside Norwich he had annihilated Kett's host (August 24).

The Norfolk rising, as a very distinguished personage, the Lady Mary, testified, "was touching no part of religion." What brought sixteen thousand men to Kett's camp were such considerations as that "All power is in the hands of the gentry . . . while nothing is left for us but the extreme of misery." What sermons were preached to him and to his men were preached by clergy of the new way.

In the west, however, although social grievances found a place in the rebels' manifestoes, the main cause was undeniably religious. The rebels demanded that the government restore all that had been changed in the last two years, that the Six Articles Act be renewed and the heretics put to death, that the English Bible be destroyed and forbidden, the statues put back in the churches; that the Mass (of course) replace the new service, which they derided as "a Christmas game." They also asked that two abbeys be refounded in every county and that Cardinal Pole, because he is "of the king's blood," be "sent for to Rome and promoted to be of the king's council."

The last act in the western tragedy was the execution of the leaders at Tyburn on January 27, 1550. Four days later, in the Parliament, the Ordinal Act went through its final stage. This act was the complement to that which imposed the new Communion Service. It abolished the old ritual for the ordination of deacons and priests and the consecration of bishops. The new rite which the act now imposed, the composition, once more, of Cranmer and his associates, was largely inspired by the liturgical work of Martin Bucer. The language was English, and, once again, every phrase or ceremony which in the old rite indicated that the purpose was to confer a power of offering a sacrifice—sacrifice in the literal sense in which the Mass was believed to be a sacrifice—was cut out. The new rite was, of course, the production of men who detested as a blasphemous human error the very idea that there could be such a sacrifice as Catholics claimed the Mass to be. The whole purpose of the rite they now devised was to dedicate the recipient as one officially authorised by the Church to preach the Gospel, and to administer the sacraments as the new theologians understood them—as the primitive Christians understood them, these Reformers claimed. Bucer's treatise, which so influenced the new rite and which was composed while he was Cranmer's guest in 1549, bears indeed the title *The Restoration in the Church of the lawful Ordination of its ministers.*

Meanwhile, a palace revolution, only a few weeks after the suppression of the risings, had displaced the Protector. He was now (January 1550) a prisoner in the Tower, and Warwick ruled in his place—a bolder villain by far, whose ambition was to lead him ultimately to an attempt upon the crown itself. The extremists among the Protestant divines found in him a steady patron. And to Bishop John Hooper, a radical indeed, this sinister adventurer is "that most faithful and intrepid soldier of Christ" and "a most holy and fearless instrument of God's word." Certainly from this moment the Reformation leapt forward ever more speedily.

The Communion Service and the ordination rite had now been dissociated from the idea of a sacrificing priesthood. There still remained in every church, however, the silent reminder of the consecrated stone called the altar—the stone of sacrifice. In the course of the year 1550 the Reformers among the bishops began to order these to be taken down. Cranmer especially was active in this new change, and Nicholas Ridley, soon (in 1551) to be named Bishop of London. On November 24, 1550, the king's council ordered all the altars to be destroyed. Every parish was now to provide a table of wood, and on communion days this was to be used by the minister. The council issued, with these orders, an official explanation which makes crystal-clear the nature of the liturgical changes since 1547. "The form of a table shall move the simple from the superstitious opinions of the Popish Mass unto the right use of the Lord's Supper. For the use of an altar is to make sacrifice upon it; the use of a table is to serve for men to eat upon."

Bishops who resisted these orders were deprived of their sees. By the end of the year 1551 the episcopate had been greatly transformed. It was now nearly five years since the death of Henry VIII. In that time there had been seven vacancies, and each had been filled by a prelate friendly to the Reformation ideas. Of the 23 bishops of 1551, no more than four could now be counted on to champion the sacramental views of the late king. Six others, of this way of thinking, had been deprived of their sees, and four of these were imprisoned.

There were Reformers whom neither the new Prayer Book nor the new Ordinal had ever satisfied. They desired, especially, a Communion Service into which no controversial ingenuity, such as that of the imprisoned Bishop Gardiner, could read any toleration of the old sacramental beliefs. Their desires were satisfied when on April 6, 1552, the second of Edward VI's Acts *for the Uniformity of Common Prayer and Administration of the Sacraments* became law. The prayers of the critic who had complained that the Book of 1549 lent itself to the perpetuation of the "gestures of the never-to-be-sufficiently-execrated Mass" were now realised. The very words "Mass" and "altar" now disappear, and the last trace of prayer for the souls of the dead. The denial of any real presence of Christ in what is given to the communicant is as explicit as words can make it, "We, receiving these thy creatures of bread and wine," "Take and eat this . . . ," "If any of the bread and wine remain . . . ," ". . . the sacramental bread and wine . . . remain still in their very natural substances, and therefore may not be adored."

This act, like that which imposed the earlier Book (of 1549), decreed heavy penalties, not only for those who publicly criticised the new services, but for the clergy who used any other service. And the act now, furthermore, enacted penalties for those who were present at any other service.

In that same year, 1552, an official catechism for children was published and ordered to be used, as Protestant a document as any Reformer could have wished. And the tireless archbishop had ready the new code of church laws—which, however, the government refused to consider, with harsh words for the simple zeal that expected the layman once more to put his neck under the yoke of the cleric. But this same government—Warwick, that is (who had himself created Duke of Northumberland)—made no objection to a theological document of high importance, a set of Articles of Religion, 42 in number, which all preachers and all priests in charge of parishes and all who took a degree in any university were commanded to accept and to sign. Just one month later than the royal mandate which imposed this statement of belief, the king died, July 6, 1553. It was to be ten years before this last of Cranmer's activities began to tell, for to this first of England's Protestant sovereigns there succeeded his elder sister, the Lady Mary, and she was just as passionately Catholic as Edward had been Protestant.

CHAPTER SIX

The Council of Trent: Calvin
1534—1552

i *Pope Paul III*

How different from all that has gone before is the picture presented by the course of events in the dominions of these kings, Henry VIII and Edward VI; how different in kind is the revolution they effect and the way it has been done! There is about it a scale and an air of planning, as an activity of state, that make the achievement curiously modern. It is all in the greatest contrast to the slow, creeping growth, in these same years, of Lutheranism from one petty state of Germany to another, progress that only comes when Catholic rulers die and are succeeded by Protestant heirs, whereupon the principality goes over to the new religion in a kind of automatic filial subjection to the new ruler—with what understanding of the differences between, say, the two theologies, with what assents of the mind, who can even guess? How could it ever be imagined that, in such revolutions, the new doctrines succeed, with the mass of mankind, by the force of their own inherent superiority as truths (whether religious or political)? That Lutheranism carried all before it by its own mere power as an evidently truer theory of grace than what it displaced?

Such success is possible, indeed, in theological conferences; but with the mass of mankind? At any time? And at a time when the mass is, for three parts out of four, an illiterate peasantry? In the sixteenth century changes so fundamental could never have been realised, of course, against the will of the governing authority—nor, even, without the governing authority's co-operation and constant support. In an age where there is no provision for the rights of minorities, nor any constitutional opposition, these new religions, vis-à-vis the state, must conquer or die. The mass of the German princes were utterly indifferent to religion as such, of any kind. But this particular change meant, incidentally, a reorganization of vast landed properties. When the monks walked out and set up as married men, the abbey, its buildings, its lands, were not left for all and sundry to occupy, one quarter of the territory of the state suddenly turned over to the bold and enterprising squatter. All this went to the prince—the process dignified with the noble-sounding word "secularisation"; the first theft, on the great scale, of a subject's property, where the state is the thief.

Wherever the Reformation succeeds it does so because a government takes it up or because the party of the Reform succeeds in displacing the government. It is significant that in Germany the first successes, after the Saxony adoption, were in the small free cities. In Switzerland, it is necessarily an affair of this kind. Between 1532 and 1540 these German principalities and cities also went over to the Reform: Anhalt-Dessau (1532); Nassau, Hanover, Frankfort-on-the-Main, Augsburg, the duchies of Württemberg and Pomerania, Albertine Saxony (stoutly Catholic—or its ruler—until now), the electorate of Brandenburg, the duchies of Mecklenburg-Schwerin, and Brunswick-Calenberg. The map will show these Lutheranised lands as a roughly triangular territory with its base on the Baltic and running across the Schleswig peninsula to the neighbourhood of Bremen, with its apex in the valley of the Main. If these states hold together they can be certain that the Catholic princes will not, of themselves, molest them, and that the emperor's diplomacy will be powerless to set the Catholic princes in movement.

In these same years a further conquest of Lutheranism must be recorded: the Scandinavian countries of Denmark, Norway, and Sweden.[1] In the years when Luther was slowly working out his theological position, these countries—which had a common sovereign, Christian II of Denmark—were the scene of an attempted revolution in which high ecclesiastics played their part. It was an attempt on the part of Sweden to liberate itself from the de facto subjection to Denmark. It was largely with the aid of the bishops of all these countries that Christian II of Denmark had put the Swedes down. In 1520, as a preventive measure, the king had eighty-two Swedish notables

[1] The total population of the three has been recorded as 1,500,000, of which 750,000 was in Denmark.

put to death, two of whom were bishops. This crime was the signal for a war of independence. Long before this had reached its peak Christian had been driven out of Denmark, and an uncle who was a Lutheran, Frederick I, had taken his place (1523). The new king moved slowly. But in a matter of four years he had managed to drive a wedge between the bishops and the temporal lords—supporting the lords in their designs on church lands. In 1527 a Diet, held at Odense decreed that Lutherans should not be molested, that the clergy, the monks, and the nuns might lawfully marry, and that bishops should be appointed without any reference to Rome. In Sweden the patriotic cause had prospered during the civil war in Denmark, and its leader, Gustavus Vasa, had been elected king. In the very year of the Diet of Odense, he too, at a similar assembly, held at Västerås, secured, after stormy debates, that all the "superfluous" property of the Church was handed over to the state; and it was settled that bishops should, from now on, be appointed by the king alone. As Norway continued to be ruled by Denmark, Lutheranism, from the year 1527, gradually mastered all these countries.

So far as events go in the main theatre of western life, the major interest in these years 1532–53 is not in this geographical expansion, nor in the dissensions about Lutheran orthodoxy which have begun to divide the chiefs. For the energy of the pioneers of the theological revolution is not any longer directed solely to the question: Has Luther the right idea of what Christianity is?—as against the Catholic critics. There are now under discussion other important questions—Has Melanchthon the right idea of what Luther is teaching? Is it Osiander who has the secret of Lutheran orthodoxy?—discussions the details of which must be sought elsewhere, which still continue among the specialists, and whose intricacy can be gauged from the query, seriously proposed: How far was Luther really a Lutheran? It is not in the life within the new movement—to which such debates testify—that the main interest lies, in the years following the surrender of 1532, but rather in the slow emergence of the papacy as the active leader of the Catholic revival. Of that revival—considered as an apostolate to revive the life of prayer—the popes, Leo X and Clement VII, for example, had inevitably been patrons and protectors. From Gaetano of Thiene to Matteo de Basci all these evangelical spirits had found encouragement and support at Rome. But now there was to be something more. How far this was related to the prayers and sacrifices of humble souls, faithful to God in the worst of times, who shall say? These are considerations that belong to the real life of the Church, and they are the secret of the Spirit. That "something more," unexpected (humanly speaking), was the papacy suddenly assuming a vigorous initiative. From it there was to come the Council of Trent.

The second main interest of these years was the emergence of Calvin.

Luther, in the weeks that followed his meeting with Cajetan in 1518, publicly, that is to say by a notarial act, appealed from the judgment of the pope to that of the next General Council —one of the classic first moves in all delaying actions against the operation of the popes' coercive authority. But twelve months later, in the Leipzig disputation, he denied that there was anything sacrosanct about even general councils. Traditionally these were reverenced as bodies whose decisions in matters of belief were, by divine guidance, infallible. And when Luther now said that some of the doctrines condemned as heresy at the General Council of Constance (1414–17) were "most Christian and most evangelical," he startled and shocked the generality of his audience. However, there was to be henceforth, on the part of the Catholics of Germany, continual talk, for the next twenty years and more, of the need for a General Council; and repeated demands, which the emperor supported, were made by the Diet that the pope should summon one. And Luther, too, was repeatedly to talk about a council.

It was not, however, until the December of 1545 that the General Council actually met, at Trent, twenty-seven years after Luther's formal appeal. For nearly eleven years of that time the pope, Clement VII, had resisted the German demand by every means open to him. In the next ten years his successor, Paul III, did all in his power to bring about its fulfilment. The long succession of disappointments through which this man had to pass, who from the first hours after his election was pledged to call the council, are testimony that, whatever the reasons for the hesitation of his predecessor, that unhappy pope cannot be accused of neglecting an opportunity that lay wide open before him.

Both these popes had to deal first with the difficulty that the

Catholics who desired the council, as a means whereby to solve the Lutheran problem, had themselves, very often, the strangest and most unorthodox ideas about the kind of thing a General Council was, about what it could be expected to accomplish, and how it did its work. They seem to have looked upon it as a kind of general assembly of the Christian people, and the task to which, above all, they expected it would attend was the reform of the central government of the Church—they looked for a general discussion at the council of what was wrong with the Curia Romana (and its head), and the formulation of practical proposals for its amendment. Into the council, as they imagined it, the Lutherans, too, would be brought and have their say. And somehow, after all the talk, agreement would be reached, a settlement devised, and Germany would be delivered from the menace that threatened the unity of its life.

Clement VII was not, for the first years of his reign, overburdened with the anxiety that the mischief latent in such ideas would soon have its chance. From 1524 to 1529 the emperor was at war with the King of France—and in any truly General Council both of these monarchs must have their part; and from 1526 to 1529 the pope was himself at war with the emperor. When, at Augsburg in 1530, the war being over and Charles V crowned by his late adversary in the field, the question of the General Council was proposed, the legate, Campeggio, shrewdly asked how anything could be hoped from the co-operation of the Lutherans since, explicitly, they repudiated the authority of the former councils. Clement VII's own reply—namely, that the Lutherans might come to the council, provided that they first returned to the Church—was not the mere "intransigence" or ingenious evasion that it may seem. It was the simple logic of the matter. Luther, for years now, had been saying that the pope was Antichrist. In what kind of mind was the possibility envisaged that the man thus described—repeatedly and passionately so described—was to sit down and, talking amiably with this zealot, devise a common *modus vivendi*? "Thou hast the words of eternal life" were the words that summed up the traditional Christian view of the rôle of the Church. "The words of eternal life" were, for Luther, written in the pages of the Bible, where every man could read them and draw his own conclusions as to their meaning. This liberty was, for Luther, the essence of the Christian life.

In later years Luther was to explain with the utmost plainness to the papal nuncio, Peter Paul Vergerio, what it was that he meant by the council that he was for ever speaking of: "Since it is the Holy Ghost who teaches us, we have certainty on all points, and stand in no need of councils. But Christendom has certainly need of a council, in order to come to a realisation of the erroneous notions which it has so long fostered." And about his own part he was no less explicit: "I certainly will go to the council, and may I lose my head if I do not there maintain my ideas, be it against the whole world. The wrath that comes forth from me is not my wrath but the wrath of God."

It is no doubt a reasonable deduction from all we know that Clement VII would never have summoned the General Council. But his own fears were not the only obstacle. History, as usual, is more complicated than small-scale résumés can show.

The successor of Clement VII, Alessandro Farnese, called Paul III, is one of the select band of really great personalities among the popes. Panegyrists are wont to measure the nineteenth-century genius, Leo XIII (1878–1903), by such sayings as that nothing equal to him had been seen since Paul III. He was sixty-six when elected,[2] and since his teens he had dwelt in the heart of the Curia Romana. Innocent VIII had given him a bishopric by the time he was twenty. Alexander VI made him a cardinal (and treasurer-general of the Church) at twenty-five. He was highly educated, bred in the family of Lorenzo de' Medici, as the companion of the two future Medici popes, Leo X and Clement VII. Michelangelo built for him the Farnese palace, which is still one of the sights of Rome, and here the wealthy young cardinal lived, as all too many cardinals lived in the time of the Borgia and della Rovere popes. He was in his forties before he turned to reform his disorderly ways. The General Council of the Lateran (1512–17), where he played a prominent part, seems to have confirmed his conversion. He held a visitation of his diocese of Parma in 1516 and a synod in 1519. In this year too, aged now fifty-one, he sought ordination and said his first Mass. From now on he is decidedly one of the band pledged to ecclesiastical reform. In the conclave of 1523 he came near to being

[2] Almost exactly the age of Erasmus.

elected. His predecessor, Paul III used to say, had stolen eleven years of the papacy from him.

What were his gifts? He was an instinctive diplomatist, possessed of a very fine and cultivated intelligence and a will of steel. He had great administrative experience, a sure judgment of men, an unerring sense of what was immediately possible, and infinite patience before the disheartening fact that to change men's ways for the better calls for years and years of labour. The best way, by far, to understand the kind of man he was is to stand for half an hour before any one of Titian's superb portraits of him. At sixty-six he was a somewhat silent old man, frail and ailing continually, but he lived to rule the Church for fifteen years and to summon the Council of Trent.

As to Paul III's good will in this matter—he was elected October 13, 1534, and it was only nineteen months later, May 29, 1536, that the bull was published calling the General Council. The interval had been occupied in dealing with the opposition in Rome—the cardinals, at their first opportunity, the consistory of January 1535, gave a majority vote against the project—and in examining the prospects of support in Germany, where the nuncio, Vergerio, made two extensive tours, interviewing princes (the princes of the League of Schmalkalden too) and prelates, and making that contact with Luther already mentioned. On these reports the cardinals again, in January 1536, showed themselves, in the majority, hostile. But four months later the bull was issued nonetheless.

It was to Mantua, for May 23, 1537, that the council was summoned, but only two months before that date the Duke of Mantua demanded that the pope subsidise a small army for the security of the council. When the pope refused "to set the bad example of a council meeting under the protection of an army" (his own words), the duke withdrew his offer. Negotiations were opened with Venice, and finally the republic invited the council to meet at Vicenza, and the date was fixed at May 12, 1538. When the three cardinals appointed to preside reached Vicenza they found five bishops only awaiting them. Another six weeks went by, and then the pope deferred the opening date, and the small company dispersed.

While the legates had been at Vicenza, Paul III had made the long journey to the French border, and at Nice had been conducting those conferences with the emperor and the King of France which brought to an end the latest phase of the war between these princes. And now, for the trial of the supporters of the council, there came the great distraction of a rival scheme to bring about religious unity. What if, from conferences between the theologians on either side, it should emerge that the different views were not irreconcilable? This was an idea that took a strong hold of Charles V, from his first hearing of it, and perhaps a stronger hold still of his brother Ferdinand, the actual ruler of the Habsburg lands within the empire and King of Bohemia and of Hungary. Ferdinand's first preoccupation was the Turks, the masters of half his kingdom of Hungary, with whom he had a long common frontier. If he could not succeed in throwing them back it would make little difference whether their victims were Catholics or Lutherans. At all costs, then—or almost all—let true unity between the princes of Germany be restored. The climax of this new "reunion" policy came at Ratisbon in the summer of 1541, when Melanchthon, Bucer, and Pistorius, for the Protestants, argued against Eck, Gropper, and Pflug, named by the emperor for the Catholics. The pope, reluctantly won over to patronise the experiment, sent—but not as a fighter in the arena—the greatest of all his cardinals, Gasparo Contarini.

The basis of the debate—made known to Contarini only after his arrival—was a series of twenty-three theses drawn up by Pflug and Gropper. Contarini made a number of alterations in these too generous surrenders, but then—despite Eck's opposition—allowed them as Catholic statements. The leading subject was the theology of justification, and Gropper now met the Protestant criticism of the Catholic teaching by a new explanation, the so-called theory of the double justification, devised by another Catholic theologian, his master, Albert Pighius. Contarini, too, accepted this theory. Presently the three Protestants and the Catholics came to a none too unequivocal formula of agreement on the basis of this theory. But Melanchthon refused to allow that decisions of General Councils were final in matters of faith, and the differences on the doctrine of Penance and the Eucharist proved insoluble. On May 22, after a month of intense work, the Colloquy of Ratisbon petered out.

The event should have demonstrated clearly to the Catholics this at least, that they could hope for nothing from any such abnormality as a General Council where the Lutherans sat on equal terms with themselves. Such a council, where the basic principles of the two sides were in plainest contradiction, could come to no conclusion save an agreement to differ—for how could the foes of Antichrist, even tacitly, allow he had rights anywhere? How could the popes surrender the right, which they claimed as fundamental, to correct false doctrine wherever found? how deny their duty to bring back the wandering sheep?

Contarini, a Venetian noble, was one of the famous men of his time long before Paul III called him into the Sacred College and the service of the Church. He had served the republic as ambassador in London and at the court of Charles V, and was actually a member of the supreme council—and of course a layman—when the pope's letter arrived announcing his coming creation. He was a finished humanist, with books to his credit on a variety of subjects, and he was well read in theology. He may stand as a symbol for one of Paul III's greatest services to the Church, his renovation of the college of cardinals. In the consistory at which Contarini was named, the pope gave the red hat to John Fisher also, prisoner of King Henry VIII, and on the eve of his martyrdom for the dogma of the divine origin of the papacy. King Henry's cousin, Reginald Pole, was another of these new cardinals, soon to be dogged by the prince's hired assassins; and Carafa, the part founder of the Theatines, and Giovanni Morone, and Cervini, whose death, within days of his election as Marcellus II, is one of the tragedies of the Catholic revival; and many another whose *gesta* in the next forty years can be descried through the thick mists of Pastor's innumerable volumes.

Paul III's cardinals were men of unusual ability, of great individuality, anything rather than stereotyped officials; and for the most part they were passionately given to the cause of reform. There were others, too, of the old sort. Politics and the wishes of princes could not yet always be disregarded. The red hat went to Bembo. And in a special first consistory it went, to the dismay of those who pinned all their hopes on the new pope, to his two young grandsons, boys of fifteen. The old leaven continued to work, and the one-time advisor of the Borgia and della Rovere was to be the last pope who busied himself—and compromised his cause—by efforts to thrust his descendants into the ranks of the reigning princes. The Farnese became, in Paul's own pontificate, dukes of Parma, to the accompaniment of thunderous censures from Carafa, and it was the pope's great-grandson who was the

Alessandro Farnese, Prince of Parma, combination of military genius and statesman, whose armies awaited only the coming of the Armada to be ferried across the Strait of Dover to the conquest of Queen Elizabeth's England; an Alessandro Farnese born just in time for the aged pope to look upon and to bless. To the very end of his great pontificate the Renaissance prelate survived, uncomfortably active, in Paul III.

To return to the Reformer, which this one-time cardinal of the Borgia truly was; in the months that followed the summons of 1536 to the General Council, Paul III had set up a commission to study and report on the general question of what was amiss. This report was as stark as the confession of Adrian VI to the princes of Germany in 1523;[3] and it went into great detail, *The Advice about Reforming the Church set before Pope Paul III by the Cardinals and other Prelates selected to study the matter*[4]–a state paper often loosely described as the agenda for the Council of Trent. It got out, fell into the enemy's hands, was printed and published by the enemy, and of course served, not as an evidence of Paul III's will to reform, but as material for slander and also, by one of the usual non-sequiturs which party spirit breeds, as justification for that repudiation of ancient beliefs which was the essence of the Reformers' achievement. Bayards are rare among revolutionaries—integrity and a sense of logic also. "A priest on the booze! The doctrine of the Trinity can hardly be true!!" He that readeth, let him substitute whatever doctrine most pleases his irony as he recalls how easily scholars have written as though they considered such reasoning serious and the reasoner sincere. It was not the bad living of clergy that first moved Luther, or Zwingli (save the mark), or the rest. But once the revolution had begun to be stabilised, at least as much was heard about this, in the propaganda, as

[3] See *infra*, p. 260.
[4] *Consilium delectorum cardinalium et aliorum praelatorum . . .* They were nine in all: the cardinals Contarini, Carafa, Sadoleto, and Pole; Fregoso, Archbishop of Salerno; Aleander, the nuncio to Germany at the time of the Diet of Worms, now Archbishop of Brindisi; Giberti, Bishop of Verona, the most experienced reformer of church life in Italy; Cortese, abbot of St. George's Venice; and a Dominican friar, Tommaso Badia, the pope's personal theologian, styled master (i.e., of theology) of the sacred palace. All these last, save Giberti, were ultimately created cardinals.

about the correct interpretation of St. Paul to the Romans. Nor is this surprising. *Cosí fan tutti.*

This document, presented to the pope on March 9, 1537, is filled with very hard sayings. And nowhere in it is there any trace of the levity that brushes inconvenient scandal aside with "How wonderfully it proves the Church is divine—that it survived all this!" Nothing short of the holy rage latent in every line of the report was called for by the spectacle of swine peacefully grubbing in the holy of holies. Anything short of this, once men had been ordered to look hard at the spectacle and report the truth, would have been a practical denial of the Gospel.[5]

The report's first statement is that the Church of Christ is almost in ruins and that in no place has evil been more active than "in this Curia Romana." As your holiness, taught by the Spirit of God, knows very well, the root of this trouble is that some of your predecessors looked about them for guides, not to what they ought to do, but to what they wanted to do, guides who would prove to be lawful whatever popes found it convenient to do; hence came the atmosphere of adulation, the all but impossibility of truth ever reaching the ears of the ruler; and also that, very speedily, learned men appeared teaching the doctrine that it was not possible for the pope to commit simony, for the owner, they said, has the right to sell what is his; and also that what the pope wants (whatever this may be) is the rule by which all his actions should be guided. "It is from this, as from the Trojan horse, holy father, that have come forth all those evils that have driven the Church almost to despair of recovery, evils the reports of which, among the infidels, have caused such mockery, and blasphemy of the very name of Christ; through our fault, our fault we repeat, holy father."

The cure must begin in the place whence the disease has come. "You have seen this, holy father, and have acted accordingly . . . by laying upon us this grave obligation to make a faithful report, binding us by a special oath, and the sanction of excommunication."

Dispensations from laws should be given for urgent reasons only; so far as possible, the law should always be followed. But there is a more serious evil than even the unlawful abun-

---

[5] The summary that follows makes use of the words of the document even when not quoting directly from it.

dance of dispensations: "It is not lawful for the pope, the vicar of Christ, to make any profit out of the use of the power of the keys granted him by Christ."

The next point—these fundamentals accepted—is the provision of good servants for the pope's task of caring for the universal Church; i.e., priests (and especially parochial priests) and, above all, bishops. As to the choice of men to be priests, at present no care whatever is taken about this matter. The most ignorant, the most wretched types, men of most abandoned lives, boys even, are nowadays ordained, and to the priesthood, "to that character in which Christ is principally represented." In the granting of ecclesiastical livings—above all, in appointments to episcopal sees—it is the convenience of the nominee that is considered, not the needs of the flock of Christ. The financial traffic in the exchanges of sees is often simony. Nothing has caused more hatred among the clergy than the way in which the common wealth of the Church has been diverted from public purposes to become the private property of individuals. There are many men who are promised a post when the present occupant is gone: they spend their lives hoping he will die soon.

Among the major scandals in this great business of ecclesiastical livings are to be placed the practices of the cardinals. These are the great sinners in the matter of holding several episcopal sees simultaneously [we may think of Albert of Brandenburg and Wolsey]. The report tells the pope that the two offices of cardinal and bishop are themselves not compatible. A cardinal's place is in the city of Rome, as the pope's aid and counsellor. A bishop must live in the place where the sheep are to whose care he is assigned. "And, holy father, how can you expect to be obeyed, and for abuses to be corrected when abuses are tolerated in these principal members of the Church? We do not think that because they are cardinals it is more lawful for them to break the law." It is plainly said that kings bribe cardinals to serve them by gifts of sees. All this should be abolished, and cardinals be provided for by the pope—equal salaries to all. Nor would this be hard, "if it is our will not to serve mammon but Christ alone."

Bishops? The worst trouble is that *most* bishops are absentees. "O God Almighty, what sight is more afflicting to a Christian man who goes about the Christian world than the solitude of the sees, whence the shepherds have departed, leaving the flock to the hirelings?" And too many of the parish priests follow their example. On the other hand, the good bishops are continually held up, in their endeavours to reform abuses, by the ease with which Rome grants permissions to persist in the abuses. "They fly to the penitentiary or the datary, where they speedily find there is a means to escape penalties, and, what is the worst of the matter, all for money. This particular scandal, holy father, is causing such an upheaval among our Catholic people that no words can describe it. By the blood of Christ, we beg of your holiness, let these horrors be removed . . . if the like practices were tolerated in any state it could not survive. And is it allowable for us to see such monstrosity installed in the Church of Christ?"

The Religious Orders? Many are so corrupted, says the report, that they are a danger to the laity. "We consider that all the Conventual Orders ought to be abolished . . . by forbidding them to receive any more novices." The Christian people are also greatly disturbed at the immorality that goes on in many of the convents where the nuns are in the care of the friars of the Conventual Orders.

Universities and schools: in Italy especially there are too many professors of philosophy who are teaching infidelity and the mockery of true religion and virtue. Greater care is needed about the books put into the hands of the pupils. The *Colloquies* of Erasmus should be forbidden to boys.

Collectors of money—e.g., "the collectors of the Holy Ghost," "the collectors of Saint Antony"—who wander about the country, deceiving the rustics and teaching them innumerable superstitions, should be done away with.

Abuses in the grants of various dispensations, of licences to clerics to make wills, and in the alteration of wills by church authority, are set out, and the report ends with some blasting remarks about the state of Rome, the pope's own city. All who visit Rome are horrified at the state of St. Peter's, where priests are to be seen saying Mass, dirty and uncouth, clad in such vestments as even in the filthiest houses would scarcely pass. Harlots, in this town, go about as ladies of distinction, with a court of attendants, clerics among them and the nobles of the cardinals' households. "In no other city have we ever seen such a corrupt sight as this." These ladies, the report notes, inhabit houses of great distinction. Rome is also the seat of endless bloody feuds. And in this city also there are hospitals, there are the poor, and it is a principal part of the

duties of the city's bishop—who is also their prince—to care for
these.

"You have taken the name Paul, holy father; you will, we
hope, imitate the charity of Paul . . . chosen, we hope, to
restore the name of Christ, forgotten by the people, and by us
the clergy, to our hearts and in our works; to heal our ailments;
to bring back the flock of Christ into the one fold; to remove
from us the wrath of God, and the punishment prepared for
our deserts, that now threatens our very necks."

The Diet of 1541, the Colloquy over, separated on the note
that differences about doctrine would be left until the General
Council, which should meet within eighteen months—i.e., by
January 29, 1543. But it was also provided that, should the
council not have met by that date, these differences should be
settled at a national council in Germany, or by the Diet. As
objective facts this last part of the decision was as remote from
Catholic teaching as anything in Luther's own theories about
the nature of the Church of Christ. Was Germany to follow
England's example and the Catholic faith to be, for the German people, whatever Germans said it was? German prelates,
or German princes, prelates and city-states combined? The
emperor was certainly captive still to the idea that there was
a way in which Protestant and Catholic could live together
peacefully, not only in the same state but in the same holy
Catholic Church, which should yet continue to be "one"; i.e.,
united in a single belief. Before Paul III had finished his
course he was to see Charles embody his desire in a practical
scheme and impose it.

Meanwhile the pope's energies were set to win back Charles
to collaborate in summoning the council. Politics now helped.
The emperor needed the pope, and so did the King of France,
and both came forward requesting the summoning of the
council. On May 22, 1542, Paul III (for the third time) issued the summons, named the legates, and chose as the place
the little city of Trent, geographically in Italy, politically a
German town, German-speaking, and the see of one of the
prince-bishops of the empire. It was convened for November
1 of the same year. Yet once again it was proved how far popes
are from being the omnipotent creatures of the legend. The
legates arrived at Trent to find, as at Vicenza in 1538, that
almost no bishops had troubled to obey the summons.

Since July 10, France and the emperor were again at war,

and Henry VIII of England was in it, as the ally of Charles—
a return, on the part of England, to the traditional diplomacy,
jettisoned these twenty years. So long as the war lasted—and
its opportunity for Lutheran princes to embarrass Charles, to
say nothing of the hazards and hindrances to travelling bishops
(even supposing any willingness to travel)—no council could
meet. In July 1543 the opening was again put off.

The General Council of Trent finally met, and the solemn
opening took place, December 13, 1545. It was just about
eleven years since Paul III, in the first hours of his reign, had
announced that to bring it about would be his first objective as
pope.

ii Calvin

In those last anxious years before Paul III's hopes of the
General Council were realised—which were also the last five
years of Luther's life[6]—there was taking place, in the city of
Geneva, one of the strangest of all the developments of this
time—the restoration, at the command of a very finished product of the University of Paris, not so much of the primitive
Church as of the régime over which Moses presided during
the forty years when Israel wandered in the desert.

The new Moses was John Calvin, thirty-two years of age in
1541. It was not, however, in any desert that his work was
done. All the West was presently feeling its effect. For the
next quarter of a century, until his death in 1564, Calvin will
be the leading figure of the whole religious world. None other,
Catholic or Protestant, approached him in immediate effec-
tiveness. In the history of the Reformation, Luther alone is
Calvin's equal in fame. For most people Luther and Calvin
are the Reformation.

Calvin was born on July 10, 1509, in the little cathedral
city of Noyon, in northeastern France, sixty miles or so from
Paris. His father, Gérard Cauvin,[7] was something of a figure
in the town, half lawyer and half man of affairs, half layman
and half cleric, for he was a kind of secretary for the non-
ecclesiastical business to the all-important bishop, who was
also the *seigneur* of the city. But Gérard Cauvin was not a

[6] He died at Eisleben, the town where he was born, February 18,
1546.
[7] In Latin, *Calvinus*; whence the new French form, *Calvin*.

native of Noyon. He came from Pont l'Evêque in Normandy, where his father had been a ferryman, and his two brothers were locksmiths. Calvin's mother was the daughter of a well-to-do hotelkeeper of Cambrai, in French Flanders. How Gérard Cauvin came to break with the artisan world in which he was bred and to acquire the professional culture necessary for his great rise in the world, we do not know. It was in the heart of the administrative side of church life that the future Reformer grew up, his father high in favour with the bishop, and the bishop one of a noble family of the region who held the see in their grasp for seventy years and more.

Calvin *fils* was the second of four sons. His mother died while he was yet a child, and his father married again. The father had the reputation that he was competent and crafty, and an awkward man when crossed. The son, when crossed, would be dangerous. It was in a strictly ruled household that he grew up, where only one will spoke. The semi-clerical father naturally destined his son for the Church. The bishop helped by providing an income—a succession of ecclesiastical livings which kept Calvin until his twenty-fifth year: at twelve, already, he was a beneficed chaplain of the cathedral.

Soon after this he left home for Paris and an education, in the company of two of the bishop's young kinsmen. At the college of La Marche he had the good fortune to have for his Latin master one of the greatest teachers of the day, Mathurin Cordier, to whom, and with reason, he never ceased to be explicitly grateful so long as he lived. It was not for scholarship alone that he was Cordier's debtor: this priest—who was to end his life among the Reformers—was passionately interested in the religious training of these boys. From La Marche the adolescent passed to Erasmus' old home, Montaigu, but—luckily for himself—as an extern student only, continuing to live with his uncle, the locksmith. Enough has already been said about this grim institution, "all fleas, and fasts and floggings," said Rabelais. Was it at Montaigu John Calvin first learned what a world of oppression men will endure if their tyrants convince them that such is the will of heaven? Discipline was certainly the main thing in the life of the college, and recreation held to be, in itself, all but a sin. Did the silent, mirthless life of these poor young men who slaved at their religious tasks leave a permanent impression on Calvin's mind of an ideal attained? It was, to Calvin, not a hard life, nor an unattractive life, but simply life. Discipline was his own ideal too; discipline, in the first place, for himself. Certainly he now saw enough of it, for at Montaigu he remained until his master's degree in 1528. Then came a dramatic change. From Noyon came the order: no more theology, law is the highroad to a good income; leave Paris, go to Orleans.

Old Calvin had been passing through some strange times, a long embroilment with the canons of the cathedral, in the course of which he fell under an excommunication. Were these experiences the reason why he had set his second son to study law, at the moment when he should have passed on to theology? Was he turning him towards a lay career? We do not know. Law, for the clerical careerist, was a more golden road than theology. But law, studied with his mind beautifully trained, was to complete Calvin's liberal education. Law meant the Roman Law, "divinely reasonable"; study of the great works produced at the will of the emperor, Justinian, a thousand years before this—the *Institutes*, for example, which are the textbook of the matter; the *Digest*, in which are collected and classified the oracles of earlier ages still, Gaius and Ulpian and Paul. Law—thus understood—was a science and a system of thought; and the education it gave, where it did not find a man a thinker, left him a thinker at the end. "The study of English Law," said that contemporary whom we seem obliged to quote at every turn of this history, Erasmus, "is as far removed as can be from true learning"; whence, he goes on, "[Thomas] More's mind, fitted for better things, naturally dreaded these studies." But the Roman Law, studied by a humanist, was also a fine training in style. Style was to be for Calvin all-important. It was through a book that he first revealed his quality, and his own *Institutes* conquered its world primarily by style; so that, by right of his French version of this book, he is among the founders of French prose.

At this moment, humanism and history had invaded the law schools and were effecting there a fruitful revolution in methods of teaching. Some of the greatest minds in legal history, Budé and Alciati, lawyers whose thoughts developed law, were at work in the universities of Orleans and Bourges, where Calvin passed the next three years. Still the scholar, for whom twenty-four hours were all too short a day, he surrendered himself wholeheartedly, not to any master, but to the law. All his books will give evidence of his legal learning, and that it came from sources known at first hand. But it is in the man's mentality that, henceforward, the legist, the jurisconsult—words not easily put into English, for that for which they stand has hardly a recognised place in this Anglo-Saxon world—is most evident. Law as an ideal, reason itself in written words, the surest instrument of peace, the very cement of social life, clear, evident, self-evidently true, fruit of reasoning; whose nature it is to come to life among men, and to rule, through the arts of reasoning and analysis: arts in which Calvin is supreme. Woe to the opponent who, in argument, concedes the most insignificant proposition.

When Calvin's father died, in 1531, the young man had taken his first degrees in law, but—his own master now—he did not continue. Nor did he proceed to theology. He went back to Paris and the classics. At Bourges, a German humanist, Melchior Wolmar, teaching Greek, had infected the finished Latinist with a new passion. And now, at the newly founded Collège de France, Calvin made new advances under the guidance of the regius professors, and he also, with them, began to study Hebrew. These are years in which Calvin's future, it seems, will be such a life as that of Erasmus. His first book appears in 1532, and it is a commentary on the *De Clementia* of Seneca. And, as he is now caught by the classic ideal, so he finds more in Erasmus than the man of letters. From the *Adagia* he proceeds to the *Enchiridion*.

What of the religious life of this serious young scholar? His moral life, in all respects, is correctness itself. What of his life with God? What was this in those Catholic days before he had even heard of the new doctrines? Would these not be very early days? Mathurin Cordier was a Lutheran, and so, too, was Melchior Wolmar. And in the circle of his student friendships at Orleans and at Bourges, humanists, lawyers, "Erasmians," enthusiasts of the school of Jacques Lefèvre of Etaples, young Catholics enthusiastic for a better world, disgusted with the clerical indifference, the incompetence, the low-mindedness to be seen on all sides—in this circle (as in similar groups all over France) there circulated the forbidden books of Luther and Melanchthon, eagerly read and debated in many a violent evening hour. Bourges had the king's sister, Marguerite de Navarre, for its patron and protector—and so had all that circle of Catholic reformers which revolved round Lefèvre and the Bishop of Meaux, Guillaume de Briçonnet; and so had the first Lutheranising writers. In these years 1531 and 1532 we are coming close to the moment when Calvin breaks with the Catholic Church. When did he first begin to resent it, and why?

There is a great contrast between our detailed knowledge of the influences that went to form Calvin's mind and our all but total ignorance of the circumstances of his conversion to the new doctrines. A few passing lines in the preface of a book written twenty years later, an allusion in the passionate letter of 1540 to Cardinal Sadoleto, Bishop of Carpentras, one of the authors—it will be recalled—of the *Report on the State of the Church*; these two fragments are almost all that we know with certainty. And we must carefully scrutinise them before we can even conjecture when it happened. But by April 1534 he had gone.

If Calvin's letter to Sadoleto is autobiographical, the first effect of the new doctrines was to annoy him by their very novelty. He found a difficulty in studying them. He fought the new ideas with all his mind. His veneration for the Church set his mind against them. In the one place, where he definitely refers to the change, he says that at first he was too deeply attached to Catholicism—"to the superstition of the papacy" are his actual words—to be easily drawn from it. It was by "a sudden change" that he passed to docile acceptance of the new. When this happened, this "sudden change," we must leave to the specialists to discuss. In November 1533, one of his friends, Nicholas Cop, was rector of the University of Paris. He opened his term of office with an inaugural address, the Lutheranism of which was unconcealed. If Calvin did not write this for him, he had a share in it. The rector fled that very night; and Calvin, too, left Paris.

For the next year or so he wandered about France, from one centre of Lutheranism to another, teaching, preaching, wholly devoted to missionary activity. In May he resigned his benefices. In October there occurred the famous affair of the *Placards*—printed sheets attacking and ridiculing Catholic teaching, often in the grossest way, discovered one morning pasted on the walls of various buildings in Paris. Raids, arrests, numerous executions followed, and in December Calvin fled from France. By January 1535 he had reached Basel, and in this literary city he devoted the next eight months to the first draft of the book that was to make him famous and a power, the book we call the *Institutes*. It was written in Latin, and its title may be translated *An Education in the Christian Reli-*

*gion, containing almost the whole sum of pious living, and
whatever is necessary to the knowledge of the doctrine of salvation; a work recently brought out and well worth reading by
all who are zealous for holy living.*

It was published in March 1536, by which time Calvin had
long left Basel. Still learning, and eager for more opportunities, he had crossed the Alps into Italy, and at her court at
Ferrara had met the French princess who was the most illustrious patron of these French heretics, Renée, daughter of
King Louis XII, now Duchess of Ferrara. Then a truce in the
persecution at home allowed a short visit to Noyon, where he
had family business to settle. He was in Paris in the summer,
and then made for Strasbourg. But the renewed war of Francis
I with Charles V blocked the direct route. Calvin went by
Lyons, and Geneva; and at Geneva, where he meant to spend
only a night in passing, he was recognised and the news was
given to Guillaume Farel, the hero, at this moment, of the
reformation just accomplished there. And by Farel, "not as by
one giving advice, or exhorting me, but calling down the anger
of God should I refuse, I was constrained to stay . . . Struck
down by the fear that what he threatened might come to pass,
I abandoned the journey I had undertaken." This was in
August 1536, and on September 5 the city authorities appointed Calvin to lecture on Sacred Scripture in the cathedral.

The Geneva to which Calvin came, at twenty-seven, was a
tiny city-state of perhaps thirteen thousand people which, for
a good twenty years now, had been the scene of endless tumult.
The "constitution" under which it was governed was a complicated business. The Bishop of Geneva was nominally the
lord, but since the year 1290 his powers had been exercised
by the princes of Savoy, as his vice-lords. Moreover, since 1409
the citizens of Geneva (i.e., the well-to-do merchants and
lawyers) had gradually won more and more control, so that
it was this oligarchy which, through various councils and the
four Syndics whom it elected, really ruled the city.[8] The
tumults which began in 1518 had nothing to do with religious
differences. They were revolts of the city against the suzerainty
of the Duke of Savoy.

The details of this struggle we must pass over, except the

---

[8] The number of those qualified to vote at the various elections
has been estimated as between 1,000 and 1,500.

fact that Geneva was able to defeat the duke only because the cantons of Freiburg and Berne came to its aid—Berne, where the government was oligarchic and which went Protestant in 1528; Freiburg, which had a popular government and which remained Catholic. Once the Reformation doctrines made a public appearance at Geneva—the *Placards* of June 1532 ridiculing a papal indulgence—the city was pulled both ways by these allies. The year 1533 was filled with riots about religion —i.e., whether the refugee evangelists from France should be allowed to preach the Lutheran doctrines. In the last weeks of the year the chief of these, Farel, driven out in 1532, was readmitted. In March 1534 the Protestants were granted a church. They were, by their own account, barely a third of the inhabitants.

As to the bishops of Geneva, there had been very little, for generations, about their rule that recalled the spirit of the Good Shepherd. That Duke of Savoy who became the last of the anti-popes (the self-styled Pope Felix V) had annexed the bishopric to his duchy—and to his family. A boy of ten (his grandson) was made Bishop of Geneva in 1451, and a boy of twelve (also a grandson) in 1460, and there was a third boy-bishop (of seven, a great-grandson) in 1495. Another of these youthful prelates, bishop from 1513–22, was the bastard son of a nobleman who was, so to speak, an ex-boy-bishop himself. For it did not follow that these children came, in later years, to ordination as priests. They were, in law, the rulers of the diocese, as the boy-kings of history were really kings. Others carried out the administration in their name. But the little bishops and their families drew the revenues. As the boys grew up to manhood they sometimes resigned the sees, became again the great lay lords they were by birth, and married.

The two years and more between the concession of a church to the Reformers at Geneva and the coming of Calvin are the history of a minority imposing its will on all. The attempts of the Duke of Savoy, in July 1534, to regain Geneva failed. At the public disputation demanded by the Catholics, in June 1535, the Reformers converted the Catholic champions to the new faith. Farel, in July, began to preach in the city churches. His sermons in St. Peter's were the occasion of riots; statues were smashed, pictures destroyed, and the treasures of the church, to the amount of ten thousand crowns, disappeared. He now asked for the abolition of the Mass, and the council, although willing, thought it better to consult their allies at Berne, since, they said, it was a general opinion that if the Mass ceased to be said the townspeople would rise. When the priests of the religious orders in the town were summoned to submit or else disprove the conclusions of the disputation, they could only answer that they were only ordinary men who knew nothing about these matters, but lived as their fathers had taught them, without making any question about such things. Their only prayer to the council was that they might be let alone. The secular clergy, likewise summoned, and lectured because they had ignored the invitation to be present at the disputation, took a firmer line with the Syndics and the council. They refused to have a summary of the proceedings read to them, or to give any opinion about the sayings of Farel. They merely wished to live as they had always lived, they said. The nuns—Poor Clares—refused to hear of submission and were turned out of their convent and, indeed, out of the town. From this time the Mass ceased to be said in Geneva (August 1535).

With the autumn the political situation changed—and in favour of the successful minority. The war which was to send Calvin to Geneva drew the Duke of Savoy away to the defence of his capital, Turin, against the French. The Bernese troops now came to Geneva in support of the Farel party and overran the whole countryside (the Pays de Vaud). After a crisis, when Geneva managed to fend off a Bernese demand that Geneva—in gratitude—should acknowledge Berne as its lord, the citizens, in a general assembly of May 21, 1536, swore to live according to the doctrine preached daily to them ever since the Mass was abolished, and declared their resolution to abandon "all masses and other ceremonies and papal abuses, images, idols and all connected with these things."

This public act took place a matter of ten weeks or so before Calvin's arrival, and no doubt he says nothing but the simple truth when he writes that matters were then still unsettled and the city divided into wicked and mischievous factions—these last being, no doubt, the Catholic majority too insignificant socially to have any say in the direction of affairs. It is a state of things which explains Farel's transports of joy on hearing that so powerful an ally as Calvin had unexpectedly arrived in Geneva, and the violence which Calvin describes when "he strained every nerve to keep me."

Calvin, twenty-five years younger than Luther or Zwingli, is a Reformer of the second generation. He is only a child of eight when Luther is nailing up his Ninety-five Theses. Never can he remember the time when there was not talk of Luther and what he had started. And Calvin's conversion is, thereby, a different kind of thing. Here is no priest or monk, dissatisfied with a religious system from within, and then worrying over his problem and working out a solution in solitary meditation on the texts of Holy Scripture. Calvin is a brilliant young layman, free to make of his life what he chooses, and when his moment comes he is familiar with all the main lines of the Reformers' solutions. He has read their books and discussed them with friends, and has read his Bible with these theories, inevitably, in his mind.

The French Reformer, then, is not wholly an original thinker. His doctrine is very largely that of Luther: the total corruption of human nature as a result of Adam's sin, the utter powerlessness of man to do good, the sinfulness of his every act, however good in itself, the impossibility of fulfilling the commandments of God, justification by faith alone (faith being the confidence that, through the imputation of the merits of Christ, man's sins are not imputed to him), the impossibility that man can merit anything in God's sight, the blasphemy of the idea that man's own good works have any value, the idea that sacraments (of which there are but two) are divine signs meant to stir up and to confirm faith, the idea that all men are predestined by God from all eternity to heaven or to hell without reference to the lives they will lead. The essence of Luther's message is the essence of Calvin's message too. And for both men, the one source of all our knowledge of God's mind and will is the text of the divinely inspired Scriptures; which, they say, all men have a right to read for themselves, which all have the duty to read. Calvin never indeed lays claim to such a specific inspiration on the part of God as the Tower incident brought forward by Luther. Nevertheless, he does not hesitate to proclaim his conviction that he is God's messenger and that he has the right to demand assent to the message he delivers.

Calvin moves away from Luther's teaching in some important doctrines. He has none of Luther's phobia at the mention of law. No religious teacher ever laid more stress on the holiness of God's law than Calvin, and as he exalts the law so does he exalt the notion of the Church of Christ as a power that actually rules the Christian's life. In the matter of ritual the changes he introduces are much more radical. Whatever finds no mention in the Scriptures must be cast out. Crucifixes and images go, and all decorations, and all vestments, along with altars and their lights. And as Calvin rejects the Mass—a blasphemous imposture, because an impossibility—he rejects also the possibility of any kind of objective presence of Christ in the Eucharist. The communion between the receiver of the Sacrament and Christ is not through any kind of presence of Christ in that which is received. It is here that the differences between Calvin and Luther is most evident. For Luther, however, Calvin had a lasting admiration, but not the sympathy which existed between himself and Melanchthon. Zwingli he abhorred, though he confessed he had not read all his writings—Calvin never learned German. Was he, nevertheless, influenced by Zwinglian ideas, mediated to him through Bucer? In later years Calvin and Zwingli's spiritual heir, Henry Bullinger, were to make a famous doctrinal treaty, the Pact of Zürich (1549).

The true source of Calvin's teaching is the Bible—"the Word of God"—to the explanation of which, book by book, he devoted the major part of his well-filled life, as the many massive volumes of his commentaries remain to show. No problems of what we call Bible scholarship troubled him. He took the authenticity and inspiration of the Bible for granted, like almost the whole of his century, and pressed forward to the task of discovering what it all meant, with a very sound knowledge of Greek and Hebrew for his principal tools, and the explanations of the great Bible scholars of the past. For two of these, Origen and St. Jerome, Calvin had little respect. But St. Augustine and St. John Chrysostom were masters well known and reverenced. But even the best of these were but servants really—never masters. His real master was the Scripture itself, understood by that special illumination which he believed was divinely given him, and Scripture, to some extent, as interpreted by Luther and Zwingli and Bucer.

It is perhaps as the inflexible teacher of a particularly horrible doctrine about predestination to hell, and of a doctrine that equates all pleasure with sin, as the prophet of holy gloom, that the memory of Calvin lingers in the popular mind.

And thence arises the modern wonder at his surprising success. How could such a message attract a following? The answer is, of course, that (apart from any such particular specialties) Calvin popularised a vast doctrinal synthesis whose purpose was to show man how to live in close communion with his Maker, and thereby live more happily—living in fidelity to high ideals, the experience of which living makes a mockery of the materialistic pleasure seekers. Calvin, whether one accepts his views or not, needs to be seen as he was in his own intentions —a great master of the spiritual life—if his attraction for thousands is to be understood, and the passionate fidelity to him. Two points should give the hasty critic to pause: the divine predestination—even to hell—was, for Calvin, an aspect of the Divine Providence, and his ideal for all his followers was a weekly reception of the Holy Communion.

As to what he desired to see done, Calvin has left us two great testimonies, his book, the *Institutes*, and the life at Geneva in the years when he ruled the city; for the absolute ruler of Geneva is what this passionate student of the Word became, who scarcely left his study save for his two weekly sermons and his three weekly lectures and the meeting of the ministers. No tyrant of our own times was more terribly the master of men's lives than was this cold, thin-faced little man with the bent shoulders and the long gray beard, old long before his time, whose eyes flashed so terribly when justly angered—and of course when angered it was always justly. From the beginning he is identified with God, in his own thought, and none attacks him save from hatred first of God.

What Calvin's power was—power of personality—and what confidence in his mission he showed are revealed in his first public encounter with the rulers of Geneva. Never did wealth influence his action, nor the prestige which the accumulation of it generally gives—any more than his senses tempted him. And as yet he had not, himself, the prestige that comes of success widely known. It was some five months after his arrival that the council was presented with a plan for the restoration of order in church affairs. System had been shattered, and now Liberty Hall and the life of Larry was the order of the day. Calvin is twenty-seven, and he proposes his doctrine of frequent communion and links with it a demand that the minister's power of excommunication shall be recognised by the state and enforced by the state. Life for the obstinately wicked shall be made intolerable—they will either reform, becoming true weekly communicants, or leave God's city for the wilds. The council, he suggests, will choose some good men in every parish, and these will keep a careful eye on the conduct of their neighbours, reporting to the ministers any notable wrong-doing. If, on the minister's kindly exhortations, the sinner refuses to amend, he is to be excommunicated, and for those who make merry over this sentence, the state will find civil penalties. There were other proposals too, of course, but this linking of the Eucharist and a *police des mœurs* is something quite new, and it will be the basis of Calvin's control.

I must not be thought to suggest that it was Calvin who invented intolerance—the general habit of mankind towards new ideas and, in those bygone centuries, an axiom for the practical men charged with government in the state as well as in the Church. Just a month before his first arrival at Geneva, the council, having adopted the Lutheran clergy's advice to the Elector of Saxony—"They must be compelled to attend the sermons, they must listen to the preachers however unwillingly"—had before them one Jean Balard, charged with absenting himself. He was not a Catholic, but, like his judges and the preachers, one liberated, as they would have said, from the papal superstition. He explained that his conscience forbade him to attend, that the Holy Ghost was his teacher and so directed him. When the council persisted, and warned him that exile was the penalty for disobedience, he made a very singular reply, which however did not avail: "And he kept on saying that we have no power to compel the citizens to go to the sermon against their conscience, since in the beginning of these changes we particularly said that no man had the power to lord it over our conscience." Calvin was to explain in later years, ". . . if authority and liberty of judging the law be left to private men, there will never be any certainty set down, but rather all religion will become doubtful."

It was in January 1537 that Calvin's plan was presented. The council did not reject the scheme but reduced the number of communion days to four a year. In the next twelve months there was much discussion whether or not to follow the system already adopted at Berne, discussions in which politics played a part. And there was, of course, resentment in some quarters about Calvin's new system. The objections to the ministers having such power came to a head in January 1538, and the council voted that no one should be refused communion. Whereupon Farel and Calvin announced that they could not in conscience celebrate the Lord's Supper. The dispute dragged on for weeks; the council finally gave the two leaders an ultimatum: to obey or leave. And, with a certain slamming of doors, they went; *"Est bien,"* they said, *"à la bonheur"*; to which Calvin added the pious remark that had they been serving men by their ministry, this would have been a poor reward, "but we serve a great master and He will reward us."

Farel returned to Neuchâtel, and in the twenty-eight years of life that remained to him never again troubled Geneva with his zeal. They both appealed to Zürich for sympathy, but were only told "to moderate their misplaced rigour and to show some Christian tender-heartedness towards a people so undisciplined." Moderate, indeed! Calvin will one day encourage his disciple, Protector Somerset, with the words, "Beware of moderation, it is the bane of all improvement." Meanwhile, he went to Strasbourg, where Bucer made him welcome and gave him the care of the French refugees. In this cosmopolitan city, placed at one of the great crossroads of European life, easy, tolerant, generous, Calvin spent three very happy years. He had his church, congenial companions, and the congenial task of preparing a new edition of the *Institutes*; the first had sold out within a twelvemonth. The new edition was a new book, four times the size of the first little tract. It appeared in 1539, and a French translation of it, made by Calvin himself, in 1541. It is with this French version—seventeen chapters in 1541, where there had been only six in 1536—that the book became a real best seller and Calvin a force that nothing could halt. It was revised in 1545, and twice again before the definitive edition of 1560, and nine times reprinted in the fourteen years 1551–64. And there were seven editions of the Latin version—also, of course, revised from time to time and enlarged. There were eighty chapters to the editions of 1559–60. There were translations too, immediately: German, English, Italian, Spanish, Hungarian, Greek, Dutch; translations also, into a dozen tongues, of another popular book based on the *Institutes*, Calvin's *Catechism*.

And it was in these years at Strasbourg that Calvin married —the widow of an Anabaptist whom he had converted, the mother of two children, who brought Calvin a son who died in his cradle years. Idelette, the mother, died in 1548: a sorrow from which the lonely Reformer never recovered.

Calvin returned to Geneva September 13, 1541, much against his inclination, urged thereto by a chorus from every Reformed church in Switzerland. It was not merely for his spiritual teaching that the Genevan authorities had so warmly invited him. The city was in a pitiable state, with only one preacher left, Peter Viret. One thing alone could halt the rot: the restoration of the discipline that was Calvin's discovery, by the discoverer himself. Calvin came back resolved, this time, to complete his task and under no illusions about his "friends." Political parties were still tearing at one another in the government, and much of Calvin's success will depend on the way the elections go.

He was immediately asked, with an abundance of compliments, to draw up a kind of constitution for the Church. His favourite scheme again had the first place. But he had to endure that the council studied the scheme and revised it. They reserved to themselves, for example, the right to punish, which is the foundation of all penal schemes; the consistory (or ecclesiastical tribunal) could only reprimand; Calvin and the preachers were not given the right to excommunicate. And the council also kept in its own hands the surveillance of sermons and of the school. Calvin bided his time. There was a majority against him for the moment. But he had a party in his favour, and soon he became its leader. Little by little refugees from France began to come in to Geneva. They were well received, given citizens' rights. And Calvin absorbed them into his party. This, in moments of crisis, would tell against him in those days when, as he recalled on his deathbed, boys followed him home, hooting "Frenchy" after him, or men set their dogs on him, or fired off guns under the windows of his modest house.

But the crises passed, and his party grew. The great weakness of his opponents—of the "national" party—was that it had no religious ideals of its own, no preacher, and no competent leader. And all this time, in the sermons and lectures delivered every week, the powerful, passionate mind of Calvin was Calvinising the minds of all his hearers. Even when the really difficult years came, 1548–53, when the "nationals" held all the offices and were steadily sapping his power in the state, they still remained captive to his religious ideas and to the formation they had received. In the end, if only Calvin lived, he was bound to be the master of all. What else could happen, when the men who most loudly cursed his despotism were yet faithful to the message he gave?

And, despite all the discontent, Calvin got his way as a practical reformer—partly because no offender was ever let off his punishment. Calvin had, to perfection, the cold ruthlessness of the righteous. Edict followed edict from the council. Playing cards were forbidden, and dice, light songs, dancing; the taverns were closed and a new species of eating-house set up where a man could read his Bible in peace. There were, of course, the five weekly sermons which all must attend. The offender's place in social life was no protection. The great ladies of the community were sent to prison as easily as their serving-girls. One man was given a spell for playing bowls during church time and another for leaving church during the sermon. The fashion of dress and of shoes, for men and for women, was regulated, and the women's hair styles also. All days but Sundays were working days, because the Scripture read, "Six days shalt thou labour." Needless to say, every least sign of the old religion was most rigorously forbidden; to say a prayer in Latin, for example, to hint a disbelief that the pope was Antichrist, or to repeat that he was said to be kind to the poor. No child was to be given any name except those found in the Bible, and a father who protested when the minister christened his son Abraham paid for his insolence in prison. Anabaptists were banished, with death as the penalty should they return. The rare atheist—the man who denied that Scripture was inspired or that the soul was immortal—was put to death, tortured and beheaded. The heretic was burned—Calvin's name is never remembered but that of Servetus comes into the memory. Few crimes were more swiftly and decisively punished than that of contradicting the master's teaching. Intellectual give-and-take had no place in Geneva. There is quite a litany of distinguished theologians—all of the Reformed school—whom he set on the road to exile for such temerity: Castellio, Bolsec, Zucchi, Carmel. And even to say that Calvin was not a good preacher could mean prison. Or, which happened to Berthelier (whom he later had beheaded), such a remark, coming from the sermon, as "Calvin doesn't like us coughing! We'll belch and make ruder noises still if we feel that way," brought a prison sentence.

Naturally there was a censorship of books—even Bullinger, *Against the Anabaptists*, was forbidden. And authors were compelled to sign each sheet of their manuscripts, which the censors countersigned in approval—and woe to the man who later slipped in any changes. Real sins, of course, were dealt with mercilessly—blaspheming, drunkenness, carousing. As to wrongdoing in matters of sex, a special prison was now built to house such offenders. And the inquisition dreamed of from the beginning became a reality. Twice a year a commission of ministers and elders descended on every house in the town to see that all was well and godly, no superstitious pictures on the walls, no wrong ideas in the minds, all diligently attending the sermons and receiving the Lord's Supper. And all this was entered in a huge register, with notes against the name, "pious," "lukewarm," "corrupt." Calvin could choose without risk of mistake the men who would do the cause service in the councils and the public offices. He would know how to block the promotion of others. Add to this the immense body of the pious who voluntarily spied on their neighbours and even drew them on in talk until they tripped. As the years went by, Geneva succumbed—for one thing, its population was radically different before the end of Calvin's personal rule; with its thirteen thousand or so native Swiss there now mingled half as many again foreign refugees, hot zealots whose prospects depended on the master alone, on their zeal and on their show of zeal.

"When I first came to the church," said Calvin to the ministers as he lay dying, April 28, 1564, "there was, as it were, no church at all. There was a little preaching, and that was all. There was indeed some hunting after idols, and they were burned. But there was no reformation. All was chaos . . . There is one point I have forgotten: I beg of you make no changes, don't bring in anything new—not that I desire what I have done to remain . . . but because all changes are dangerous and sometimes harmful."

The student, contemplating this pitiful picture of Calvin's preoccupation with these petty tyrannies in a small Alpine town, may need vigorously to remind himself that the great man of this petty world was a great man in his own right, and that long before he died, all Europe, outside Spain, was feeling his power and in some measure responding to it.

Calvin was a man universally consulted on religious problems of every kind, the regular correspondent of the Reformation leaders of various schools, and the correspondent also, when need arose, of the great personages of this world. But it was really through the army of disciples whom he taught and trained in his own academy, whom he formed as ministers of the Word, and with whom he never ceased to keep in touch, that Calvin became a kind of pope in the Reformation world, and his work international in a way that no other of the Reformation churches has ever been. Anglicanism is what its name declares it to be; Lutheranism is German and Scandinavian. But the Presbyterians are no more or less Scots than they are Dutch or French or Swiss, Welsh or American. The students for the ministry to whom Calvin lectured were of all nations. Of the ninety-five on the rolls in the last year of his life, eighty-five came from outside Switzerland; there were even Russians among them.

The numerous churches which they served in all these countries were not bound to Geneva by any formal link. But all had the Calvinist doctrine—they lived on the *Institutes*, taken in first by means of the *Catechism*. All had the Genevan liturgies. All were most faithful to the *Discipline*. All churches were organised on the same pattern—the minister, the elders, the deacons. Everywhere that this was possible the ministers of the locality met for a weekly conference of prayer and study. And with all of the churches Calvin kept in touch in that vast correspondence the surviving remains of which fill ten folio volumes of print.

Slowly the Calvinist churches—Calvin would, of course, have rejected all such use of his own name—began to form: in France, in Bohemia, in Poland, in southern Germany—Bavaria and Württemberg—in the Rhine principalities, in Flanders, in Holland, in the England of Edward VI, in the Scotland of Mary Stewart. They have to meet the stormy and persistent opposition of the Lutherans. They come to a doctrinal understanding with Zwingli's people. But not all the Swiss will join with them.

Did this form of the Christian religion make a universal appeal in these countries where it now began to take root? Are all classes of society found at the sermon? Is the congregation more particularly of one class? And is it this same class which everywhere constitutes the strength of Calvinism? All these first Calvinists are, of course, ex-Catholics. And many of the Calvinist ministers are, unlike Calvin himself, one-time Catholic priests. Do we know anything about their antecedents —their "professional" antecedents, so to speak? In France, at any rate, few of the upper ranks of the secular clergy—the

innumerable canons of the cathedrals and collegiate churches
—went over. The chapters were, indeed, usually more militant
against the new movement than the bishops. Of the parish
clergy, again comparatively few of the town clergy became
Calvinists. Some of the country priests did. But the great
source of what priests Calvin recruited was the group of
mendicant orders, Dominicans, Franciscans, Augustinians—
the only trained, professional preachers whom the Catholic
Church of those days knew. The first of the Reformation
preachers to be burnt in France as heretics were one-time
friars. Many of these recruits were, it seems, rebels by nature,
men hostile to all authority, and Calvin had as many difficulties with these as, in days gone by, their old superiors had
experienced.

As to the laity: in France the nobles properly so called and
that summit of the *bourgeoisie* whence the great lawyers and
administrators came, surrendered very few of their numbers
to Calvin in these formative years. The professionals of lower
degree were more affected, but the mass of the converts were
the ordinary people of the towns, the artisans who worked the
looms, for example, and with them their artisan-masters who
owned the looms. It is out of this class that the first *groups*
are formed; it is they who are the stuff of the first secret
churches. The main attractiveness of the new thing was the
preaching: the message, in season, out of season, delivered in
terms of ordinary speech, devoid of the technical, stereotyped words never heard save from the pulpit—the message
that each listener matters intensely to God his Father, that he
is one of the elect, marked by God, the special care of God's
providence: this and the new simplicity of religious practice—
a sermon of this sort, hymns or psalms in the native tongue,
almost no rites, no more confession of sins to a priest, no more
submitting to any man's judgment about such matters, no
more complications; and the consolation of feeling certain that
one is saved and that, once saved, one cannot be lost.

But the new preachers never won over the peasants—except
in those regions of the south which had once been the haunt
of the Albigenses. Other things apart, the peasant—it has been
argued—recognised in the new religion the foe to two of the
dearest and most instinctive practices of his life, the cult of
the saints, which canonised the very "localism" of his life, and
the cult of the memory of his dead, who lay in their humble
graves or whose bones came to fill the charnel house and for

whom, in the little church where they had prayed and made
their peace with God, the Mass was offered that put the seal
on all, and reminded the survivors that between them and that
other world there was the bond of a present mutual activity
—that the dead do not sleep but are in real contact with ourselves, the communion of saints, the most real consolation of
life. Before this faith, to which the supernatural was as "concrete" as the world of the fields and the woods and the cattle,
the new offer of salvation through the reading of books and
the speeches of men and community hymns had no attraction.
"All changes are dangerous." This alone, of Calvin, would
the peasant have understood. It would have had his heartfelt
agreement.

This is all said of France—a country where Calvinism had,
for a long time, nothing but its own merits to aid it; and where
the government was, from the beginning, hostile, and, very
soon, busy with the work of suppression. Calvinism is no exception to the rule that in no country did any of the Reformation doctrines succeed where the government was resolutely
opposed to them. In no country did they ever succeed where
the government did not make them its own—whether the
government was a petty German prince, a Scandinavian king,
or a tiny city-republic.

iii *Trent I:* 1545–1552

The General Council, which at last opened at Trent in
December 1545, was not to hold its final session until nearly
eighteen years later. It did not, of course, sit continuously for
anything like that period. The times were stormy, and if the
history of the council is a history of crises, it is in this a faithful
reflection of the history of the times. It is a history which,
incidentally, brings home vividly how central to international
life the question of religious differences then was and how
central, also, the action of the popes.

There are three easily distinguished periods in the story of
Trent. In the reign of Paul III, who summoned the council, it
sat from December 13, 1545, to September 17, 1549. In the
reign of his successor, Julius III, the sessions were resumed,
from May 1, 1551, to April 28, 1552. And ten years later Pius
IV brought the council to a conclusion, in sittings which lasted
from January 18, 1562, to December 4, 1563. In this chapter
the activities of the first two periods will be surveyed and

something said of the never-ceasing interaction of politics upon the council.

To preside over the council the pope appointed three cardinals with the faculties of legates *a latere*, Gian Maria del Monte, fifty-eight years old and a most experienced administrator; Marcello Cervini, a scholarly theologian, forty-five; and Reginald Pole, who was forty-six. Their first task was to organise the procedure of the hundred or so ecclesiastics (some sixty bishops and between forty and fifty theological experts, all but four of them friars) who were to take an active part in the council. Among them were scholars and lawyers, of the first eminence in their specialties, and ecclesiastical diplomatists with personal experience of all the problems—and the personalities—that had so long tormented Europe. The council was fortunate in its secretary, a layman of thirty-five, Angelo Massarelli, a tireless worker and a master organiser. For the great contentment of future historians he was to be the secretary through all the sessions of the council, 1545–63—and he kept a day-to-day diary. As the years went by he became a priest, and in 1557 Paul IV made him Bishop of Telese.

What ultimately emerged from their preliminary discussions was that each problem—whether of defining doctrine or of the particular reforms to be enacted—should first of all be discussed by the professional theologians or canonists, the bishops attending as silent spectators. This meeting was called a "particular congregation." Next, the conclusions of the particular congregation were debated by the bishops sitting alone—this was called a "general congregation." When the general congregation had arrived at its conclusions and fixed the text of the decree, this was promulgated in a solemn ceremony called a "session." It is in these sessions that the council is formally in being. They were held in the Cathedral of Trent[9] and preceded by a High Mass. The congregations took place in one of the great mansions of the little city.

Every care was taken that the council's work should proceed in a truly religious atmosphere. The little world of clerics lived under a kind of rule, and for Trent itself special prayer services and processions were the order of the day. And in a strong opening address on January 7, 1546, Reginald Pole, in the name of the legates, reminded the bishops of the nature of the duty that had brought them together. One who was

9 In the third period of the council, the sessions took place in the church of S. Maria Maggiore.

present has recorded that hardly had the secretary read through the first paragraph of this searing recall to realities when, as by instinct, the whole audience turned to Pole. His purpose is to force on the minds of the council what it is that Christendom is now expecting; and he invites the assembled bishops to begin by reflecting that it is bishops who are most responsible for all the evils "now burdening the flock of Christ. . . . We cannot even name any other cause than ourselves. . . . If God punished us as we deserved, we should have been long since as Sodom and Gomorrah"—this, after listing some of the abuses. Why dwell on this shameful subject? says his critic. Because, Pole replies, unless we place our own sinful responsibility in the front of our minds, "it is useless to call upon the Holy Spirit for help."[10]

One most important question which the council had to decide in these preliminary weeks was whether or not to be guided by the often expressed views of the emperor, that there should be no discussions about religious doctrine until after the council had enacted a detailed reform of prevailing abuses. The pope, on the other hand, was no less firm for the principle that what mattered first of all was the restatement of belief on all those doctrines about which the Reformers, for thirty years now, had been preaching a new theology. At the council— but not in the council—there were present ambassadors from the emperor, sent to secure that nothing it did should interfere with his schemes for the reorganisation of Germany. And there were within the council quite a body of bishops from his various kingdoms—from Spain, for example, and from the kingdom of Naples—who automatically supported him. The council decided, on the proposition of Tommaso Campeggio, that it would deal simultaneously with the questions of belief and with the specific reforms, and issue, at the various sessions, decrees treating of both.

There are four sessions in the first period of the council at which such decrees were promulgated, reckoned as the fourth, fifth, sixth, and seventh sessions of the council, and held on April 8 and June 17, 1546, on January 13 and March 3, 1547.

The actual history of what went on in these meetings at Trent has hardly been studied at all by English-speaking historians, partly, it may be, because the abundant documents

[10] An admirable translation of this address, by Fr. Vincent McNabb, O.P., was printed in *The Dublin Review*, January 1936.

made available to scholars by the popes in the last seventy years, and (so far as the official records go) all now in print, confront a generation to which the technical study of theology is less and less congenial. One unfortunate result is that the masters in Israel are only too often content to reproduce the judgments (and the wit!) of the great writers of the past, who could study barely a dozen documents where today hundreds are available.[11] To the ordinary man—by which I mean all those who, having a living to earn, cannot in the one lifetime be professional scholars also—the best way to become acquainted with the great council is to read, what has long been available in English, the text of the decrees the council promulgated; a book half as long, perhaps, as this present work. It would be folly to attempt more here than to list the subjects of which the decrees treated and to give some idea of the circumstances under which they were debated. Let us begin with the doctrinal task accomplished in these four sessions.

In the first place we shall note—not without astonishment, Trent being an event that overshadows all subsequent history —that the attendance of bishops was very small indeed. There were then, in one country and another, round about seven hundred bishops. In the first of these sessions we are considering there were present fifty-one bishops; in the second, fifty-eight; in the third, fifty-nine; and in the fourth, sixty-two. And there was the staff of forty-eight theologians and canonists. It is indeed a small assembly, and we might hope it had been larger, although the cynical-sounding remark of the modern French historian, recording the fact, has point—*heureusement*. One thinks of the Vatican Council of 1870, of the freedom of speech, and of the debates that went on for weeks, until the bishops, bored with the repetition (at endless length) of what rapidly became commonplaces, began to shout the speakers down and to vote that no more be heard. Even in general councils bishops will be human, and their *modus operandi* is itself but a natural thing. And certainly at Trent there was all the liberty anyone could desire, but only one real scene, where, as the prelates streamed out after a stormy debate, the Bishop of Chioggia took the Bishop of La Cava violently by the beard, and they had to be parted. Next day there were solemn words from the president, and due apologies, and warm embraces between the two.

11 I am thinking, of course, of Ranke and Paolo Sarpi.

It was no part of the council's design to restate the whole belief of the Church, nor even to restate its whole belief on the doctrines controverted. All it proposed to do was to restate clearly the Catholic doctrine with regard to those particular points where the Reformers had offered a new teaching. And in the decrees there are no arguments. The decrees of Chalcedon are not a compendium of the case against Eutyches. And the decrees of Trent do not contain a single argument in confutation of Luther or Calvin. All decrees of general councils called in consequence of some movement to promote new versions of the traditional belief are of this same character—in face of the new, they reassert the old. The councils are not conferences where theologians beat out an understanding, a *modus vivendi*. They are assemblies where authorised, or rather authoritative, witnesses testify to what the Church actually believes on the point at issue. As to the Reformers of the sixteenth century, Paul III instructed the council that its business was to condemn not individuals, but wrong doctrines. Nowhere, in any of the acts, is there any reference to a particular Reformer.

The council began at the foundations. On April 8, 1546, the decree on the Scriptures, stating that the first objective of the council was to "*preserve*" (italics mine), not to *restore* "the purity of the gospel," and declaring that the truth and the way of living made known by Christ, the Son of God, "were contained both in the written scriptures and in the unwritten tradition, which received by the Apostles from the lips of Christ had been handed on by them and so came to us," it listed the names of the books of the Old and New Testament as the sacred and canonical scriptures. In a second decree it set up a censorship for religious books, and especially for editions of the Bible, stating clearly its principle; namely, "to decide the true meaning and interpretation of the Holy Scriptures is the business" of the Church. In preparation for these two decrees, there were ten preparatory congregations.

In the session of June 17 the council promulgated its decree on original sin, and four days later took up the question of justification, so clearly related to this in all men's minds for thirty years now. The discussions here were long indeed. There were forty-four meetings of the theologians and sixty-one of the bishops. It was not until December that the final text—nine pages of closely knit Latin—was ready, and with the decree there appeared the new feature, a list of canons; i.e., statements of the position of one or other of the Reformers, set out in a lapidary style and explicitly condemned: thirty-three canons in all. This was promulgated on January 13, 1547.

But in the six months during which the council was at work on this decree, the world outside was otherwise engaged than in speculations about Trent. War had at last broken out in Germany, and now the Protestant princes were at one another's throats.

Seven months before the council opened—i.e., in May 1545—Charles V sent to the pope the exciting news that he was now in a position to take the field against the princes of the League of Schmalkalden. He did not tell the wary Paul III the whole of what was in his mind—that his ally in the coming war was to be the new Protestant Duke of Saxony, Maurice. Nor, when the next bombshell came from the imperial court, did it explained to the pope that this was part of the plan—"this" being the emperor's announcement that in February next (i.e., three months after the council would have opened) there would be held at Passau a joint conference of Catholics and Protestants to settle the religious affairs of Germany. This "colloquy" came to nothing; not a single Protestant of any importance attended. When in May 1546 the Bishop of Trent (Cardinal Madruzzo) went to Ratisbon for the Diet, the emperor gave him, in the utmost secrecy, a message for the pope: he desired to make a military alliance and to begin the war. Paul III finally consented, and on June 26 (nine days later than the council's decree on original sin) he signed the treaty. Charles V had already signed two other treaties, one with the Duke of Bavaria, who was a Catholic, on June 7, and one with Maurice of Saxony on June 19.

It was the League that attacked, and at first victoriously, so that at Trent—with only 120 miles between themselves and the victorious Protestants—some of the bishops nervously proposed to transfer the council to an Italian city farther to the south. And Charles (in July) urged that there should be a suspension of doctrinal decrees. In August the papal troops—the Italians hired with papal ducats—arrived in Germany; the Elector of Saxony and Philip II of Hesse, the chiefs of the Schmalkalden League, were put to the ban; and a victory at Ingoldstadt, north of Munich, made Charles master of southern Germany, and Trent once more a safe town for Catholic bishops. October saw the rival Saxony princes at war, ravag-

ing and laying waste, and meanwhile the plague arrived and
the Italians died like flies. When the pope decided to recall
his army, January 22, 1547, only two thousand were left of the
twenty thousand he had despatched. This act of Paul III, need
it be said, brought the emperor to one of his cold cynical rages.
No doubt he had learned by then that, just nine days before,
the council had gone to the very heart of the differences with
the Protestants and published the decree on justification.

The council's next session was fixed for March 3, and the
decree it then put out had the sacraments for its subject matter
—the sacraments in general, the two sacraments of Baptism
and Confirmation in particular. By now the plague had
reached Trent. One of the bishops died of it in the night of
March 6, in circumstances that left the whole place shaking.
The bishops demanded an open discussion on whether or not
to move away from Trent, and on March 10, despite the
legates, they voted to transfer the council to Bologna, to meet
there on April 21. This was eventually to prove to be the end
of the council's usefulness for some years.

At Rome the effect of this news was general consternation.
The pope had not been consulted: but Charles would never
believe that the move to Bologna was not his work. They were
already on the coldest terms since the withdrawal of the papal
troops, and now the emperor's ambassador (March 24) denounced the old pope to his face in language Luther might
have envied. It moved him not at all. The council had been
free to decide. The pope had approved the decision—carried
into execution before even he had news of it. He could not
give directions to the council according to the good pleasure
of the emperor. As it was, a thousand tongues denounced the
council as a farce arranged between the two of them. There
was a stormy scene in Germany, too, between Charles and the
nuncio that ended with a filthy remark from the emperor about
the pope and a crude "Get out, nuncio. And when next you
have any business take it to my chancellor." This was on
April 14, 1547. Ten days later, at Mühlberg, halfway between
Dresden and Wittenberg, Charles (or rather the Duke of
Alva) annihilated the Elector of Saxony's army. The elector
was his prisoner, and soon Philip of Hesse would also be in
his hands. Maurice received his reward—the dignity of elector
and the lands of his cousin.

Who would now put bounds to what Charles might not do?
He had forbidden the bishops who were his subjects to leave

Trent for Bologna, and the thirteen of them stayed on, "the true council." And Charles and his court theologians worked out his plan, the temporary settlement about religion, about beliefs and about rites, which he would impose on Catholics as well as Protestants. To Paul III before the scheme was published his ambassador said, "The emperor will use his imperial powers, and will save the Catholic Church in spite of the Holy See." Meanwhile the council remained inactive at Bologna, this terrible crisis growing more and more acute—to be complicated, September 10, 1547, by a dreadful crime, the assassination of the Duke of Parma, Paul III's son, by the orders of the emperor's lieutenant in Milan, Ferrante Gonzaga: not a crime ordered by Charles, but an incident growing out of a conspiracy to overthrow the duke, which Charles had sanctioned as far back as January 14.

Here, brought into the open by the murder, was one of the hidden considerations which, for years, to the despair almost of the Catholic Reformers, had bedevilled the pope's dealings with the emperor. It was the mania of the Borgia and the della Rovere returned in force, the passion of a pope to see his descendants sovereign princes. This son, Pierluigi, was a worthless blackguard stained with every kind of vice, whose disappearance none—outside his own family—made even a show of regretting. The pope, after long and hopeless efforts to persuade Charles to grant him the Duchy of Milan—the key province, in time of war with France, of the hold of a king of Spain on his Netherlands—had managed to win from Charles his natural daughter Margaret as a bride for Pierluigi's son Ottavio, some years before. And then on August 26, 1545 just a matter of three months before the council opened at Trent, the pope, in spite of the undisguised condemnation of his cardinals, had made over to Pierluigi, in fief, the duchies of Parma and Piacenza, conquered fifty years before by Julius II.

And now it had all ended like this, after just two years, and if the pope's conscience was troubled, there was certainly an added *malaise* on the somewhat charged memory of Charles V—and the prospect of war. For Pierluigi's son had thrown himself into Parma with troops and planned to bring the French back into Italy. This story must be read elsewhere, and how the discovery of Ottavio's double-dealing next year and of the sympathy and assistance his brother, Cardinal Alessandro, was giving him against the pope finally broke the old man.

He died, eighty-one years of age, on November 10, 1549. But before he died he had to face the extraordinary settlement of religion called the *Interim*, and to approve the indefinite suspension of the Council of Trent.

The *Interim* of 1548 was foolish in itself—in the way in which the intermeddling of civilian politicians in strategy and tactics is foolish. But the circumstances in which it was devised made it a most mischievous anti-papal and anti-Catholic action. For example, when the council now at Bologna declared that they would not return to Trent unless the imperial bishops there first came to Bologna as a public testimony that they did not consider themselves to be the General Council, and unless it was understood that the decrees about belief already passed were final—this against the demands of the last Diet[12] —the emperor made a protest which revived an ancient heresy as mischievous as any of Luther's. On January 16, 1548, his ambassadors appeared before the assembled bishops, then engaged in a discussion about the sacrament of Penance, and, in the emperor's name, made a protest about the actions of "an assembly calling itself a General Council" and certain persons who had usurped the style of papal legates. Thereupon the ambassadors summoned the bishops to return to Trent, saying, "We are here acting as the legitimate agents of our master the Roman Emperor." To which the presiding legate, del Monte, replied, "And I am here in my office of legate of the true, undoubted pope, Paul, the successor of Peter and the vicar of our Saviour Jesus Christ." The emperor must lower his tone, the legate gave warning, for there are terrible punishments for those who oppose general councils and scheme to usurp their rôle.

After twenty-eight years Charles V had reached the point made by Luther in his *Appeal to the Christian nobles of Germany*, that the pope is really, and rightly, the emperor's subject. The discussion went on for the whole of the day between the two companies of lawyers—the legates, that is, and the ambassadors. The emperor is the child of the Church, the cardinals repeated, not its master. Death would be preferable to accepting the position that the state can deprive the council of its freedom.

The *Interim* of May 15, 1548, is a statement of belief and a

[12] Augsburg, September 1547.

direction about rites. On all the points about which the controversies had raged, although it stated always the Catholic doctrine, it did so in language studiously vague. It said nothing about purgatory, and it revived the theological theory of the double justification which the council had just repudiated. It demanded no change in the outward ritual of the Mass and the sacraments. The fasts were to be retained—and for utilitarian reasons. The images of the saints were to remain in the churches, but as memorials merely. Where the use of the chalice had been introduced, in the rite of Holy Communion, it could be retained. The priests who had married were not to be disturbed. *Nec alteri alteros perturbent*[13]—these words, from the ruling about Holy Communion, sum up the whole motive of the emperor's policy.

All the efforts of Paul III to change this last manifestation of that policy failed entirely. He did not threaten Charles, as his fiery grandson would have liked. Charles was demanding still more urgently that the pope leave the settlement of Germany to him. And his bishops at Trent again claimed, in a letter to the pope, to be the real council. Charles was actually talking to the nuncio of schism, threatening an appeal from the pope to the council—to his council at Trent, no doubt. Whereupon the pope brought one occasion of the quarrel to an end by allowing the bishops at Bologna, who had never proceeded to any public act in two years, to return to their sees, September 17, 1549.

What had the Council of Trent accomplished, in these first sessions, towards the reform of abuses?

In the fifth session, June 17, 1546, two decrees were published. The first was about education; the education, primarily, of the future priests. It repeated laws that went back nearly four hundred years when it prescribed that to every cathedral there should be attached a learned priest who would teach theology and lecture on the Scriptures, "that heavenly treasury, which the divine liberality has given to mankind." Lectureships in Scripture are also to be founded in all churches which are served by a college of secular priests. The decree specifies how these foundations are to be financed. In the smaller towns, where such chairs cannot be established, there must at least be provided a trained priest who will teach the liberal arts,

13 Nor shall the one party trouble the other.

and free of charge. Monasteries, too, are to provide themselves with a theological lecturer, and abbots neglectful in this are to be corrected by the bishop of the diocese, who is given for this purpose the status of a delegate of the apostolic see. The decree ends with the demand that rulers will see to it that in all schools and universities instruction in the Sacred Scriptures shall be provided, for this is "the most necessary instruction of all." The second decree concerns preaching. And therefore, in its very first sentence, we meet the word bishop, for, says the council, "preaching is the chief of all a bishop's duties." The decree follows well-worn lines and orders the parish priests to preach every Sunday and on all feast days, giving their people the message of salvation as best they are able, and according to their people's understanding. There are provisions which give the bishops more control over the sermons preached by the friars, and power to restrain the operation of special privileges that are alleged to exempt individuals from this supervision. Finally, preaching is absolutely forbidden to priests who go about collecting alms. They must not preach, nor must others preach on their behalf—all privileges to the contrary notwithstanding, those who break this rule are to be punished by the bishop.

To work through codes of this kind is indeed yawn-provoking. There is never the excitement of novelty in reading that authority does not approve of disorder, that the preacher, as a famous man once said, is "against sin." All that can ever have been said in denunciation of sin has already been said centuries ago. The exhortations fail to move the mind, and always there seem to be, in the stern laws, the same old loopholes about which the lawyers for the defence will soon be active: "except for grave and legitimate causes," and the like. And at times one has this impression of the Tridentine laws also. But there are some new features, and they are all important for the future. The law now begins to provide penalties that are automatic; it finds a way round exemptions by clothing the bishop with the pope's own authority, and in general, at Trent the bishop's office begins to recover from the parlous state to which a mass of special privileges had for centuries reduced it—particularly with regard to certain classes of clerics. The accepted idea that Trent is the beginning of the age of centralisation in the Catholic Church, since when the bishops are mere instruments of higher powers, is as much in need of revision as the related idea that only from Trent begins the Church's understanding of its own nature and beliefs.

None of the Catholic reformers, as we have noted, ever made any secret that what was principally wrong with the Church was bad bishops. On January 17, 1547, the council promulgated its will about the duties of bishops. It began by quoting the pope, St. Leo the Great, to the effect that "integrity in the ruler is the secret of well-being in the subjects," and in language of studied restraint it explains the gravity of the bishop's obligation to live in the diocese committed to his care. It says that the laws about this have almost dropped out of memory and that ecclesiastical discipline is everywhere in ruins. And it then proceeds to enact automatic penalties—loss of revenues—for offenders; and automatic penalties also for those whose duty it is to keep the pope informed about non-resident bishops if they allow three months to go by without doing so. Then follow regulations about appointments —"the conferring of ecclesiastical benefices"—a subject taken up again in the reform decree of the session of March 3. Benefices—appointments to sees, to canonries, to parishes—the institution where more than in any other there had raged for centuries a kind of licenced anarchy and civil war; the subject of masses of legislation, the source of the fortunes of armies of ecclesiastical lawyers; the source of more scandals than we can comprehend. Only a lawyer—which this writer is not—could describe the precise effects of Trent with regard to the benefice system. One thing, however, is very evident: the determination to strengthen the hands of the local bishops, and (to this end) the devising of ways round the elaborately developed strategy of appeals against his sentences.

It is with these same disciplinary problems—not merely with reminding bishops how they *ought* to rule, but providing that the very laws will cease to be a jungle where the wicked can find shelter from justice—that the reformation canons of the next phase of the council are concerned, sessions XIII and XIV, held October 11, and November 25, 1551.

A new pope was now reigning, Julius III, no other than the Cardinal del Monte who had guided the council through its first difficult years. He had been elected to succeed Paul III after a long conclave of seventy-one days whose history epitomises the struggles which, for another fifty years, were to be a principal occupation of all popes, the fight to preserve the

freedom of religion from the patronage and protection of the
Catholic princes.

Julius III was sixty-two years old at his election. His forte
was ecclesiastical administration, and he had the reputation
of being one of the leading canon lawyers of his time. At Trent
he had deserved very well of the council, and of the pope who
had set him to preside. Now, placed where no weaknesses
could be concealed, his less favourable parts were bound to
influence events. But they hardly concern the history of Trent.
The most unexpected weakness was a return to the Renaissance, to the Rome of his own ecclesiastical youth, in the
matter of recreations and amusements, and the long periods
of retirement to that Villa di Papa Giulio which is one of
the show places of Rome. And there cannot be passed over
the admission to the college of cardinals of the wretched
Innocenzo del Monte, a lad of seventeen, who steadily went
from bad to worse until, in the time of Pius IV, he committed
a couple of murders and had to be locked up.

For all this—for the rough peasant crudity of his life and
appearance, for the weakness of his intervention in the Habs-
burg-Valois wars, for the way in which, after a short twelve
months, he seemingly lost interest in the council—Julius III
has been one of the popes generally condemned by the historians. But in one respect he has been greatly maligned. He
did not suddenly lose, at sixty-two, the industrious habits of a
lifetime. In addition to setting the council moving once more,
he organised vast preparatory research work that produced
results when Pius IV came to wind up the council ten years
later. And certainly he was no less plain-spoken as pope than
he had been as the Cardinal del Monte. "The reasons why
princes hate the Church are threefold," he said to the cardinals
in his first consistory. "In the first place, the greed of the
Roman Curia; next, the levity with which ecclesiastical appointments are made; finally, the outrageous luxury in which
the clergy live."

Julius III began with an attempt to complete his predecessor's work by the reform of the great office called the *Dataria*,
whose business it was to issue the formal grants of papal favours. It has been truly said that the favours—exemptions from
ecclesiastical regulations—were so many that, in practice, many
laws seemed to have been dissolved into thin air. The officials,
who, like almost all public officials in every state, had paid
money down for their appointments, lived by a percentage on

the fees paid by petitioners. Every new law was to them simply an occasion for a host of new dispensations. And the *Dataria* fees were one of the most important sources of the Holy See's revenue. Julius III did not finish this job—nor a good score of others: for one thing, he died after a short five years of rule. It was not until there arrived as pope a reformer who really struck terror into the professional cleric that the problem of the *Dataria* was solved. This reformer was Carafa, the co-founder with St. Gaetano of the order of Theatines, now seventy-four years of age and condemned to yet another five years before the whip would be put into his hands.

The bull of Julius III summoning the council to resume its labours at Trent was published December 27, 1550. Charles V was of course far from pleased when his old adversary thus renewed the battle. The King of France was openly hostile to the council. He had taken up the defence of the Farnese claim to Parma and within a few months would be at war with the pope. Meanwhile the various French ambassadors in Switzerland were commissioned to do all in their power to hinder the council. A French schism was not an impossibility. What saved Henry II from this last criminal folly was the influence of the youthful Cardinal Charles de Guise, better known for the next quarter of a century as the Cardinal de Lorraine.

The council was to meet on May 1, 1551, and, true to time, the first session was held on the appointed day. Only one of the legates was a cardinal, Marcello Crescenzi; the others were the Archbishop of Siponto and the Bishop of Verona. A new feature was the appearance of bishops from Germany, the electors of Cologne, Mainz, and Trier leading them. But the total number of bishops remained low.

There were two sessions only at which decrees were promulgated, those of October 11 and November 25, 1551 (counted as sessions XIII and XIV of the council), which have already been mentioned in connection with the decrees reforming the Canon Law so as to make the bishops' authority more of a reality. In the first of these sessions the subject was the sacrament of the Holy Eucharist, and the fourteen canons which pointed out the erroneous novelties of Luther and Zwingli and Melanchthon were preceded by an elaborate exposition of the Catholic belief, which the bishops were careful to set out in ordinary language and not in the technicalities of scholastic theology, lest Catholic doctrine might seem to be a mere matter of debatable science. At this session there were forty-three bishops, and in the preparatory work forty-eight theological experts shared.

The doctrine that the Mass is a sacrifice, and the judgment on the Reformers' treatment of this, had not been dealt with in this decree on the Holy Eucharist. Nor was it taken up in the next session, set for November 25. Instead, possibly to save time, the council now proceeded to a topic for which all the preparatory work had been done, at Trent and at Bologna, three or four years before—the sacraments of Penance and Extreme Unction. Once again the specialist historians can tell us what works of the Reformers the council had in mind when, in the nineteen canons, it signalled capital departures from the tradition and condemned them: Luther's *Babylonian Captivity*, for example, Melanchthon's *Loci Communes*, Calvin's *Institutes*. The subject of the Mass and the sacrament of Holy Orders would be dealt with, it was announced, in a session to be held on January 25 of the new year 1552. But by that time the winds of war were once more rising. And meanwhile there had arrived at Trent the official envoys from some of the Protestant princes and cities of Germany.

The Reformers had, from the beginning, appealed, as in a conventional gesture, to the judgment of the next General Council. Luther, some weeks after his famous meeting with Cajetan at Augsburg, had even made a formal appeal, November 28, 1518[14]—thereby offending against the famous law *Execrabilis* of Pope Pius II (1459), which regarded such an act as a kind of high treason in religion. But the council which they all had in mind, henceforth, was not what the word had always meant hitherto; Luther, in 1519, had expressly denied at Leipzig that general councils enjoyed any divine prerogative which preserved from error their judgment about the articles of Christian belief. In a religious system which denies that there is any real distinction between clergy and laymen, and holds that all Christians are equally priests; denies that the Church alone has the right to decide the meaning of Scripture, and denies that the pope, exclusively, has the right to summon a General Council—in such a system the word "council" refers to another sort of assembly altogether from what Paul III had in view (and Charles also) in all the long years when he strove to get Trent into movement.

14 See p. 111, *supra*.

Without going through the evolution of the new idea in the thirty years since Luther's revolutionary address to the German Nobles, it may be said that when the Diet met at Augsburg in 1547, after the emperor's victory of Mühlberg, the Protestant princes, asking for a council that should be "free and apostolic," explained this to mean a council where it would be acknowledged that the pope is subject to the council's decisions, and where the bishops—before the council met—would be released from their obedience to the pope, and in which the Protestant theologians would sit as equal in authority to the bishops. And this was still the idea in their minds in 1551, when (October 22 and November 11) the envoys arrived of the Duke of Württemberg and the towns of southern Germany, two very prominent Reformers, Johann Brenz and Johann Sleidan; the envoys of Maurice of Saxony did not come until January 9 following.

These envoys came to arrange the conditions on which the Protestant princes would participate. They were officially received by the council on January 24, 1552. What they proposed were the three points mentioned and also that all the council's decisions previous to this date should be regarded as null and the whole work begun again. They received the formal answer that their proposals would be carefully considered. Nothing but further bitterness could possibly have come from meetings of men so diametrically opposed and so passionately attached to their own beliefs. In March the war called the second war of Schmalkalden broke out: Maurice of Saxony against the emperor this time, and the King of France invading the Rhineland as the ally of the Protestants, and about to lay hands on the spoil promised him in advance of victory, the cities of Metz, Toul, and Verdun. How Maurice was victorious at Rettau (May 18, 1552), and how he all but captured the emperor, is what every school history tells. If the emperor, at Innsbruck, was not safe and was saved only by a rapid flight to the south, it was time for the council also to move. By its own vote, on April 28, 1552, it brought to an end this second phase of its activities.

The war continued in a desultory fashion for another year or more. The allies—Maurice and the French king—were, very reasonably, thoroughly suspicious of each other. The emperor was giving every sign that he was, as we say, losing his grip. He now definitely left the conduct of German affairs to his brother Ferdinand, and it was he who, on the Catholic side, was the principal force in the Peace of Augsburg of September 25, 1555, which brought the war to an end—and the Reformation also, as a phase of international history. What a handful of princes had accomplished at Nuremberg in 1532 was now accepted by the empire as a permanent state of things: the division of Germany into a Lutheran region and a Catholic region, with equal rights to remain Lutheran or Catholic according to the religion of the ruling prince. It was only "the two above-named religions," said the treaty, which were to profit from the pledge that states were henceforth free in the management of their religious affairs. Both Catholic and Lutheran were at liberty to oppose the efforts of any state to go over to Calvinism. And while, in spirit at least, the Catholic war against Calvinism never ceased, relations with the Lutherans were more in the nature of an armed neutrality. Those subjects who preferred not to live in a state where the ruler did not profess their religion were to be free to move out with all their goods. Also, by an act which was not the outcome of a debate in the Diet but done by the emperor as emperor, if any Catholic bishop or abbot who was thereby the civil ruler, also, changed his religion, he was to lose his rights to the see and to the principality; and the chapter with whom the right lay to elect to the see was to elect always a Catholic.

The treaty of 1555 is a recognition in public law that over an immense territory of Christendom there has come to an end what had been vital for more than a thousand years, the rôle of the Catholic Church in public life, the right of religion to a place in public life—for to the place of the Church in public life none of the new establishments even professes to succeed. The ideal of religion as the partner of the state, the supernatural complementing the natural, may rarely have been attained in practice. Henceforth it will cease to have any meaning. Appeals to it will simply not be understood.

CHAPTER SEVEN

Trent: Queen Elizabeth: Knox
1552—1567

i *Trent II: 1562—1563*

One of the illusions to which the historian is always liable
is to think that "history" actually happened in the more or less
orderly way in which he is narrating it—to take it for granted,
unconsciously of course, that this is how it looked to the actors
in the events, that (for example) when the Peace of Augsburg
was signed everyone said to his neighbour: "A new age has
begun. This is the end of the old order." And even if it really
was so, common sense should tell us that there can never be
any really clean breaks in such a complicated business as the
interrelations of those masses of mankind we call nations or
states, or religions. An age had closed? No doubt. Nevertheless,
in 1555 the completion of the Council of Trent is eight years
away; Calvin has still nine years of activity in front of him,
his supremacy at Geneva has only just begun; Charles V, this
very year, will abdicate as Duke of Burgundy, and next year
as king of his Spanish domains, and lastly as emperor, and the
new King of Spain will be almost purely the Spaniard in his
outlook; in the Netherlands the political conflict is preparing
out of which will come the Eighty Years' War (1568–1648),
in part a Protestant *vs.* Catholic war, as in France there are
imminent those Wars of Religion (1562–98) which are so very
largely a political fight; in England, in 1555, the heretic rule
of twenty years is over, Henry VIII's Catholic daughter Mary
has reversed all that he and his little Protestant successor had
achieved, and she is married to Charles V's son and heir,
known, from 1556, as Philip II of Spain—a régime around
which *we* can see the fates hovering (the marriage being child-
less), Mary's enigmatic Protestant sister in patient, cautious

attendance, and the Elizabethan Settlement, in fact, imminent; the continuity of holy living is maintained with St. Peter
of Alcantara and St. Teresa in Spain, St. Philip Neri in Italy,
St. Peter Canisius in the empire, St. Francis Xavier in the
Indies, and—as one born out of due time—St. Ignatius Loyola
somehow simultaneously effective in all these places. The latest born of all these personages was twenty-four at the time of
the peace of 1555. That year is truly a terminal date—if we
will recall with it those other years also, 1556 and 1558, 1562
and 1563 and 1564. The last is the year in which Calvin died,
by which time the chronic troubles of the Age of the Reformation are become the troubles of its successor, for which no one
has yet found a suitable name, an "age" which existed nonetheless. For no "age" has had to await the historian's label
before it could come into being.

The successor of Julius III was one of his colleagues as
legate at Trent, Marcello Cervini. He reigned only twenty days.
Then, on Ascension Day, 1555, Carafa was chosen, to his own
vast surprise. "This must be the will of God," he is reported as
saying, "for never in my life have I done any man a favour."
The prospects that the council would be reassembled dropped
to zero, Carafa—Paul IV, we must now call him—never having
made a secret of his views that there were more direct ways
of reforming bad clerics than through these weeks and months
of discussions; also, he thought it akin to treason for popes
to descend to persuade and coax Catholic princes to do what
was their obvious duty. Politics he abhorred, and one of his
first acts was to hand over the administration of the Papal
State and all its international relations to others. The pope
would give himself wholly to the reformation of abuses.

The reign of Paul IV (1555–59) has been described as disastrous, and the condemnation is understandable, for he was
a pure despot in mentality and in methods, and the mistakes
of such rulers wreck much more than their own peace of mind.
But on the other hand, his severity towards the incorrigible,
his indifference to the rank or social position of the offender,
his inflexibility, the four years of iron rule, of dismissals, of
imprisonments, of clerics sent to row in the galleys alongside
the thieves and the murderers—all this so thoroughly cleared
the sink that never again has any pope had to face, even in his
nightmares, what still confronted at his accession the author
of the *Consilium* of 1537. "It is a miracle that the Holy See has

survived all that our predecessors have done to ruin it," he said on one occasion. The *Dataria* was now at last reformed, the pope scorning the objection that he risked losing the best part of his income. Wandering monks were an especial object of his attention. One raid, in the night of August 22, 1558, rounded up a hundred of them in Rome itself, some of whom went to prison, others to the galleys. Yet another hundred were arrested a few days later.

Another plague, thought incurable, was the host of bishops who, deserting their sees, hung round Rome in the hope of favours. It had been with the greatest difficulty that Julius III had got a few of them to travel as far as Trent for the council. In 1556 there were as many as 113 of these personages in Rome. Paul IV somehow got rid of them all before he died, August 18, 1559.

As after the death of Paul III, so now there was a long interval—three months and three weeks—before the cardinals could agree. In the last two days of the conclave the votes suddenly swung to Gian Angelo Medici, a Lombard of sixty, a level-headed canonist, experienced, cautious, sparing of speech.[1] He took the name Pius IV and immediately made it known that he meant to reassemble the council.

All the wonted opposition reappeared. Ferdinand—now the emperor—thought, first of all, how irritated the Protestants would be at the news. If the pope were first to announce that priests might marry and that the Holy Communion would be administered under both species, it might smooth the way. From France came the demand that the council should be a new council—that all done hitherto should be ignored and, the Protestants co-operating, a new beginning be made. Meanwhile the king had already summoned a national council to settle the problems of the Church in France. With what a wealth of patience the new pope worked through all the first year of his reign can be guessed, but on April 16, 1561, the legates once more made their entry into Trent.

They found there awaiting them, besides the Bishop of Trent, nine others, bishops only. It was not until nine months later, January 18, 1562, that the solemn opening took place. There were then present 113 bishops. In this last phase of the

[1] Elected December 25, 1559.

council the attendance was quite another thing from what had been seen in the times of Paul III and Julius III.

The doctrinal task was now completed by statements on the Mass, Holy Orders and Matrimony, on Purgatory, the cult of the saints, and Indulgences—sessions of July 16 and September 17, 1562; of July 15, November 11, and December 4, 1563.

As to the council's other activities in the many "congregations" that filled the years 1562–63, it was now that the bulk of the great constructive legislation was worked out upon which the Catholic Church has lived right down to our own time—*ius novissimum* of the Canon Law writers. No further time was wasted on schemes to reconcile "Yes" and "No" in the interests of the emperor's German policies. And through stormy scenes the legates steered the council past thorny questions that set the Spanish and Italian bishops fighting in massed array, or the French to ally themselves with the imperialists (again in the interest of the schemes of princes). Nor did the legates insist when the council shrank before the tumult caused by the appearance of the draft scheme for the "Reformation of the Christian Prince." But a vast work of constructive reform was done, amid what plain speaking may be well believed.

From it all there needs to be singled out what, more than anything else, has made all the difference between the health of the Church in the last four centuries and its chronic state in the Middle Ages—the law of Trent that in every diocese there must be founded a college where aspirants to the priesthood will be taught and also trained. From that time the parochial clergy have been not only a body professionally instructed, but (to use an expression which, taken literally, is wholly inaccurate) a kind of new religious order. These new diocesan colleges are the seminaries, the best-known work of the council.

There also calls for especial notice one of the few changes made by the council in the matter of sacramental discipline—and of something more important still. This was the decree about the sacrament of Matrimony, known from its first word as *Tametsi*, of November 11, 1563, which decided that, for the future, marriages technically called "clandestine" would be, by the fact, null and void. Marriage is a sacrament where the contracting parties are the ministers, the very pact they make—which is the marriage—being also the matter and the form which constitutes the sacrament. *Consensus facit matri-*

monium (it is the consent that makes the marriage), the adage of the canonists, might also be rendered, "It is the consent that is the sacrament." This being so, whenever a man and woman in the way of whose marriage there stood no natural or legal impediment exchanged the pledge to take each other for wife and husband, wherever they did so, whether before witnesses or in a solitude, husband and wife they then became.

There is no record of any civilisation that was content with this—let us call it natural—way and procedure. For obvious reasons humanity in general, society, has called for a certain publicity in the pact-making. And from the beginning, Christians made their marriage-effecting pacts, *in facie ecclesiae*, "with the Church looking on." Despite the laws of the Church which came to demand this as a duty, the evil persisted that people married in secret, sometimes with witnesses or a single witness to the pact, sometimes with no witness at all. Time and again, in the visitation of parishes in the Middle Ages, a couple is brought before the bishop, living together and, as they allege and swear, married by a secret pact. They are made to do penance for the scandal they have caused and they renew their pact in the proper way. Now, at Trent, after strenuous debates, the Church takes the strong line of declaring that henceforth clandestine marriages are void of effect. All Catholics, for the future, must make their pact of marriage in the presence of the parish priest and two witnesses at least.

Finally, in the concluding, twenty-fifth, session the council decreed that never again were money offerings to be stipulated as a condition for gaining indulgences—with terse and terrible words about the abuses this had led to, and the scandal thereby given.

The Council of Trent came to an end, by its own act, on December 4, 1563. Pius IV confirmed all its decrees by a bull dated January 26, 1564, and he ordered that the laws should come into operation on May 1 following. By a third bull, of February 17, that same year, he abolished all privileges, exemptions, faculties, dispensations, and indults, no matter to whom accorded or to what place, however holy, which were contrary to what the council had decided. For the determination of the doubts that would arise once the decrees began to be applied, a special commission of cardinals was set up, the Congregation of the Council. And in the next six years four tasks which the council had handed over to the Holy See were carried through, the publication of an index of books forbidden to be read (1564), of a catechism for the use of parish priests (1566), a revised breviary (1568), and a revised missal (1570).

All that now remained was that the council should be obeyed, that its decrees should not remain a dead letter, and especially that the popes should set an example in this. The pope to whose patience and determination we owe the major part of what the council achieved, Pius IV, was not another Carafa and, by his natural disposition, he was easygoing with others rather than exacting. He had chosen as his secretary of state (a modern description of the post) a nephew of twenty-one, who, six months before, had still been a student of law at Pavia and who was to be the great Archbishop of Milan revered as St. Charles Borromeo. For much of the short time that Pius IV survived his council (he died December 9, 1565) the observance was in safe hands. But with the next pope, Pius V, the least of its laws had the sacredness of the rules of the religious order which had formed him.[2] At last an actual saint was seen in the see of St. Peter, and an example given, not in the personal life alone, but in the exercise of the public office; an example so powerful, so long-lasting, that to carry out the law became the unconscious habit of popes henceforward. And the terrible judgment of the pope of forty years before was most mercifully reversed, the words of Adrian VI in 1523 to the princes of Germany that "the disease has spread from the head to the members, from the popes to the prelates of lesser degree."

In the spring of the year 1521, when Luther was preparing for the Diet at which Charles V put him to the ban, a war was raging between that prince and the allied kings of France and Navarre. In the assault on the citadel of the Spanish town of Pampeluna, the chief stronghold of the kingdom, just one week before the Edict of Worms was published, an officer of the garrison, thirty years of age, was badly wounded (May 20, 1521). He was the future founder of the Society of Jesus, known to us as Ignatius Loyola. The long and boring convalescence that followed the healing of his terrible wounds

[2] The Order of Preachers, commonly called Dominicans.

was the turning point in his life—his conversion, in the first place, from an utterly worldly and sinful existence.

The curious coincidence in time, almost to the day, of events that thus brought together the lives of these two subjects of Charles V has often been remarked. But it was many years before the Basque had reason to pay any attention whatever to what the Saxon was then engaged in, and Luther's career no more influenced Loyola than Loyola influenced Luther. It is also of interest that with Loyola, Luther, and Zwingli there lay, in the foundations of the historical career, the resolution of the personal problem of their own fidelity to God's will. With Loyola, as with Zwingli, it was the uncomplicated, if grave, business of lack of control where women were concerned—gaming, also, and duels. Zwingli, the priest, explicitly declared his surrender to the habit. Loyola, the layman, once crisis came, when God had touched his life, thought, in the spirit of a penitent sinner, of nothing else but wholehearted reform. Luther's solution for his own private problem involved the denial that the authority acknowledged until now has any rights over men; Loyola's is to submit himself to that authority completely, as to a man's only security that he will not perish. Calvin? To leave history for the moment, and to conjecture merely, the French heresiarch seems never to have suspected that there could be ought amiss with himself in God's sight, except as all mankind is necessarily imperfect and damnable apart even from its own activities.

Once Ignatius Loyola is well enough for normal life, his one thought is a pilgrimage to a great shrine of Our Lady—Montserrat—a general confession of the sins of all his life, the distribution to the poor of all he has, and for the rest of his life the service of God in the poor. It is, as with others we have seen, in the hospitals that we next find him. And like another Don Quixote, taking literally all that the biographers had recounted of the saintly heroes now his models, Ignatius endeavours to combine all that they had ever accomplished in the way of prayer and penance: a continual fast (Sundays excepted), severe scourgings, the vilest rags of clothing, seven hours prayer a day on his knees—while all the town regards this haughty noblemen as mad, mocking as they pass the man whose natural self itched to run them through, as in days gone by.

The mind, however, was singularly lucid. It was in these

months of 1522 that Ignatius began to piece together out of
his personal experiences, and with the help of a special heavenly guidance that was not—he insists—a vision, the book that
we know as the *Spiritual Exercises*. His initial, if comprehen-
sible, mistake, that sanctity consists in material austerities, that
the tale of penance done, of prayers said, is a measure of holiness—an error which, in 1522, Luther is dishonestly identifying
with Catholicism itself—Ignatius managed to correct by the
simple process of listening to his directors and obeying their
instructions. He is as traditional in all this as Thomas More.
Again, after months of such a life, he fell ill, of course, and
all but died; troubled, not only by physical weakness, but with
the nervous crises that might have been expected, and all that
tangle we call "scrupulosity"—anxiety whether one has sinned
this time, anxiety whether the director whom one consults and
who is reassuring has really understood, or whether one has
not misled him, so that he was reassuring where, properly informed, he would have been severe: all this, and hell-fire
flaming in the background. And again the way out was the
same, disregard of one's own less experienced diagnosis of oneself, submission to the fact that others are better judges, surrender of the luxury that one is a special case, acceptance to
be one of the millions of the ordinary.

As with Luther, so with Ignatius, the personal crisis experienced will serve, when it comes to preaching a message to the
generality. And the message of Ignatius will be to stand to the
tradition, to act as Catholics have always been bidden by the
Church to act. *Stare super vias antiquas*, indeed. Never from
his revelations—if that word, not really correct, perhaps, be
allowed to pass—did Ignatius learn what hitherto had seemed
white was really black; never did he learn any new interpretation of fundamental Christian truth. His mission—from
any knowledge of which he is still seventeen years away—
will be to save men by conserving every scrap of the tradition, by urging only that every scrap of it be lived. He has no
fundamental "correction" to propose, whether on the authority of his own exceptional studies or of secret words, which it
is not lawful for a man to speak. In every respect Ignatius is,
very strikingly, the antithesis of all that is going on in his own
time in the lands beyond the Alps. The *Babylonian Captivity*
and the *Spiritual Exercises* were, almost exactly, contemporary
works, the products of two men born within the same ten

years.[3] And yet to Germany and the religious revolution Ignatius seems never to have given a thought.

The leading idea in the mind of the knight of God was clear, the purpose strong, to go off to the Holy Land and for the rest of his days preach Christ to the Mohammedan. Towards the end of February 1523 he left Manresa, trudged to Barcelona—lamed since Pampeluna and for life, of course—begging his food and an alms towards his fare, finding a captain who would take him gratis if he saw to his own food, reaching Gaeta on the Neapolitan coast, March 25. Then—still on foot, and a beggar—to Rome for the papal licence without which no pilgrim's life would have been safe once he reached the Turks; on again to Venice, two months' wait, an unexpected place on one of the government's galleys, and, on September 1, Jaffa. To find, after all, that his apostolic idea was looked on by the friars responsible for the conduct of pilgrims as naïve and mischievous. In these days it was a favour that Christians were allowed in the country at all. Ignatius was now all but expelled. By February 1524 he had got back to Spain, and at Barcelona put himself to school—to learn the elements of Latin with the little boys of eleven. For all his rank, he had known no more than how to read and write.

For five years he laboured at his desk, at Barcelona, in the universities of Alcalá and Salamanca. And, as he never ceased to do since his reconciliation to God at Montserrat, everywhere he evangelised, speaking of God, teaching the elements of the catechism. "Manresa," said a witness at the canonisation, "had forgotten there was a God" until Ignatius came there. So, a train of converted Catholics—since he was barred from Turks —in Barcelona, Alcalá, Salamanca, converted after the thought-out method enshrined in the *Exercises*; formed Catholics whose principles had become resolutions and, acted on, had produced habits: real apprehensions, then real assents. And trouble everywhere, too. In both these university towns Ignatius was arrested by the Inquisition and imprisoned, questioned rigorously about his teaching, then approved as orthodox, and most strictly forbidden to preach again, since he had had no theolog-

[3] The first appeared in 1520. The *Spiritual Exercises* begins to be put together (and used as a means of converting Catholics to a proper view of their life) in 1522. We hear of the manuscript in 1527 from the Inquisition at Alcalá, and in 1535, from the same source, at Paris. It is first printed in 1548.

ical training. Obey the law of the Church he must—and he must also go on with his mission (and learn theology). He left his native land (for ever, as it turned out) for Paris in 1528, and in the great university he learned his theology and also found the six associates with whom, making a joint vow on August 15, 1534, he took the step which led to the new religious order, the heart of which (as an order differing from any other) is the *Spiritual Exercises*.

The years Ignatius spent at Paris, 1528–34, are filled with alarums and excursions, in the history that tells of the spread of Lutheran ideas to France. But there is not the slightest reflection of this turmoil—the heretical discourse of the very rector of the university, his flight and Calvin's, in this very year 1533–34—in the lives of these seven men. Their vow is to lives of absolute poverty and chastity, and to give themselves to the conversion of the Mohammedans in the Holy Land: unless the pope otherwise directs. But first they will finish their professional studies. The six are all younger than Ignatius, now forty-three; four are Spaniards, one a Savoyard, one a Portuguese. All have come to be attached to Ignatius through the *Exercises*. There is no common life, no superior, no obedience. But the same rule of life which each one lives.

It was three years before they met Paul III (April 3, 1537), who gave them leave to be ordained, leave to go to the Holy Land, with a word that he thought it most unlikely they would find a ship—the naval war of Charles V with the Turks was still lashing the Eastern seas. The pope was right. While they waited, they gave themselves to evangelical preaching in the cities of northern Italy and, once they were ordained, to hearing confessions also; another wave of Clerks Regular in process of formation, it would seem, ten of them now. At the end of 1538 they went back to Rome, and the pope suggested they should fix their ideas in a new religious order. Between themselves the ten thrashed the matter out in long detailed discussions, from which—after much criticism, from the pope's canonists—there emerged the solemn sanction of the bull *Regimini Militantis Ecclesiae* of September 27, 1540, the foundation charter of the religious order long called by everyone the Jesuits.

The reluctance of the professionals whose business it was to draft such bulls as these was due in large part, no doubt, to the array of novelties in the organisation: an additional year of novitiate, vows first taken being simple vows (and not binding for life), a long interval between these first vows and the perpetual vows (years when the professional sciences of philosophy and theology would be studied and a certain amount of time spent in the practical apostolate), no elections, save for the rare general congregation that would elect the general, in whose hands were all the appointments. There were no limitations to the kind of work the society was prepared to do if commanded. And there was a fourth vow, by which the Jesuit bound himself to go wherever the Pope ordered him and for whatever task—a feature much criticised before the approval was given, but which is really no more than the supreme consecration of the underlying principle of the whole, that the Jesuit, wherever he is and whatever he does, goes in the spirit of the missionary, trained, detached, wholly dedicated to the allotted task. And wherever there is as much as one Jesuit at work, there the order is, in all its unique quality.

The number of Jesuits was restricted to sixty by the bull, but in 1544 this was removed. By the time Ignatius died, July 31, 1556, there were one thousand of them, and they were at work all over the world, the Indies, the New World, Spain, Italy, Germany, the Netherlands. They had appeared at Trent from the beginning as theological experts sent by the pope himself, and in the last stages of the council the successor of Ignatius, Diego Lainez (one of the original seven), played a most important part, not in any preparatory committee, but in the council itself, where, as general of his order, he had voice and vote like the bishops. To the missions of the East—to India, Cochin China, and Japan—Ignatius in 1540 had sent perhaps the greatest of them all, Francis Xavier, to labour heroically there until death came in 1552. Holland produced St. Peter Canisius (1521–97) who, if any, was the spiritual genius that halted the Lutheran flood at the point it had reached by 1555, and then began the restoration of Catholicism within the Catholic states. From Italy the society drew into it one of the hideously tainted Gonzaga clan, to be the famous St. Aloysius (1568–91); and from Spain the great-grandson of Alexander VI,[4] to be the third general and St. Francis Borgia (1510–72).

What are the *Spiritual Exercises?* Not a book to be read— if an answer to the question is really sought—but a programme

4 And of Ferdinand and Isabella.

to be worked through, of which the book is the *aide mémoire* for the experienced Jesuit who is the guide; thirty days of continuous, carefully planned, ordered meditations, on the Gospels primarily, and other exercises, made in a complete silence, in a house apart from all distractions, as a result of which the will, freed from all earthly influences save that of the instructed reason, makes a firm and lasting choice to serve God always, in every act of life. Order, light, definition, peace.

"*Digitus Dei hic*," Paul III is supposed to have said as he studied the plans from which came the Society of Jesus; "God's finger is here." It is proverbial that the Jesuits were a principal instrument of the popes at every turn of that vast and varied business, the restoration of Catholic life, and already within the lifetime of the founder Jesuits had given their lives for the faith. There remains to be mentioned another spiritual influence of these same years whose memory has long passed away with the generality even of historical students, which was never, in scale or variety, comparable for an instant with the great society but which was the agent whereby was wrought the conversion of the Curia Romana and of the city of Rome. It was the influence, radically, of a single man, the Florentine, St. Philip Neri, an utterly unusual, unconventional character who, as he had no predecessors in his particular way, so also he left no successors. The providence of God sent him a long life, and until the age of eighty he continued to be himself and to be active, and then, with a Clement VIII reigning and a régime which offered in every respect the greatest of contrasts to what had obtained under Clement VII, the saint died, 1595.

It was in the time of Clement VII that Philip Neri came to Rome, a lad of seventeen, in 1532. His father was a notary, far from well-to-do, and there were other children, girls. The family's spiritual relations, in the father's younger days, had been with Savonarola and his disciples. The young Neri was a good-looking, unusually intelligent, artistic boy, irrepressibly gay, *trés farceur*, excellent company, and never so pressed for time that he could not give friends another couple of hours. It seemed an agreeable anarchy of a life with this lad who would say "No" to nothing except to sin—for he was innocence itself—and who, though he yielded always, was somehow ever found to be leading. The innocence was no natural gift alone. When Philip Neri came to Rome it was not with any idea of a career or a profession, but as one mysteriously led by God for purposes not yet made clear, except to live every day as God willed and to trust to God alone. For years he was little more than a vagabond who lived in the streets, on the streets, and slept where night found him—what part of the night he did not give to prayer. His associates were all those with whom chance threw him, but men always, of all kinds, nobles, plebeians, students, painters, musicians, and, in large measure, the moral riffraff of the Renaissance capital.

He was already a force, someone to whom (as all this world knew) a man could open his heart, to whom a man found himself opening his heart before he knew what he was doing; a strength that never lectured, that communicated through sheer friendliness the attractiveness of the good in itself; a saint, but so rarely serious that this seemed incredible. Philip Neri was already something very evidently fashioned by grace, as well as by nature in an unusual mood, when a priest, Persiano Rosa, insisted with him that he be ordained (1550).

There is little to be told of the life that went on for the next forty-five years, of the bands who, in each generation, continued to follow the leader through the Roman streets in these expeditions, half pilgrimage, half picnic, to one shrine or another; of the meetings for prayer, extempore prayer and extempore sermons, which might also be extempore lectures, given at the bidding of the leader, with music and stories as diversions; Mass, of course, and the sacraments, very, very frequently; direction through a discernment beyond the possibility of the natural, discernment of desires and inhibitions; conversions from which there was never any relapse; the saint in his room by the little church in the Via de Monserrato, the door never closed, a whole world passing through it day and night; the mysticism of the saint's own Mass when, after the Consecration, the server would leave, locking the door, not to return for an hour or so; there is little but this, and of organisation just nothing. But gradually the grandees of the Curia were caught, like all the rest, and presently from among Philip Neri's disciples there were cardinals, not a few, and popes, Gregory XIV certainly, and Clement VIII and Leo XI. And the *doctrina* below it all and supporting it? The Gospel merely, the traditional axioms, the traditional sacraments, humility, obedience, charity, submission when trials came—and is there need to speak of the opposition, of misrepresentation in the early years from the vested interests of professional

ecclesiasticism? Nor is it all improvisation, with the leader.
Throughout the saint's life the Dominican attachment is
evident, the contact with the friars, the never-ending study of
St. Thomas, the mystical relation with the Florentine Dominican whom he never saw, St. Catherine de Ricci.

After a hundred years of continuous activity, what first had
shown in St. Catherine of Genoa and the Oratories of the
Divine Love is finally conquering in the most hardened hearts
of all. But with the thought of conversions we come to the
limits of the historian's field. Not to his skills does the ultimate
truth reveal itself.

ii *"Bloody Mary" and "Good Queen Bess"*

By the time that Pius IV confirmed the work of the Council
of Trent, England had been definitely and finally linked with
the Reformation by the action of its government. The death
of King Edward VI, July 6, 1553, found the country completely "Reformed," so far as laws could do this; the basis of
the new arrangement being the unique English doctrine that
kings are, by God's appointment, the heads of the Church of
Christ within their own realms, and the oath to the king as
"Supreme Head of the Church after God" which every in-
habitant had to swear on reaching the age of fourteen—which
beginning and foundation went back now nineteen years.

King Edward VI's heir, his sister Mary, was notoriously a
most zealous Catholic, who had defied her brother's ministers
to do their worst when she refused to allow the new Communion Service to be used in her chapel and persisted in having the Mass said. The ambition of the chief of the council,
John Dudley, Duke of Northumberland since 1552 and the
real ruler of England, now set up in opposition to Mary the
claims of her cousin, the Lady Jane Dudley, whose marriage
to one of his sons he had just brought about. Mary's energy
and the national detestation of the tyrant Dudley ended this
tragic farce in nine days. Among its most zealous promoters,
while it lasted, had been sundry of the leading Reformers,
especially the Bishop of London, Nicholas Ridley, who had
preached at Paul's Cross that neither Mary nor Henry VIII's
other daughter, Elizabeth, could reign for that they were both
of them bastards—an insult from the brethren which Elizabeth never forgot and never forgave. Cranmer, the Archbishop
of Canterbury, had gone no further than to set his signa-

ture, as a member of the council, to the treasonable documents setting up Jane and summoning Mary to surrender.

London, at this time, was as plagued with Protestant fanatics as Paris had been twenty years before. The queen had barely taken possession of her capital when the outrages began, attempts to murder priests preaching once more Catholic doctrine or saying Mass, shows in mockery of the Mass, manifestoes calling on Israel to rise, and the like. The better-class Protestants left the country, with as many of the clergy who had "reformed" as could go, finding new homes in all the main continental centres of the Reformation, Strasbourg, Zürich, and Geneva, but not in Wittenberg—being, in fact, chased away from the Lutheran holy land, where they were held in as much detestation as the Papists, because of their doctrine of the Eucharist. In these towns they settled down, training the students among their clergy for the coming day when England would again be open to them, fighting not a little among themselves over rites, managing their affairs much as the churches called Congregational were to do in later generations, and utterly undisturbed by such features of their religious life as the absence of episcopal jurisdiction among them, of the possibility of episcopal ordinations or of the rite of confirmation. Those who could write gave Mary's government the benefit, in tracts that urged the godly to resist, to revel, and even to murder the idolatrous bastard.

For some time there was little to resist, except the restored Catholic worship, decreed by Mary's first Parliament in the autumn of 1553, a restoration which, as might be expected, after no more than four years of the new rite (and only a few months of the newest), met with no opposition save from the half-crazed who saw Antichrist everywhere outside their own particular solution. Soon there were to be a certain number of the Reformed party in gaol, for causes connected with religion; and to the scandal of the brethren without, there were doctrinal feuds between the confessors. Bishop Ridley's reconciliation with Bishop Hooper was a minor miracle.

This is not written as though to suggest, by implied contrast, that all was well spiritually with the queen's party. Almost nothing was well with them, save the repentance of highly placed apostates who for twenty years or so had sworn a denial that the papal authority was divinely founded while, in their hearts, they still believed this to be true.

If Mary had had the powers of the King of France she would

have annulled the whole of the religious legislation of the last two reigns on the day she took possession of her throne. But acts of Parliament can be repealed only by other acts of Parliament. And when the Parliament elected in the fall of 1553 met, while there was no real difficulty about securing a majority for the restoration of the Mass, there were ominous signs that members were not so friendly to the proposal to "bring back the pope." For months yet to come Mary was in the curious position of being personally recognised by the pope as a Catholic queen, while in law she was the ruler of a people to whom she was the supreme head of the Church of Christ and who had sworn oaths repudiating as a fraud the pope's claim to that same authority.

How far there really need have been this extraordinary delay, one may doubt. Our knowledge of the detailed history of these months comes, in large measure, from the correspondence of rival ambassadors at Mary's court, from France and from the emperor, who were not only deadly enemies but neither of them interested really in Mary or in the Catholic Church.

Mary's life, from the day when Henry VIII announced to her mother that he did not believe she was his wife—when Mary was a child of eleven—down to the day ten years later when, after the death of her mother, he reduced her to signing an acknowledgement that she too did not believe it, was such that it is marvellous the adolescent girl came out of it with her reason. That these terrible years took their toll in physical and emotional ailments that were permanent is matter of history. At thirty-seven she was already ageing.

From the moment the news came that she was the queen, Mary needed nothing so much as a man she could trust. It was to be her sister's predicament five years later. There was not a man in the council Mary met who had not shared in the plot to dethrone her. There was not one on whose word, on whose very oath, any sensible man would have relied for a moment. And Mary was not, of course, taken in. Nor was she ever able to find any better men, possessed of real ability—Gardiner excepted; and he had been a principal agent in the tragedy of her life.

Across the seas was that first cousin whom she had never seen since childhood, the emperor, the gallant defender (to Mary) of her mother in the divorce affair—a Charles V seen through the passionate devotion to Catherine of his ambassador Chapuys. It was on Charles' advice, and taking his word that what she did was well, that Mary had signed all that Cromwell put before her in 1536. He had later intervened, with effective threats, when Dudley and the rest had thought to force the new religion on her. In the recent crisis he had been less helpful. The embassy he had sent over, anticipating that Edward was about to die, had been instructed to recommend caution to Mary, submission, and caution again: her cause was now hopeless, the emperor thought, and he was anxious she should not make an enemy for life of the new régime. He did not, of course, understand England, though to deal with bad men and rascally politicians had been his lifetime's occupation. But he might have recalled the woman whose blood he and Mary shared, Isabella. Mary, despite the ambassadors, acted and came through; to present, in Charles' eyes, problems no less acute.

Let us not blame Charles too readily. It is August 1553; he is at Brussels, barely a year away from that hasty flight from Innsbruck over the Brenner that followed Maurice's victory at Reutte, and the news of Maurice's death is not yet a month old. The emperor is only fifty-three, but he has suddenly aged. The first question is Mary's marriage, he says very truly; and because he feels at the end of things he sets aside his first idea, to propose himself as her husband. Instead he thinks of Philip, his son, now twenty-six and ruling Spain during these last seven years that he has been absent.

This section of my book may seem to have left the Reformation for the tangle of general English history. But the emperor's anxiety that Mary should seem to herself really to choose for herself when she chose Philip, set him to keep out, at all costs, the one man who might claim from him the first place in the queen's confidence. This was her other cousin, Reginald Pole, the son of her mother's closest friend, who because of that friendship (very largely) her father had sent to the block; also fifty-three years of age and also elderly, and lately, of course, the legate presiding at Trent. Pole's word to the queen will be not to marry, and to trust herself as an Englishwoman to her people; and it is also his principle that the best thing to do, always, is the right thing—and therefore, for Mary, to proclaim the whole Catholic faith directly and trust in God alone. And there are people in London to say that if only Pole were home the whole country would support him.

There is one difficulty about keeping this formidable rival out of England that seems insuperable. Within a matter of hours of the news reaching Rome that Mary really was queen the pope—Julius III—had commissioned Pole as legate, with the widest powers, to go to England and do all that could be done to restore the Catholic religion there. Such was the skill of Charles that the difficulty yielded to his first touch. It was not until October 1554 that Pole reached England.

And by that time Mary was safely married to Philip and a good part of her subjects alienated for ever. And only now was it found possible to steer through Parliament to repeal of all the laws of Henry VIII that set the English sovereign in the place created by God for the popes.

Mary reigned for five years and four months only (July 1553–November 1558). She had been queen a year when her marriage took place. Another year and, the Peace of Augsburg signed, Philip left her for the business of his father's several abdications (October 1555, February 1556). It proved to be the end of their married life. In November 1555 the queen lost her one strong advisor who was genuinely a Catholic, Stephen Gardiner. In August 1556 war broke out between Philip, as King of Spain, and the pope, Paul IV—Carafa—in which Philip was not the aggressor. In January 1557 the King of France, the pope's ally, declared war on Spain, and in April Paul IV cancelled Pole's appointment as legate—he was to return to Rome, where the Inquisition was beginning an enquiry as to whether he was not a heretic. In June, that same year, England declared war on France, and though the Spaniards won a great victory at St. Quentin on August 7, the French, in January 1558, took Calais, the last remnant of the English possessions in France. From that blow the queen never recovered, and after a long dragging illness she died, November 17, 1558. On that same day, at Lambeth, just across the river from St. James', Pole died too. Such is the political background against which we must set the only thing for which Mary is ever remembered, the repression of heresy which brought 273 of her subjects to the stake between February 1555 and November 1558.

The Marian Persecution: here is a subject around which the ground is still hot for miles. We can still read in the latest history that "Gardiner and Bonner . . . went to it with a will," and of "the fires of Smithfield and the like places all over Southern England"—this in a history utterly devoid of religious prejudice. And merely to analyse the statistics can be held, on the other hand, an apologia for the horrors, unless one writes as though 1557 were 1957.

Of the 273, fifty-one were women; there were five bishops, among them Cranmer, sixteen other clergy; nine are listed as gentlemen; the rest were peasants and labourers. And all this was done in a country where the Catholic religion had ceased to exist, by a national consent, for a good twenty years before the executions began, the judges being, to a man, men who had apostatised, or had appeared to apostatise, through all that period. Again, we know no more than a kind of ledger entry about 169 of the 273: neither what they were, what the heresies were of which they are accused, nor how they came to be arrested, nor how they were tried. And the principal source of our knowledge is an industrious contemporary, a man in his forties at the time of the burnings, for whom all he could find was valuable material as confirming the rightness of the judgment of such as himself that the Catholic Church was the Church of Antichrist. The great bulk of the victims, 235 out of 273, were put to death in London and in the neighbouring counties; Essex, Kent, and Sussex particularly.

There had never been anything like this before in England; there has never been anything like it since, except the executions for witchcraft in the next two generations.[5] Nor did these amount to an average of seventy executions a year.

But the picture of Mary as a gloomy bigot, consoling herself for the disappointments of her life by the thought of the pleasure she occasioned Almighty God each time a heretic was burned, is legend.

It needs to be remembered—and this may be as shocking to the reader as the fact of the executions—that the "heretic," to all sects or churches, at that time, was simply a criminal, rightly treated as we treat wilful murderers. There is scarcely one of the leading Reformers who would not agree to that proposition. Their case against Mary was not: How horrible to burn heretics, but: How wicked to treat as heretics the followers of the Gospel. This is not apologetic—it is history; the reconstruction, from the sources, of the mentality of the past. Heresy was a fact which the Elizabethan Settlement of the national religion in 1559 could not ignore. The statutes

[5] That is, in England down to 1604. In Scotland, 1560–1600 (then Calvinist), some 8,000 women were burnt as witches—the total population was around 600,000.

about burning heretics, revived under Mary, were indeed repealed by Elizabeth. And her statute enacted a definition of
heresy that made life safe for all who believed in the Trinity
and the Incarnation. But the statute left intact that heresy
was, at common law, an offence punishable by death. An
English Servetus could have been burned under Elizabeth,
and, in fact, in 1589 she burned an Arian.[6]

Queen Mary Tudor can be described by the historian of
today[7] as "personally gentle and inclined to mercy," despite
experiences which "ought to have turned her into a fearsome
instrument of hatred and vengeance. She was also sensible and
generous—altogether of a better character than was common
in her family." But she was no administrator, she was badly
served, and the reign was one long disaster, in which the drift
towards the brink, perceptible since Cromwell disappeared,
continued steadily. One of the claims the new régime would
have upon the ordinary man was that the country was once
more being governed.

There was one matter, however, in which Mary's brief reign
was far from an ineffectual failure. It gave the Catholics who
were conscientious—I speak of the leaders, clerical and lay—
a second chance. When the new assault is delivered, under
Elizabeth, there is no repetition of the tame, universal surrender of 1534. The story of that *résistance* does not belong to
this book. But the pioneers who led it were men formed anew
during the breathing space of Mary's reign. With the general
acknowledgement, then made even publicly, on the part of
such bishops as Stephen Gardiner and Edmund Bonner, that
their acceptance of the royal supremacy, and the régime based
on it, as the true religion of Christ had been feigned—a lie
told in order to escape what befell Fisher and More—there
disappeared the party seemingly contented to abjure the pope
provided the Mass was retained.

The effect upon religion in England of the succession to
Mary Tudor of her sister Elizabeth can be stated, with substantial accuracy, very simply: the restoration of all that Henry
VIII and Edward VI had accomplished. But Protestantism
did not, upon that November 17, 1558, displace Catholicism
as the night succeeds the day, or the day the night. There fol-

[6] It was not until 1679 that the death penalty for heresy was abolished, by an act of Parliament of Charles II.

[7] G. R. Elton, *England under the Tudors* (1955), p. 214.

lowed months of continuous anxiety for the new ruler, which lasted until the consecration of Dr. Matthew Parker as Archbishop of Canterbury, December 17, 1559.

The new sovereign, the child of Henry's union with Anne Boleyn, was just past her twenty-fifth birthday. In blood Elizabeth was the most purely English of all the English sovereigns—a great contrast to the half-Spaniard who had just died. She had never, since her early childhood—so far as we know—had any religious formation but what was favourable to the Reformation ideas, speaking generally. During her sister's reign she had gone through the form of living like a Catholic. What her own personal ideas were about religious dogma is a secret none has ever penetrated. In such a matter, above all, was she the daughter of the man who would burn his cap if he felt it knew his thoughts. Like many another, it may be hazarded, she believed in God and had a religion of her own, making use of the forms around her as it suited her own ideas. Never was she anything but anti-papal; and never did she for a moment show any sympathy for those forms of the Reformed religion which gave anyone the right to look into his neighbour's soul. Of that horror of the pope as Antichrist, and of the Mass as blasphemy—the two leading propaganda themes of "the queen's religion" in the coming years—Elizabeth had not a trace. About nothing was she fanatical, except the obedience and reverence due to herself, separated by her position and set apart from all mortal men save other sovereign princes. She had a most lucid intelligence, trained by the best education her time could give. She had a will of steel and a real she-devil's temper. And, having lived since her sixteenth year in close proximity to the block, stained with the blood of more than one of her near kinsfolk and associates, Elizabeth had learned to defend herself: in an age when these abounded she was a most consummate and successful liar.

The new queen seems not to have had the faintest anxiety about her own position, from the beginning. Within the week she was securing a prompter obedience than ever Mary had been given, and people were recalling the time when her father ruled. What were her anxieties? Not, certainly, whether her advisors were competent; Sir William Cecil, first of all, with five or six years of administrative experience in the heart of the government, caution itself, a very paragon of methodical industry; his brother-in-law, the lawyer Nicholas Bacon; and the financial wizard of the day, Sir Thomas Gresham. All these had something else in common with the queen—they were *not* Catholics. And this was something the sovereign shared with all her council, save those brought in by Mary and now slowly discarded.

One uncertainty was how much change the country would stand at the first move. Another was the possible reaction of foreign powers—all of them still Catholic powers. Not the pope perhaps, Paul IV, broken by the fiasco of the war against Spain and by the terrible revelation that the cardinal-nephew was one of the great blackguards of the day. But what of the French, with whom a peace was in negotiation but whose king had bidden his daughter-in-law, the young Queen of Scots, married to the Dauphin, to set up the arms of England on Mary's death, proclaiming herself Mary's true successor? What of the King of Spain, who had just ceased to be King of England (or the Queen of England's husband)? What of the power of these princes to intrigue with those whom the changes would antagonise? Elizabeth knew all this well from personal experience. This same King of France, only five years before, had intrigued in this way, and all to set Elizabeth on her sister's throne. And with the result that a formidable rebellion had been within an ace of doing the trick. The anxieties of November and December 1558 were far from childish. Never, certainly, was England more likely to lie at the proud foot of a conqueror should one of these princes choose to venture, and manage to survive the hazards of the Channel.

Mercifully, for the plans of Elizabeth, the energies of Spain and France were directed at this moment to making a peace. Had either of them moved on England, the other must—in theory—have moved to defend it. Actually, the two years' war had exhausted both. France, within three years, was to begin the thirty years' tragedy of the Wars of Religion. Spain had just received as its sovereign the man whose genius for over-long consideration of the problem before him none has ever exceeded. Before the weaknesses which thus crippled Spain and France for the next generation, the most political-minded of popes could be no more than the "poor chaplain" that one of the Queen's advisors in 1558 described him.

It had taken Henry VIII nearly five years of manoeuvring, propaganda, and pressure to secure from Parliament the laws which built up the new religious edifice in which his rôle was so singularly like that of a local pope; and Edward VI's guardians had spent another five years replacing the traditional doctrines and rites with the latest from the Reformation studios. All this Mary had torn down in two great repealing statutes, in 1553 and 1554. How should Elizabeth now go to work? Very simply, in a single act she repealed the Marian statutes and revived almost the whole of the Reformation laws of Henry VIII and Edward VI. And in another act she revived the Protestant liturgy of Edward VI. But to get these acts through Parliament was far from simple. It took nearly the whole of four months, from January 25, 1559, to May 8. As to the reasons for the delay, historians can still do no more than conjecture; details of the debates, the parliamentary time-table, itself, are lost. We have references to the long-drawn-out battle in the correspondence of various foreign ambassadors, and in the correspondence of Reformers now returned to London with their erstwhile hosts of Strasbourg and Zürich; we have references in later controversial exchanges between Catholic and Protestant divines. And we have the statutes as they emerged—not the printed statutes only, but the parchment which actually lay on the table of the house that was debating it, from the erasures in which the lawyer-historian whose account is still the most masterly of all has, with the lightest of humour, made a wealth of suggestive criticisms.

The controversies between scholars about the events of these crucial four months I must pass over, merely drawing attention to the important fact that this was a triangular fight. There were the Catholics, whose religious rites were about to be proscribed; there were the Protestants; and there was the queen. For the first time the Reformation was about to find itself facing a protector and patron who was really powerful —not the senate of some city-republic of less than ten thousand people, nor a princeling like the Elector of Saxony, powerful only because there were so many scores of princes less important than himself in that truly "ramshackle" affair, the Holy Roman Empire. The English state was something of a different order, and with the intelligent, imperious Elizabeth in the first flush of possession, a Baal before which all but the stoutest would bow down instinctively.

If there were any Catholics who were uncertain what was in store for Mary's work of restoration, their doubts were speedily resolved. The new queen, the day after her accession, did indeed issue a proclamation forbidding anyone to introduce changes into the order now established, but two days later still—Sunday, November 20—the sermon at Paul's Cross was preached by Dr. William Bill, one of Elizabeth's chaplains, a well-known Edwardian divine who had officially approved Cranmer's draft of articles six years before this. On November 27 the Bishop of Chichester, John Christopherson, replied to him, was summoned before the council, and put under house arrest. Meanwhile, in the palace the Mass was said as usual and Elizabeth assisted at it as Mary had done. On December 5 the writs summoning the new Parliament (to meet on January 23) were sent out. Nine days later Mary was buried at Westminster, and again a bishop was in trouble. This time it was John White, Bishop of Winchester, and his offence was his praise of the dead queen for her deliverance of England from the yoke of the heretics, and his blunt warning that dangers once more threatened. "The wolves are coming out of Geneva," he said, referring to the Marian exiles now finding their way back to England.

On Christmas Day, Elizabeth, after five weeks of Catholic appearances, gave at last an unmistakable sign of her Protestant intentions. To the Bishop of Carlisle, Owen Oglethorpe, as he was vesting to say, or to sing, the Mass in her chapel, the queen sent word that he was not to elevate the Blessed Sacrament after the Consecration. Oglethorpe was by no means one of the Hildebrands. He had wavered under Edward VI, not in his belief, but in fidelity to it; and this, it would seem, simply through fear of losing his university preferment. However, he now made a stand, making the reply (it is said) that in this matter the queen had no authority to command him. The Mass began with Elizabeth present, but after the Gospel she rose and left the chapel. On her first Christmas Day as queen, Elizabeth had, as Catholics say, "missed Mass."

Two days after this a second proclamation appeared. It was more stringent than the first, though its purpose was the same —to make it clear that the government would not tolerate any initiative in the way of reforms on the part of private individuals. Parliament had been summoned, and it was for Parliament to decide about these matters. Let no man presume, meanwhile, to decide for himself. The proclamation itself, however, made some changes—the Epistle and the Gospel at Mass were to be read in English; also, all sermons were forbidden. The proclamation was addressed, in the first place, to the clergy dispossessed by Mary; it was they who were explicitly forbidden to clamber into their old pulpits; the government desired nothing less, at this moment, than that they should loose upon the capital (that was not obviously yearning for it) a flood of the wild, meaningless hate which had been the staple of their propaganda for twenty years.

The Reformers were far from pleased: were definitely uneasy, indeed, as their correspondence shows. Their anxiety is a faint first sign of what was to be a leading feature of English life for another hundred years—conflict between the gospel-men's ideal of a Reformation that should root out the traditional religion as thoroughly as at Zürich or Geneva, and the government's decision that the movement had gone far enough, that whatever happened from now on would depend on its initiative and remain under its control. To obey the government, the first duty of every good subject—and in the organisation of religious life as in all else: the ideal was no invention of Elizabeth, nor peculiar to England. It was everywhere the unstated axiomatic common sense of the business of rulership. If theologians had achieved so much, so easily, in the reign of Edward VI, it was only because the government had given them a free hand, the politicians as such being indifferent to the details and leaving it to the archbishop —to Cranmer—as to the professional competent to deal with them. But from henceforth no man's private judgment, whatever his rank or office, was to be given such scope. There was to be a law, made, like all English law, in Parliament; and the designated officials—clerical or lay—would obediently administer the law and the subjects submit to their administration, with, always, recourse to the crown as the remedy when administration was thought to be unjust.

The general election began on the day following this proclamation, and on Sunday, January 15, 1559, the queen was crowned. Once again there was a liturgical crisis, and a scene. By this time, after two months of "incident," the bishops were in no doubt about the queen's intentions. The Church as it had been for a thousand years—doctrine, discipline, rites—was to go, and in its place they were to see restored something resembling what had obtained between 1534 and 1553. At the coronation the sovereign swears to protect and defend the Church in all its rights—how could the bishop who crowned Elizabeth take from her, or administer to her, an oath which, if it meant anything, was a pledge on her part to destroy what the rite supposed she was pledging herself to defend? Show, "form," mockery—politic, and therefore of course permissible at all times, "understandable"; but mockery, and calling on God to back up mockery, making God partner in a perjury; Elizabeth herself faced Cranmer's dilemma of 1533 all over again. And she demurred. It is supposedly Cecil who was her casuist and persuaded her to go through with the "form."

But the bishops had resolved that the queen should not be given the chance. The details are obscure. To how many of them pressure was applied—whether pressure was indeed applied—we do not know. We know their first resolution. We know that Oglethorpe then consented to act, that he had not with him his episcopal vestments—*pontificalia*—and that the government asked Bonner to lend his; that the Mass (which in the English practice followed the crowning) was not sung by the consecrating bishop, but by one of the queen's chaplains, a married priest, Dr. George Carew; and that is all. One account says that the queen withdrew after the coronation to her "traverse"—a half-screened gallery from which she could see but not be seen. Apparently she did not receive Holy Communion, the only sovereign, except William Rufus, to be crowned without.

Parliament met on January 25. It was no doubt fairly representative of the classes who brought about the election of members of Parliament, as most sixteenth-century parliaments were. That a Catholic majority was jockeyed out of its legitimate influence by the Protestant government's unscrupulous intrigues and pressures is mere assertion and provokes the question: What is meant by "a Catholic majority," and what was the quality of its Catholicism?

England in 1559 was undoubtedly not a Protestant country —not, by any means, a country where the mass of the inhabitants, or even an appreciable proportion of them, had gone over to the Reformation in conscientious conviction that its theological solutions were true. It was not a country "yearning for the light," as used to be said. But in the class which then elected the mass of the House of Commons there was a very high proportion with which, for a good thirty years now, religion had been a secondary consideration—the men, for example, who would have fought to the last Mary's restoration of Catholicism had it involved any obligation to restore the abbey lands which they held. There were also in this Parliament Catholics of another sort, who fought the government from love of what it proposed to destroy. And there was a small band of Protestants, no less conscientious, and no less hostile to the government's claim to have the last word in deciding the country's religion: returned exiles among them, who had enjoyed the unusual experience, for the sixteenth century, of a life where they worshipped God as they chose without the fear of any punishment except the displeasure of their equals.

The principal statutes of this Parliament are the two known as the Elizabethan Acts of Supremacy and Uniformity. In their parliamentary history there are three stages: (*i*) February 9–28, (*ii*) March 14–24, (*iii*) April 3–29. On February 9 a bill appeared in the Commons of which we know nothing except its purpose, to repudiate the papal supremacy over religion in England. It was debated for three days (February 13, 14, 15) and then committed to Sir Francis Knollys and Sir Antony Cook for revision. The first of these was married to a first cousin of the queen on the Boleyn side; the second was the father-in-law of both Cecil and Nicholas Bacon. Both were Protestants of the type which, in later years, it became fashionable to call Puritans; both had spent Mary's reign in exile. What they did to the bill is not known, but it reappeared in the House on February 21,[8] and as revised it was passed (Saturday) February 25, described, in the *Journals* of the House of Commons, as "the Bill for Supremacy of the Churches of England and Ireland, and abolishing of the Bishop of Rome." It appeared in the Lords, February 28, and we hear no more of it then until March 13.

The Spanish ambassador, Feria, is authority for the statement that the bill only passed in the Commons thanks to some "management" (my own word) on the part of Cecil. The bill, according to the same letter, provided an oath to the queen as supreme in religious affairs which all should take under pain of high treason.

On the day when the bill first passed the Lords something else happened. The Lower House of Convocation made a strong protest denying that the Parliament has any "authority to treat of or to define whatever concerns the faith, the sacraments and ecclesiastical discipline." These matters belong only "to the pastors of the Church, whom the Holy Ghost has placed in the Church of God for this purpose, and not to laymen." That a doctrine is an innovation, they say, has from all time been regarded as proof that it is false. Finally they sol-

---

[8] According to one interpretation of the *Journals* of the House of Commons this bill of February 21 is a new bill.

emnly profess their faith in transubstantiation, in the doctrine that the Mass is a true propitiatory sacrifice in which Christ is offered, for the living and the dead; that to the pope, because he is the successor of St. Peter, belongs the supreme power over the Church of Christ in this world. This was presented to the bishops, and by their president, Edmund Bonner, the Bishop of London, was handed to Sir Nicholas Bacon, Lord Keeper of the Great Seal. No reply, or acknowledgement of it, was made. But it was a fact before the minds of all as, in the fortnight about which the *Journals* say nothing, the bishops fought the government in the House of Lords—a piece of information we owe to the envoy of the Duke of Mantua. He also reveals that the ban on controversial preaching had now been removed, and the violent sermons against the pope were being delivered everywhere by the court preachers. "We are thundering in pulpits, especially before our queen . . . that the pope is Antichrist," said one whom Elizabeth was shortly to make a bishop.

On March 13 the bill was made over for revision to a committee of fifteen—two bishops, seven pro-Catholic lords, and six pro-Reform lords. Again we know no details except what a foreign ambassador wrote home to his government, to the effect that the bill restored the Communion Service of Edward VI and that the Catholics had brought about the defeat of this part of the project. On March 18 the revised bill passed its third reading in the Lords, as a Supremacy Bill pure and simple, so it would seem, twelve voting against it; namely, the Earl of Shrewsbury, Viscount Montague, the Abbot of Westminster, and nine bishops.[9] For the bill were thirty-five lay lords, present and voting. It was in these debates that the Archbishop of York, Nicholas Heath,[10] and the Bishop of

[9] There were 26 sees in England and Wales, each represented in the House of Lords. Why did only nine bishops register their vote? To begin with, when this Parliament assembled, January 25, 1559, there were 10 sees vacant. Between May 21, 1558, and January 2, 1559, no fewer than eight bishops died: two other sees had fallen vacant in 1557. Of the seven bishops alive and not present on March 18, 1559, two had not been summoned to the Parliament (Tunstall and Goldwell); one (Thirlby) was away at Cateau-Cambrésis, the queen's ambassador at the peace conference; three had been ill for months and unable to travel (Bourne, Morgan, and David Poole); Watson of Lincoln, one of the leaders in the fight, had fallen suddenly ill.

[10] Lord chancellor 1555–58, who, as such, had proclaimed Elizabeth's accession.

Chester, Cuthbert Scott, made the great speeches which (with Abbot Feckenham's speech at a later stage) are the sole oratorical relics of this long parliamentary fight.

The bill as the Lords had amended it now went back to the Commons, who reinserted what the Lords' revising committee had deleted and returned it thus to the Lords. And the Lords, this time, passed it without any change, three readings (it seems) in one day, Wednesday, March 22. Only the royal assent was needed, and in one act of Parliament the pope's authority would have been destroyed, the crown put in its place, and the Mass abolished. It was now Holy Week; the Easter recess was at hand. It was arranged that on the Friday, Good Friday, March 24, the queen should give the royal assent and Parliament be dissolved. Instead of that, on March 24 the Parliament was merely adjourned, to meet again on April 3, the Monday in Low Week. And a week after the reassembly the Commons took up once more this business of the settlement of religion. It is with the puzzle of this extraordinary change of mind between the Wednesday and the Friday of Holy Week, about a government bill which had at last been got through all its stages, that the learned studies of Professor Neale deal, which have caused such interest in recent years.

What now happened on Monday, April 10, was that Cecil told the House of Commons that the queen, out of humility, did not wish to be styled head of the Church, while thanking members for their good will, and they were ordered to devise some other way of expressing her supremacy over religion. The none-too-pleased majority complained, it seems, that the secretary should come to them daily with new and contradictory proposals; so the Spanish ambassador, once more.

The real business was the introduction of a new bill to establish the supremacy. It went through the Commons without incident, so far as we know, and on Saturday, April 15, it was read in the Lords, who, on the seventeenth, made it over to a committee of fifteen—two bishops, six Catholic peers, seven pro-Reformers. They worked at it for nine days; the Lords passed it on the twenty-sixth—by what votes, we do not know. A little more is known about the "Bill for Uniformity of Common Prayer and the Administration of the Sacraments," which made its appearance in the Commons on April 18 and had passed through its various stages by the twentieth. In the Lords, too, it had a swift passage (April 26, 27, 29). But we have the speeches against it of the Bishop of Chester and of the Abbot of Westminster. We also know that it passed its final stage—this bill that abolished the Mass—by three votes only, there voting against it the nine bishops free to vote (two were by now in prison) and nine lay lords.[11]

On May 8 both bills received the royal assent. The act about worship was to come into force on June 24 next, the Feast of St. John the Baptist. Once again the sovereign was supreme head of the Church—even though the statute said no more than "Supreme Governor of this realm . . . as well in all spiritual . . . causes as temporal." Once again there was an oath testifying to one's acceptance of this, and that no foreign prelate has any spiritual jurisdiction in the realm, and that one does "utterly renounce and forsake all foreign jurisdictions." Once again there are penalties for denying the royal supremacy and for refusing to take the oath. A further statute of 1563 will extend the obligation to take the oath and will sharpen the penalties. From that date all candidates for holy orders in the Church of England—deacons, priests, bishops— took this oath as part of the ordination ceremony: it was of obligation for all in Holy Orders, all members of the House of Commons, all who took degrees at a university, all officers of the crown, all judges, justices of the peace, mayors, and all who at the moment were in office—all must take the oath or *ipso facto* lose their appointment. As to defending, or up-holding in writing, printing, preaching, teaching, or by express words or act, the spiritual jurisdiction of the pope, for this on a first conviction the offender is to lose all his property; on a second, to be imprisoned for life; on a third, to be put to death as a traitor. In this very first statute of the reign there is a death sentence for the crime of saying that the pope is the head of the Church of Christ.

As to the second statute, it forbids the use of any other form of public prayer, or of administering sacraments, but that which is contained in the Prayer Book authorised by

---

[11] These nine were the Marquis of Winchester (the lord treasurer, and by rank the queen's principal minister), the Earl of Shrewsbury, Viscount Montague, and the Lords Morley, Sheffield, Dudley, Wharton, Rich, and North. Shrewsbury and Montague were the two lay lords who on March 18 had, with the ten prelates, voted against the supremacy. Winchester (*olim* Sir William Paulet), the oldest man so far in public life, born the year of Bosworth, 1485, was the expert who had played a leading part in remodelling the financial department of the administration. Rich was the one-time attorney general whose rascality More had denounced at his trial.

Parliament in 1552; whether in churches or in any other places. From the Litany there has been struck out the Cranmerian petition, "From the Tyranny of the Bishop of Rome and all his detestable enormities"; and the baldness of the (1552) form used in administering the Lord's Supper to the communicant is relieved by adding to this the form used in the Prayer Book of 1549. The penalties for clergy who use any other services rise, with the repetition of the convictions, from loss of one year's income and six months' imprisonment to deprivation together with imprisonment for life. Critics of the Book and those who make free of it in songs or rhymes or who interfere with the clergy carrying out the new rites or who persuade the clergy to use other rites are to be fined, progressively, 100 marks and 400 marks, and, on a third conviction, to lose all their moveable property and go to prison for life. Moreover, the legal obligation to attend service on Sundays and holy days, enacted in 1552, is revived, and for each non-attendance there is a fine of 12 pence, to be collected by the churchwardens of the parish and to go to the relief of the poor.[12] To encourage the bishops to enforce this act—i.e., to ferret out offenders and bring them to punishment—the statute enacted that, all laws to the contrary notwithstanding, they could make full use of their episcopal powers. One interesting omission from this regulation of public worship is that there is no provision in the Prayer Book for the coronation of kings, nor any allowance in the statute for the use of the books that contain such rites. Maybe there were to be no more such ceremonies? Cranmer certainly had thought the rite an idle show, as he made clear in his sermon at the crowning of Edward VI.

It can hardly have been the episcopate which had fought the bill tooth and nail, that the government had in mind when it thus licensed this wholehearted pursuit of offenders. Within three weeks of the royal assent to the Supremacy Act the new oath had been tendered to Bonner, and he had refused it. And as he refused, so did all. By the beginning of November 1559, all the English sees stood empty. "The spiritual juris-

---

12 There is a tendency to smile if this "trivial" fine is described as persecution. Yet one in three of the beneficed clergy (the parish priests, that is to say) drew only twice twelve pence a week as total income.

diction originated by St. Augustine, nearly a thousand years before, had come to an abrupt termination."

And while this was in process another task had to be carried through, to bring home to the seven or eight thousand parish clergy that they must never again say Mass and must pledge themselves to take the queen as their pope for the future—to whom, by virtue of a third statute of this same parliamentary session, they would, for the future, pay an annual tax of 10 per cent of their miserable incomes, and upon appointments to a benefice a tax called first-fruits: those annates about which the layman once waxed so wroth when bishops had to pay them to the pope of Rome. The most obvious means of carrying out this plan was a general visitation of the whole of the Church, after the precedents of 1536 and 1547, done simultaneously by six groups of royal commissioners: doctors of theology, doctors of the civil law, and the local gentry or peers, to whom Elizabeth granted "in our place full faculties in the Lord." Into the long tale of matters into which they are to enquire, and of all that they are sent to correct, there is inserted a discreet reference to the recent changes, the offence of "those who obstinately and peremptorily refuse to subscribe to the religion that has been established." There is no mention of the oath of supremacy in the commission, neither a command to tender it nor powers to do so—all in the greatest contrast to the commission by virtue of which the oath was offered to the bishops. Between June 24 and the end of August all these commissions had been started on their courses.

One of the most extraordinary lacunae in the documents of this period is the disappearance of all but one of the reports of these six commissions. The one which has survived is that for the province of York, the four sees of York, Durham, Carlisle, and Chester.[13] Here there were 968 parish churches. In 31 session days between August 22 and October 26, the commission sat in 24 different towns, to which the clergy of adjacent deaneries or archdeaconries were summoned. The record tells that 314 priests failed to appear. Also that 90 were deprived. This is all that we possess of the documents of the six visitations, except a collection of 1,804 signatures of priests accepting the new state of things, which came from the six sees of London, Norwich, Ely, Lincoln, Coventry and Lich-

[13] The following counties: Northumberland, Cumberland, Westmorland, Durham, Lancashire, Yorkshire, Cheshire, Nottingham.

field, Oxford: sees where the total of parishes reached 3,669. What happened in the 3,472 parishes of the other 12 sees of England, and in the 735 parishes of Wales, no one knows. We do know that the Reformers habitually spoke of all this mass of clergy with the greatest contempt, as to their education and as to their fitness to preach the new doctrines, to say nothing of their interest in these. And we know that for years to come, in every part of England, these clergy of pre-Elizabethan vintage were the chronic torment of the lives of the new bishops, as men it was impossible to interest, let alone to trust, in the task of turning the English into "good and devout Gospellers."

Would any of the zealous men who so earnestly worked and prayed for the downfall of the old religion in England have been seriously unhappy had there disappeared with it the whole idea of episcopal government? Exiles who would greatly have preferred a continuation at home of that liberty they had enjoyed in Frankfort, say? Some there certainly were of this mind, and anxious also for the legal establishment of the "disciple" whose presence, with Calvin, was almost a mark of the true Church. Whatever their desires, they were not to be consulted. The architects of the Elizabethan Settlement were laymen. They cast out the old despite the unanimous opposition of every one of its "constitutional organs." They installed the new, arranged exactly as they wished it. In the new the cleric was to serve, servant of the servants of God indeed! That story lies, however, with other books than this.

But although Elizabeth had determined there should be bishops, by November 1559 there was not one left to serve her.[14] Actually, since the first deprivations of May and June, the government had been actively choosing likely men for the vacant sees. There remained before it a twofold problem, first how to arrange that the formalities, of election and confirmation of the election, would meet the requirements of the statute about episcopal appointments just revived, and then where to find the bishops who would perform the rite of consecration. As to the rite, the traditional rite was forbidden by the recent statute that imposed the exclusive use of the Prayer Book of 1552, and no other rite was authorised; the ordinal of

14 Anthony Kitchin, Bishop of Llandaff, signed a promise not to work against the new arrangement; whether he took the oath is not known. He was not deprived, although he refused to consecrate Parker.

1552, so Cecil noted, "was not established by parliament." The seemingly insuperable difficulties about the formalities and the rite—i.e., the direct prohibition of penal statutes—were overcome by a unique royal act, a special clause in the queen's commission addressed to the consecrators, "Supplying, nevertheless, by our supreme regal authority" whatever is lacking of those things required by statute or by church law; which commission the government took care to have warranted as good by six doctors of the civil law, who signed their names to their opinion.

The government's first move was the consecration of its candidate for Canterbury—Dr. Matthew Parker, a one-time president of Corpus Christi College, Cambridge; in his younger days a chaplain to Anne Boleyn and, at fifty-four or fifty-five, a taciturn, enduring character, loyal, reliable, a disciplinarian; and a convinced Protestant to whom the "Genevan" fanaticism now to be fashionable was extremely repugnant. During the summer of 1559 commissions to consecrate him were made out to various bishops still in possession of their sees, to whom the supremacy oath had not yet been tendered. All refused—inevitably. For one thing, it was a serious offence to consecrate a bishop without a special authorisation from the pope. The very first words spoken in the ceremony by a Catholic bishop about to consecrate the elect are, "Has the apostolic mandate been received?" and the next, "Let it be read." For a Catholic bishop to consecrate one whom the pope has not appointed is tantamount to an act of schism. In the second place, Parker, in these bishops' eyes, was not of the same religion as themselves. On their part, it would have been a sacrilegious farce to go through the motions of handing on to a man spiritual powers which he himself did not believe existed, which he did not believe he could receive or the consecrating prelate confer. Only statesmen to whom these rites were a mere solemn formality, of the same kind as the president of a college fixing the new doctors' hoods at a commencement, could ever have thought of such a conjunction as papist and heretic so linked. No bishop in possession of his see would in 1559 consent, and presently all the sees were empty save one, Llandaff in Wales, and even here the bishop, a venerable ruin said to be in his nineties, refused. The government turned to a group of survivors of the episcopate of Henry VIII's and Edward VI's creation: to William Barlow, one-time Bishop of Bath and Wells;

John Hodgkin, one-time Suffragan (that is, assistant) Bishop of Bedford; John Scory, one-time Bishop of Chichester; and Miles Coverdale, one-time Bishop of Exeter. None of these had ever had any authorisation from Rome to become bishops. All had been, even before their promotion, active Reformers. The first two were appointed under Henry VIII and consecrated by the ancient rite of the Catholic *pontificale*. The others had been given their sees by Edward VI and consecrated according to the new rite of 1550. Barlow, the Elizabethan government had designed to fill the see of Chichester; Scory was to go to Hereford. Neither of the others was to be further used. On December 17, 1559, these four consecrated Matthew Parker in the chapel of the archbishop's palace at Lambeth, using the rite of Edward VI's Ordinal. And in the ensuing months Parker consecrated the other men whom the queen had chosen.

It is around the ceremony of December 17, 1559, that the complex controversy of the reality of Anglican orders has developed—a problem that is theological rather than historical, and no real concern of such a book as this. One, historical, element in that controversy was the question whether Barlow himself, bishop since 1536, had ever received episcopal consecration. The theological questions are whether Barlow conceived himself to be doing to and for Parker what Catholic bishops intend to do, and believe they are doing, for the priests whom they consecrate as bishops; whether what Barlow meant to do, and conceived himself to be doing, made any difference to the kind of effect his action was producing upon the soul of Matthew Parker; whether the rite used, taken in conjunction with the fact of Barlow's known disbelief that such a gift existed as Catholics conceived the episcopal character, could bring about in Parker's soul the changes meant to be brought about by the Catholic rite when used by a bishop who believed what it meant and himself meant to do all that the rite supposed.

By the end of 1562 all the sees but Oxford had been filled, and all was ready for the next session of Parliament—unthinkable with the bishops' benches untenanted—and therefore of Convocation also. The principal business of this first Convocation after the Settlement of 1559 was to sanction a kind of test of belief for all in Holy Orders. To prepare such a test had been one of the preoccupations of Cranmer in the last years of Edward VI, and only a month before the king died the archbishop had secured his authorisation for what he had produced —a list of forty-two propositions or, to use the word so favoured in the sixteenth century, Forty-two Articles of Religion. It was these Forty-two Articles fashioned by Cranmer that the Convocation of 1563 now revived. Changes were made; the number was reduced to thirty-nine and they were imposed as a test in this way: all future candidates for ordination were to declare their belief in them by signing them; all appointed to a parish were, on the first Sunday after taking possession, publicly, during the service, to read out the Thirty-nine Articles and to declare their acceptance of them. They are not a creed, but they are a statement of the position of the Church of England, at this date, in relation to the religion which these divines had once professed and to various other versions of the Reformation active everywhere. The articles were reimposed by Convocation in 1571, and in that same year they were imposed also by act of Parliament. With that statute we may, perhaps, consider that the "formative" period of the new Church of England ends.

What of the content of these Thirty-nine Articles? Confining our attention to the thirty-one which have reference to the controversies since 1517, fourteen are as Cranmer published them in 1553, fourteen have been modified, three are new. Seven of Cranmer's forty-two were discarded.[15] Holy Scripture, it is taught, contains all things necessary for salvation, and the fourteen deutero-canonical books, which the article names, are not sources of doctrine. The Church of Christ is not infallibly safeguarded from error in its teaching, although it has authority in controversies about faith. General councils, which can be assembled only at the commandment of princes, may err, and have erred, even in things pertaining to God. Every national church has authority to change those rites which are not divinely ordained.

Preaching, or ministry of the sacraments, by the self-appointed is condemned. The proof of a lawful minister is that he is called to this work by men who have public authority given to them in the congregation to call ministers into the Lord's vineyard. The bishops, priests, and deacons may marry. The ritual for their consecration or ordination set forth by

[15] The Thirty-nine Articles are the most accessible of all Reformation documents, for they are printed in every copy of the Book of Common Prayer.

Edward VI, and confirmed by Parliament at that time, is a sufficient rite, and it is in no way superstitious or ungodly. The Church has the power to excommunicate, and so long as the wrongdoer is not openly reconciled by penance and received back by the authorised judge, he is to be utterly avoided by the faithful. The chief government of clergy and laity, in all causes, belongs to the queen's majesty. Her power is not subject to any foreign jurisdiction. It is a slander to say that the queen is given the right to preach or to administer the sacraments, and the article repeats the disingenuous *Admonition to simple men*, of 1559, to the effect that the royal supremacy means no more than that the clergy are as much the queen's subjects as the laymen.

"The Bishop of Rome hath no jurisdiction in this realm of England."

The *Homilies* of Edward VI's time, now reimposed and completed by a second volume, are commended as containing good and wholesome doctrine. It is, on every point at issue, the pure doctrine of one or other of the Reformers. Transubstantiation is condemned as "repugnant to the plain words of Holy Scripture." The Sacrament is not to be worshipped. "The Cup of the Lord" is not to be denied to the laity, and "the sacrifices of Masses . . . [are] blasphemous fables and dangerous deceits." The wicked who receive Holy Communion do not receive Christ, but only the sign or sacrament.

As to sacraments in general, there are only two commanded by Christ our Lord in the Gospel—Baptism and the Supper of the Lord. The five others which are commonly called sacraments—Confirmation, Penance, Orders, Matrimony, and Extreme Unction—are partly misunderstandings of what the Apostles did, partly states of life. These two sacraments established in the Gospel are not mere tokens to the world that a man is a Christian. They are signs by which God brings about a strengthening of a Christian's faith in him. If the minister of the sacraments should chance to be an evil-living man, this in no way diminishes the grace that God gives.

There are eight articles on the related subjects of original sin, justification, good works, and predestination, the teaching of which is that of the Confession of Augsburg, very largely.

Finally, the articles deal with those Reformers and their followers whose private judgment about the Gospel in its social implications had roused general opposition from princes, Protestant as well as Catholic, the so-called Anabap-

tists. The articles declare, for example, that it is an accursed
theory which holds that whatever a man believes, whatever
the sect to which he adheres, he will be saved if he consci-
entiously lives according to its teaching; that it is lawful for
rulers to inflict the death penalty on heinous criminals, and
lawful for men to fight in the wars at the government's command; that riches and goods are not rightly to be held as common property; that the Christian religion does not forbid the
taking of oaths.

iii *John Knox*

When in the Convocation of 1563 the new bishops completed their work on the Articles of Religion and, by the nar-
row majority of one, the "Primitive" party received its first
check, Elizabeth had been four years on the throne. In all that
time her unpredictable wilfulness had been a source of continual anxiety to her chief advisors. If Elizabeth died unmar-
ried, what would happen to the settlement of religion? Who
would rule in her place? And in the autumn of 1562 the small-
pox brought the queen very near to death; so near that she
made a solemn protestation that her relations with Lord Robert Dudley—not yet Earl of Leicester—had been wholly innocent. Who, if she had died, would have reigned in her
place? If the last will and testament of Henry VIII were followed, it would have been the Lady Catherine Grey, sister of
the ill-fated Lady Jane, and now in the Tower for marrying
without the queen's consent. If the rules of inheritance by
descent had been followed, it would have been the young
Queen of Scots, just a year or so returned from France—whom
no one of the council, it seems, ever spoke of in the discussions that, privately, took place.

Elizabeth recovered, but the anxiety of the ministers persisted. Nothing so moved the queen's anger as their attempts
to discuss with her this question of the succession. Yet the
whole future of the country might turn on this, and the future
of the Protestant cause throughout the world—if the historians
are right who hold that a Catholic England, in the twenty
years following 1559, would have meant French victories over
the Protestants of France, and Spanish victories over the Protestants of the Low Countries in those years: the end of Protestantism outside Lutheran Germany. And there is a corollary
to this belief—"belief" because, after all, it is but one of the

"ifs" of history—namely, that England could not have remained Protestant after 1559 if Scotland had not, about that time, itself ceased to be Catholic. Scotland, by the time when Elizabeth was thought to be dying, in 1562, had ceased to be one of William Cecil's crucial worries; the Protestant cause in that country was now where it needed to be for the maintenance of his own achievement. The action of the new Catholic sovereign, aged twenty, of this newly Protestantised state would, of course, call for careful study. But the state had been successfully Protestantised, and Cecil had played a decisive part in this at a critical moment. The legal extinction of Catholicism wrought by the Scottish Parliament in 1560 was, in fact, Protestantism's last conquest of a Catholic country; the last—which was also, according to the historical theory just spoken of, the most important, the "crowning mercy," as that notable Protestant, Oliver Cromwell, was to say of one of his own victories.

It seems agreed that in the early years of the sixteenth century Scotland, a poor and very backward country, with a population of perhaps 500,000, offered one of the worst evidences of what the main weakness of Catholicism as a general religion could produce—the weakness, that is to say, of the churchmen's neglect of Catholic doctrine, ignorance of it, indifference to their ignorance, and of their assumption that the doctrine must somehow continue present to men's minds and function in their lives. What the general history of Scotland was in the years since the murder of King James I in 1437, Maitland has described in a brilliant passage[16] which defies summary, the tale of five kings successively cut off by violent deaths in their early manhood and leaving children as their heirs. This in a country still so primitive in its organisation that no king was ever truly independent of the nobles, but must contrive to rule by playing off one faction against another; where feuds were frequent and bloody; with the wild life of the Highland nobles amid their Gaelic-speaking clansmen, the scarcely less wild life of the nobles of the English border, the intervening territory where a few towns struggled with difficulty into a semblance of corporate influence—Edinburgh, the largest of them, and the king's capital, rising to no more than a population of 9,000.

[16] See the *Cambridge Modern History*, Vol. II, pp. 551–52.

Of the religious organisation, with its abbeys and friaries, its thousand or so parishes, and its hierarchy of thirteen bishops, the most important feature is that, for seventy years before the day when the week-old Mary Stewart succeeded her father, James V (1542), it had been entirely in the power of the king and his nobles. This James V, whose lax morals won him the name of "the Red Fox," had provided for five of his bastard sons by appointments to well-endowed abbeys—young lords never in Holy Orders and never meaning to receive them. The bishops were taken from the families powerful enough to dominate the see, and they were not a whit different in their lives from the other men of their house. Ladies of the same noble rank lived openly with them as their mistresses. Cardinal Beaton is reported to have had ten bastard children, and another bishop a dozen, each by a different mother. Nothing could describe more starkly this terrible state of things than the declaration of the synod of 1549, introducing some salutary laws of reform, the bishops then saying, "The two chief root-causes of our ills, which have provoked such trouble and given rise to so many heresies, are firstly, the corruption of morals and the profane impurity of the lives of ecclesiastics of all ranks, and secondly their crass ignorance of the rudiments of learning—of secular learning and the arts. It is from these two sources that many abuses have flowed."

These terrible facts are not of course the whole story. Then, as in our own hypocritical century, there were found courageous individuals to rise and rebuke the age. It is from the lips of good-living Catholics that the most stringent language comes about these sinners, and this in days long before these aberrations became part of the new preachers' stock in trade —which new preachers did not, of course, descend upon the country from another planet, but were themselves ex-Catholics, "hungry sheep," when not disgruntled shepherds, driven half out of their minds by a lifetime of seeing nothing but lip service to reform on the part of superiors "corrupted and content." But there was still sufficient confidence for Catholics to continue the work of pious foundations, not monasteries any longer but collegiate churches, to which were attached what we should call high schools. In the hundred years 1450–1550, fourteen of these were established—let us remember the exiguous scale of Scottish life—and in 1494 a bishop of most exemplary life, William Elphinstone (1431–

1514), founded the University of Aberdeen, and under his auspices the famous Aberdeen Breviary was printed in the opening years of the sixteenth century. Another remarkable prelate was Robert Reid, Bishop of the Orkneys, who died in 1558, as the first assaults on all he strove to repair were being organised. He too founded schools and left funds to the town of Edinburgh for the foundation of a school in the capital. The list is not too long, even when we add to it two abbots, Quintin Kennedy and Alexander Milne; and the last writer to publish works in the Scots version of the language the country shared with the English, Ninian Winzet, schoolmaster and priest and a model of Catholic candour in calling sin by its true name wherever he found it. The list of distinguished Catholics, in the fifty years before Knox and his political allies raised the whirlwind, is short, and, it has to be admitted, the scholars have paid more attention to the whirlwind than to the more arduous task of recovering the detail of the age in which the prophet was born and bred.

In no country was the first victory of the new religion more nearly a purely political affair than in Scotland. Would we expect that a country, *ex hypothesi* so morally rotten, would hear with wild enthusiasm that a new, most rigorous form of Christianity was now to be offered to it? Would the ordinary man be a man religiously inclined, in a country where for generations the clergy had been exemplars of every kind of loose-living and hypocrisy? Ready to stand by and see the said clergy dispossessed, to see monasteries tumbled down by the mob, churches sacked and looted, perhaps; not interested to prevent the breakup of the old? But religiously interested in the new, anxious to be pious? And in a couple of years to have become a fervent whatever-it-was-called? The average man? The generality of the populace?

The new Reformed doctrines first came into Scotland within ten years of Luther's manifestation in the matter of indulgences. The first propagandist, Patrick Hamilton, a young man of noble birth, was burned as a heretic in 1528. Between that date and the last execution of the sort, in 1558, there were ten other victims. Protestants in these years were few and far between, and the government of James V had other more pressing interests than to seek them out and destroy them. The chronic problem, abroad, was England; the England of Henry VIII, whose nephew James V was. James had come to the throne, a mere child, when his father was killed in the great English victory of Flodden. He died, of a broken heart it is said, at the news of the great Scottish disaster of Solway Moss. In a loose, general kind of way those two tragic facts epitomise the leading anxiety of whoever it was ruled Scotland—king, regent, cardinal, queen—in this violent, lawless century.

The regent—for the week-old baby sovereign—was her father's closest male relation on the Scottish side, his third cousin, James Hamilton, Earl of Arran, and, if the baby died, King James VI. The cardinal was David Beaton, Archbishop of St. Andrew's and primate of Scotland, a most capable administrator and a strong man (where Arran was weakness itself) and the late king's most confidential advisor. The queen, the baby's mother, was the French princess Mary of Guise, sister of two men who in another ten years will be in the first places at the French court: Francis, Duke of Guise, and Charles, the Cardinal of Lorraine. Arran's attempt at an independent policy was soon over. In a year he had succumbed to the powerful mind of the cardinal of St. Andrew's. In 1546 there fell into the cardinal's hands the most dangerous propagandist of Protestantism that had so far appeared—the ex-priest George Wishart, a man of fiery character, like his disciple John Knox, and fitted by natural temperament for the rôle he felt bound to assume, the Hebrew prophet in the denunciatory phases of his mission.

Wishart was a man who had seen many lands in the course of his apostolate. Only a timely recantation had saved him from the attentions of the Supreme Head of the Church south of the border, for a sermon at Bristol against devotion to the Blessed Virgin. Switzerland had known him, and Germany too. By all accounts he was a courteous, learned person who lived the life of an ascetic. But for two years after he returned to Scotland, in 1544, he preached a gospel where the threats of what God would do to the unheeding were never veiled. Nor does he seem to have greatly succeeded. At the stake, March 1, 1546, he called on the bystanders to teach the bishops the Word of God. If they refuse to learn, he said, the anger of God will surely strike. "They cannot escape it." The city of St. Andrew's is so small that the fancy is legitimate that the cardinal who had sentenced him could not but hear. Just three months later, on May 29, a band of bravos, subsidised by Henry VIII, broke into the castle of St. Andrew's, and presently the corpse of the cardinal, pierced with a score of wounds, was dangling from a window. John Knox was not among these men, but he hurried to join them, as a kind of chaplain, and he shared their fate when on July 30, 1547, a French army captured the castle. With the rest, Knox went to the hideous life of a rower in the French king's galleys.

After Beaton's murder a great change came over the spirit of the government of Scotland. The strong mind that was native had gone; the strong mind that replaced it (ultimately) was foreign, French, the mind of the queen mother, Mary of Guise. In the year after the murder, the English king who had had a hand in it died, and in his place there ruled the ineffective Duke of Somerset, protector of the child sovereign, Edward VI. In that same year, 1547, the King of France also died, Francis I. The new king, Henry II, was much more interested than his father in Scottish affairs—in the use of Scotland, as French tradition had used it for a long time now, as a base of operations against the common enemy, England. He sent welcome help to the Scots, money and troops, in the winter after yet another English invasion and victory—Pinkie —and in 1548 the Scots consented that their queen, now five years old, should be betrothed to the king's heir, Francis, two years younger still, and be sent to France to be bred at the court with her future husband. If all went well the two kingdoms of France and Scotland would one day be united under a single ruler.

With the increased French aid and the new future which the marriage treaty promised, the French influence grew stronger and stronger. In 1554 Arran was induced to lay down the regency, and Mary of Guise became the actual ruler of the country, with Frenchmen in all the positions of trust, and a supply of trained French troops. The Protestants of Scotland had had it against them, hitherto, that they were antinational because pro-English. The tide now flowed the other way. England was Catholic again, from 1553, and persecuting Protestants; Scottish Protestantism lost its pro-English taint. France, not England, was the threat to the independence of Scottish life. The Protestants, in opposing the French "occupation," could be super-nationalist and good Protestants too.

At this moment, in 1555, Knox returned to Scotland. He had been freed from the galleys in 1547, had evangelised in England (where there had been talk of making him Bishop of Rochester), had then gone abroad, *Maria regnante*, and played a great part in the theological controversies that divided the exiles. He came back at the invitation of a small group of Protestant nobles, and he stayed less than a year. What he is credited with accomplishing was the forming of these very different and none-too-friendly men into a party. Some of them were sincere; others, it is no less certain, were simply drawn by the desire for church lands. But Knox united them, inspired them with a common spirit of aggression, and gave them a simple rallying principle, "No more Mass, death to the priesthood." He returned to Geneva in 1556, where Calvin held him in the highest esteem and where he ministered to a congregation of English exiles that included such fanatics as Christopher Goodman, who sang the praises of assassination as the remedy for idolatrous tyrants; William Whittingham, the main force behind the Geneva version of the English Bible; and Antony Gilby. In this sanctuary of learned fanatics Knox wrote his own tract, with the actual—Catholic—rulers of Scotland and England in view, *The First Blast from the Trumpet against the Monstrous Regiment of Women*; its argument, that a woman ruler was an indecency, permanently alienated the great man from the woman who would be ruling England at the moment when Knox's Scotland stood most in need of England.

Five of the lords whom he had influenced in those meetings of 1555–56 pledged themselves in December, 1557 to "establish the most blessed word of God and his Congregation," even at the cost of their lives, declaring that they also forsook and renounced "the Congregation of Satan, with all the superstition, abominations and idolatry thereof." It was notice to all that a party had been formed and that it meant to act, "the Lords of the Congregation."

By December 1558, there had been great changes. The Queen of Scots had married the dauphin (April 24), the bishops had burnt the heretic Walter Milne (April), there had been a Protestant riot in Edinburgh on the Feast of St. Giles (September 1), and when the Estates met in December a strong anti-Catholic petition was presented to the queen-regent: in England (November 17) Elizabeth's reign had begun, this at the time when Mary of Guise might have hoped to change successfully her policy of merely enduring all things and hoping.

Knox returned from Geneva in the spring of 1559. On May

10 he preached the famous sermon at Perth, the town[17] filled with the armed followers of the Protestant lords, come in from all parts of the Lowlands to demonstrate in favour of two arrested preachers. And the crowd passed out to sack the monasteries in the town. On June 11, with pilgrims of the same sort at his heels, he repeated the process at St. Andrew's. On the twenty-ninth the Lords were in possession of Edinburgh. But they had no deepness of earth, general feeling was not in their favour, and in three weeks they had abandoned the capital. Meanwhile, on July 10, their queen had become Queen of France, the King of France was now the King of Scotland; and August brought more French troops. It was time for the foreign ally of the Lords to act, if another foreigner was not to make Scotland his own. While in Scotland the regent and the Lords agree to an uneasy truce, Sir William Cecil advanced from private encouraging notes to Knox to the despatch of a veteran diplomatist, thoroughly Protestant this many a year, Sir Ralph Sadler, with funds, and the mission to encourage the divisions between the regent and the Lords. The war—the movement of troops, rather—took up again, and in October the Lords, possessed once more of Edinburgh, "deposed" the regent in the name of the king and the queen, and laid siege to Leith.[18] The French twice drove them off with ease; and their followers, as before, melting away, the Lords again fled from the capital.

It was now November 1559, and in their desperate situation the rebels sent an agent to London to make a personal appeal for real intervention, an army. This agent was William Maitland, master of Lethington, the shrewdest Scot of his day, the peer of Cecil himself. In this matter Cecil and he were agreed. The real difficulty was Elizabeth, in one of those moods when "the cat would have fish but not wet her paw." Finally she yielded. The Duke of Norfolk was sent to organise an army, Lord Grey to command it, and a fleet under Admiral Winter was despatched to the Forth. We must leave the war to history books of another kind, which tell it in all its dramatic detail. But after the storms of the North Sea it was Winter's ships that mattered most. The English queen and the rebel Lords came together in the Treaty of Berwick (February 27,

17 What was the size of Perth? Had it as many as 2,000 inhabitants? The monasteries were Franciscan and Dominican friaries and a house of Carthusian monks.
18 The port of Edinburgh.

1560)—a pact for mutual defence against France. The English army arrived, and another siege of Leith began, to be once more disastrous for the besiegers; and then the valiant Mary of Guise took ill and died, June 10. It was the end, for the time, of the Stewart authority in Scotland. Six days later Cecil arrived and negotiations with the French were opened.

The result was a Franco-English treaty, which hardly concerns this story, and a Franco-Scottish treaty (July 6, 1560) which is of the first importance to it, for although it did not contain any "settlement" of religion, it gave the Lords of the Congregation a means whereby—with a certain dishonesty—they took over the government of Scotland in the name of the king and queen. This Treaty of Edinburgh provided that a Parliament was to be held when the sovereigns had consented to this, and that it was to choose twenty-four men, from whom the sovereigns should select seven and the Parliament five, and these twelve should rule in the sovereigns' name. The Lords did not wait for any parliamentary sanction. They proceeded immediately to reorganise the Church. And the Parliament met, without any reference to the sovereigns.

Was it a legal Parliament? Were its acts good in law? The historians still debate this. Knox addressed it in a petition calling for the destruction of popery and the establishment of the religion of the Gospel. "Establishment" was a word that made those nobles anxious whose one interest was to grab the church properties for themselves. This part of Knox's desires was, for the moment, left unfulfilled. A Confession of Faith was adopted that has been described as the Calvinism of Calvin's last period. Another act abolished the jurisdiction of the pope, the heresy laws also. It was moreover forbidden to say Mass or to be present at Mass, with the punishment for a first offence of loss of all goods and a flogging; for the second offence, banishment; for the third, death. When the news reached France, the king and queen refused to recognise the Parliament as a legal assembly, and they refused to ratify the Franco-Scottish treaty of July 6. But the Lords were in possession. And the appearance of legality invested their "settlement." Less than four months after this the happy days of Mary Queen of Scots were suddenly and tragically brought to an end when the boy to whom she was married, Francis II of France, died, at sixteen years of age.

And in August 1561, Mary returned to Scotland.

The mind and will of this girl not yet nineteen was the sole hope of the old religion. For this young French queen was almost alone, among the great personages of the kingdom, in her attachment to the Catholic Church as a religion. And her chances of peacefully reversing the event of 1560 were simply nil. She had neither the ability nor the experience to form a party from among the factions, to keep it loyal to herself and to use it to overthrow the victorious Protestant lords. As a Catholic ruler Mary was doomed from the day she landed at Leith. Nor did her own ideal of toleration in religious affairs in the least avail her. And such as her power was, the time left for any exercise of it was to be brief indeed. The English concern that the hold of the Protestant lords upon the government should continue was of course a main factor in her fate, and the manœuvres between Edinburgh and London were ceaseless. Only three and a half years after her return Mary met her cousin Henry Lennox, Lord Darnley. He was to prove himself as worthless as he was handsome.

In less than six months they were married (July 29, 1565). The marriage, Mary wrote to the pope, was an important move in her scheme for the restoration of the Catholic religion. The queen ventured to forbid Knox to preach. A Catholic was installed as provost of the capital. Aid was sought from Spain and from France. In October 1565 the leading Protestant lord, the queen's half-brother, James Stewart, Earl of Moray, defeated in an attempted rebellion, fled to England. His place as Mary's chief advisor was taken by a Catholic, David Riccio, her Italian private secretary. The hour was critical, and not for Scotland only.[19]

What happened next was that Darnley, alienated from his wife since the first weeks after the marriage, angered by her refusal to make him king in fact, jealous of her reliance on Riccio, joined with the Protestant lords to destroy the secretary. They forestalled the queen's action against Moray through the Parliament of 1566, by murdering Riccio in her very presence, March 9, 1566, Darnley looking on. Eleven months later it was Darnley who was murdered February 10,

[19] "It is not too much to say that the course of events in Scotland in the winter of 1565–66, which culminated in the ruin of Mary's plans, was one of the decisive factors in assuring the survival of British, and hence of European, Protestantism." *James Stewart, Earl of Moray*, by Maurice Lee, Jr. (1953)—a refreshingly detached account of a story where every detail is passionately contested—p. 157.

1567, and in the following June came the surrender of the helpless queen to the lords, her imprisonment at Loch Leven and abdication. Mary was not yet 25. There lay ahead of her twenty years of life as a prisoner.

It was, however, the murder of Riccio, which, for the modern historian, "spelled the ruin of the old religion in Scotland." The last convinced Catholic to control the government of Scotland had lost the last Catholic capable of advising her and also loyal to her ideas, as well as to her person. The end of Catholic control in Scotland "meant that England too was safe," says the same writer. "It was a decisive event in British history."[20] And, of course, in much else.

[20] *Op. cit.*, p. 170, for both quotations.

INDEX

Absenteeism, of priests and bishops, 48

Abuses. *See* Scandals; Superstition

Adrian VI, pope, 215, 260

Albert of Brandenburg, Archbishop of Mainz, 100–1, 108–9, 122, 123, 170; his instructions for indulgence preachers, 102

Albert of Hohenzollern, Grand Master of Teutonic Knights, 123–24

Albert the Great, St., 24

Alcalá, university, 71

Alexander III, pope, 41, 42

America, missions to, 71–72; first sees founded, 72

Amsdorf, Nicholas, 99 *n.*, 129

Anabaptists, 120, 140–43, 150, 291–92

Anne Boleyn, 155, 156, 158–59, 164–65, 169, 172, 182 *n.*, 186

Anne of Cleves, 194

Aquinas, St. Thomas, 24, 25, 26, 84, 110, 153

Articles (of religion): the Ten Articles (1536), 187–88; the Six Articles (1539), 193, 195; the 42 Articles (1553), 205, 290; the 39 Articles (1563), 290–92

Aske, Robert, 189, 190

Augsburg, Confession of, 125–30, 187; *Confutation of the,* 127

Augsburg, Peace of (1555), 254, 255

Augustine, St., 26, 99, 229

Augustinian Friars, 24, 89

Ballard, Jean, 231

Baptism in primitive Church, 16, 33

Barbarian Invasions, influence on Church life, 18 ff.

Barnabites, religious order, 84 ff.

Barnes, Robert, reformer, 150, 187

Basci, Matteo da, 86

Battista of Crema. *See* Carioni

Beaton, David, cardinal, 294, 296–97

Belief, unity and content of, traditional before Reformation, 14–18

Benedict XIII (Peter de Luna), 21, 22, 44

Berwick, Treaty of (1560), 299

Bible: universally taken as inspired, 15; various vernacular translations of, 68; polyglot edition of Alcalá, 71; Erasmus' New Testament, 76; Luther's, 116; Tyndale's, 151; English translation authorised (1538), 191–92

Bishops: belief the office of is God's creation, 16; role and reverence for in primitive Church, 16; social importance of in Middle Ages, 19; right to appoint is central to pope *vs* emperor struggles of Middle Ages, 41; number of and distribution in 15th century, 46–47; character of majority in later Middle Ages, 46–49; abuses in the system, 48–49; English, surrender to Henry VIII, 178, 181; official report on abuses by, 217–18; Trent's laws about, 240, 248–49

Bishops' Book, 191

Image Books

. . . MAKING THE WORLD'S FINEST
CATHOLIC LITERATURE AVAILABLE TO ALL

Image Books

... MAKING THE WORLD'S FINEST
CATHOLIC LITERATURE AVAILABLE TO ALL

11

Image Books

...making the world's finest Catholic literature available to all

VIPERS' TANGLE
by *François Mauriac*   D51—75¢

THE MANNER IS ORDINARY
by *John LaFarge, S.J.* D52—95¢

MY LIFE FOR MY SHEEP
by *Alfred Duggan*   D53—90¢

THE CHURCH AND THE RECONSTRUCTION OF THE MODERN WORLD: *The Social Encyclicals of Pius XI.* Edited by T. P. McLaughlin, C.S.B.   D54—$1.25

A GILSON READER: *Selections from the Writings of Etienne Gilson.* Edited by Anton C. Pegis.
D55—95¢

THE AUTOBIOGRAPHY OF ST. THERESE OF LISIEUX: *The Story of a Soul.* A new translation by John Beevers.   D56—65¢

HELENA
by *Evelyn Waugh*   D57—65¢

THE GREATEST BIBLE STORIES
A Catholic Anthology from World Literature. Edited by Anne Fremantle.   D58—75¢

THE CITY OF GOD—St. Augustine.
Edited with Intro. by Vernon J. Bourke. Foreword by Etienne Gilson.   D59—$1.45

SUPERSTITION CORNER
by *Sheila Kaye-Smith* D60—65¢

SAINTS AND OURSELVES
Ed. by *Philip Caraman, S.J.*
D61—95¢

CANA IS FOREVER
by *Charles Hugo Doyle*
D62—75¢

ASCENT OF MOUNT CARMEL—St. John of the Cross. Translated and Edited by E. Allison Peers.
D63—$1.25

RELIGION AND THE RISE OF WESTERN CULTURE
by *Christopher Dawson*
D64—85¢

PRINCE OF DARKNESS AND OTHER STORIES
by *J. F. Powers*   D65—85¢

ST. THOMAS MORE
by *E. E. Reynolds*   D66—95¢

JESUS AND HIS TIMES
2 Volumes   D67A—95¢
by *Daniel-Rops*   D67B—95¢

ST. BENEDICT
by *Justin McCann, O.S.B.*
D68—85¢

THE LITTLE FLOWERS OF ST. FRANCIS
Edited and Translated by Raphael Brown.   D69—95¢

THE QUIET LIGHT
by *Louis de Wohl*   D70—95¢

CHARACTERS OF THE REFORMATION
by *Hilaire Belloc*   D71—85¢

THE BELIEF OF CATHOLICS
by *Ronald Knox*   D72—75¢

FAITH AND FREEDOM
by *Barbara Ward*   D73—95¢

GOD AND INTELLIGENCE IN MODERN PHILOSOPHY
by *Fulton J. Sheen* D74—$1.25

If your bookseller is unable to supply certain titles, write to Image Books, Department MIB, Garden City, New York, stating the titles you desire and enclosing the price of each book (plus 5¢ per book to cover cost of postage and handling). Prices are subject to change without notice.   21

Image Books

... MAKING THE WORLD'S FINEST CATHOLIC LITERATURE AVAILABLE TO ALL

THE IDEA OF A UNIVERSITY
By John Henry Cardinal Newman. Introduction by George N. Shuster   **D75—$1.35**

PLAYED BY EAR: The Autobiography of Father Daniel A. Lord, S.J.   **D76—95¢**

MY BELOVED: The Story of a Carmelite Nun. By Mother Catherine Thomas   **D77—75¢**

DARK NIGHT OF THE SOUL
By St. John of the Cross. Edited and translated by E. Allison Peers   **D78—75¢**

TERESA OF AVILA
By Marcelle Auclair. Translated by Kathleen Pond   **D79—$1.35**

SAINT PETER THE APOSTLE
By William Thomas Walsh   **D80—95¢**

THE LOVE OF GOD
By Dom Aelred Graham, O.S.B.   **D81—85¢**

WOMAN OF THE PHARISEES
By François Mauriac. Translated by Gerard Hopkins   **D82—75¢**

THE PILLAR OF FIRE
By Karl Stern   **D83—85¢**

ORTHODOXY
By G. K. Chesterton   **D84—75¢**

THIS IS CATHOLICISM
By John J. Walsh   **D85—$1.25**

MEDIEVAL ESSAYS
By Christopher Dawson   **D86—95¢**

VESSEL OF CLAY
By Leo Trese   **D87—65¢**

SAINTS FOR SINNERS
By Alban Goodier, S.J.   **D88—65¢**

THE LONG LONELINESS
By Dorothy Day   **D89—85¢**

THIS IS THE MASS
By Henri Daniel-Rops. Photographs of Bishop Fulton J. Sheen by Karsh   **D90—95¢**

THE ORIGIN OF THE JESUITS
By James Brodrick, S.J.   **D91—85¢**

A POPULAR HISTORY OF THE REFORMATION
By Philip Hughes   **D92—95¢**

THE RESTLESS FLAME
By Louis de Wohl   **D93—85¢**

PROGRESS AND RELIGION
By Christopher Dawson   **D94—85¢**

THE CATHOLIC CHURCH IN THE MODERN WORLD
By E. E. Y. Hales   **D95—95¢**

THE LIFE OF TERESA OF JESUS: The Autobiography of St. Teresa of Avila. Translated and with an introduction by E. Allison Peers   **D96—$1.25**

GIANTS OF THE FAITH
By John A. O'Brien   **D97—95¢**

SCHOLASTICISM AND POLITICS
By Jacques Maritain   **D98—95¢**

THE SON OF GOD
By Karl Adam   **D99—85¢**

THE MAN WHO WAS CHESTERTON
Edited by Raymond T. Bond   **D100—$1.45**

Image Books

**. . . MAKING THE WORLD'S FINEST
CATHOLIC LITERATURE AVAILABLE TO ALL**

Image Books

. . . making the world's finest Catholic literature available to all

A HISTORY OF PHILOSOPHY, Vol. 3:

Late Mediaeval and Renaissance Philosophy, Parts I & II
By Frederick Copleston, S.J.

A magnificent exposition of philosophical thought from Ockham to the Speculative Mystics (Part I), and from the Revival of Platonism to Suarez (Part II).
D136A & D136B—95¢ ea. vol.

CATHOLIC VIEWPOINT ON EDUCATION

By Neil McCluskey, S.J.

A complete, authoritative, and clear-cut presentation of the Catholic viewpoint on a vitally urgent national issue. "Required reading"—*N.Y. Times.*
D149—75¢

MIRACLE AT CARVILLE

By Betty Martin

The story of a courageous girl's triumph over the world's most feared malady. **D150—85¢**

CATHEDRAL AND CRUSADE
(2 volumes)

By Henri Daniel-Rops

A history of the stirring age between the eleventh and fourteenth centuries. "An important work of Catholic scholarship."—*The Saturday Review.*
D154A & D154B—$1.35 ea. vol.

SEARCHING THE SCRIPTURES

By John J. Dougherty

A popular and lucid guide to the reading and study of the Bible, giving historical background and theological explanations. **D151—75¢**

TRANSFORMATION IN CHRIST

By Dietrich von Hildebrand

Presents a profound analysis of the Christian experience and offers a rich new insight into the reality of the Christian life.
D152—$1.35

SECRETS OF THE SAINTS

By Henri Gheon

Four complete biographies in one volume: the Curé of Ars, the Little Flower, St. Margaret Mary, and St. John Bosco.
D153—$1.25

A DOCTOR AT CALVARY

By Pierre Barbet, M.D.

The classic and moving account of the Passion of Our Lord as described by a physician.
D155—75¢

MARY IN OUR LIFE

By William G. Most

A comprehensive and beautifully written study of Mary's importance in one's faith. **D156—95¢**

If your bookseller is unable to supply certain titles, write to Image Books, Department MIB, Garden City, New York, stating the titles you desire and enclosing the price of each book (plus 5¢ per book to cover cost of postage and handling). Prices are subject to change without notice.

Image Books

. . . making the world's finest Catholic literature available to all

ON THE LOVE OF GOD
(2 volumes)
by St. Francis de Sales
Trans., with an Introduction by John K. Ryan
The great spiritual classic—often called a companion volume to *Introduction to the Devout Life* —in a distinguished new translation.
D164A & 164B   95¢ ea. vol.

THE SANDS OF TAMANRASSET
by Marion Mill Preminger
The exciting story of Charles de Foucauld—playboy, soldier, aristocrat—who became a true hero of God.   **D160   85¢**

BLITHE SPIRITS: An Anthology of Catholic Humor
Edited by Dan Herr and Joel Wells
A sparkling collection of witty and humorous pieces on some lighthearted aspects of modern Catholic life by 25 celebrated authors.   **D163   85¢**

A HISTORY OF PHILOSOPHY, Volume 4
Modern Philosophy: Descartes to Leibniz
by Frederick Copleston, S.J.
Another volume in the celebrated history of philosophy described by Blackfriars as "the standard history of philosophy for many years to come."
D137 $1.35

WE LIVE WITH OUR EYES OPEN
by Dom Hubert van Zeller, O.S.B.
Stimulating and rewarding meditations on the spiritual life for today's lay men and women.
D162   75¢

THE PROTESTANT REFORMATION
(2 volumes)
by Henri Daniel-Rops
"An excellent and moving synthesis of one of the most critical periods in the history of the Church."—*The Sign*
D159A & 159B $1.35 ea. vol.

YOUR CHILD'S WORLD: From Infancy through Adolescence
by Robert Odenwald, M.D.
A new handbook of practical advice and guidance by a leading Catholic psychiatrist.
D161   75¢

THE BOOK OF MARY
by Henri Daniel-Rops
An absorbing account of the life and times of "the most appealing of all figures in the Gospels," the Mother of God.
D158   75¢

PRAYER IN PRACTICE
by Romano Guardini
A practical and luminous introduction to prayer by an eminent theologian.   **D157   75¢**